Comparative ethnic and race relations series

Racism and equal opportunity policies in the 1980s

SECOND EDITION

This book looks at the problems of racism and equal opportunity in employment and government policies towards them in Britain. It brings together a group of specialist contributors and covers the major areas of debate, including the law, policies towards unemployment, job training and the labour market, the role of the public and private sectors, the role of trade unions, the gap between policies and pronouncements on equal opportunity and their implementation, and the related issue of sectarian discrimination in Northern Ireland. It looks at the future prospects for equal opportunities and provides conclusions for policy.

In particular, it aims to address important topics such as the assumptions underlying current policies, and whether they realistically reflect reality, the actual effect of legislation, and the relationship between power disparities in society as a whole and racial inequality.

The book will make a major contribution to the debate about equal opportunity in employment, and will be of interest to a readership ranging from students and teachers, to policy makers, administrators and professionals who confront 'race' problems in everyday situations.

Comparative ethnic and race relations

Published for the Centre for Research in Ethnic Relations at the University of Warwick

Senior Editor
Professor John Rex *Associate Director & Research Professor of Ethnic Relations, University of Warwick*

Editors
Professor Robin Cohen *Executive Director & Professor of Sociology, University of Warwick*
Mr Malcolm Cross *Principal Research Fellow, University of Warwick*
Dr Robin Ward *Head of Ethnic Business Research Unit, University of Aston*

This series has been formed to publish works of original theory, empirical research, and texts on the problems of racially mixed societies. It is based on the work of the Centre for Research in Ethnic Relations, a Designated Research Centre of the Economic and Social Research Council, and the main centre for the study of race relations in Britain.

The series will continue to draw on the work produced at the Centre, though the editors encourage manuscripts from scholars whose work has been associated with the Centre, or whose research lies in similar fields. Future titles will concentrate on anti-racist issues in education, on the organisation and political demands of ethnic minorities, on migration patterns, changes in immigration policies in relation to migrants and refugees, and on questions relating to employment, welfare and urban restructuring as these affect minority communities.

The books will appeal to an international readership of scholars, students and professionals concerned with racial issues, across a wide range of disciplines (such as sociology, anthropology, social policy, politics, economics, education and law), as well as among professional social administrators, teachers, government officials, health service workers and others.

Other books in this series:
Michael Banton: *Racial and ethnic competition* (issued in hardcover and as a paperback).
Thomas Hammar (ed.): *European immigration policy.*
Frank Reeves: *British racial discourse.*
Robin Ward and Richard Jenkins (eds.): *Ethnic communities in business.*
Richard Jenkins: *Racism and recruitment: managers, organisations and equal opportunity in the labour market.*
Paul B. Rich: *Race and empire in British politics.*
John Rex and David Mason (eds.): *Theories of race and ethnic relations.*
Roger Hewitt: *White talk black talk: inter-racial friendship and communication amongst adolescents.*

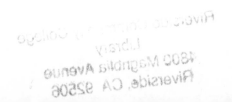

Racism and equal opportunity policies in the 1980s

SECOND EDITION

edited by

RICHARD JENKINS AND JOHN SOLOMOS

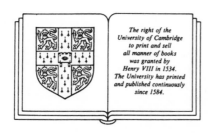

The right of the
University of Cambridge
to print and sell
all manner of books
was granted by
Henry VIII in 1534.
The University has printed
and published continuously
since 1584.

CAMBRIDGE UNIVERSITY PRESS

Cambridge
New York   Port Chester
Melbourne   Sydney

Published by the Press Syndicate of the University of Cambridge
The Pitt Building, Trumpington Street, Cambridge CB2 1RP
40 West 20th Street, New York, NY 10011, USA
10 Stamford Road, Oakleigh, Melbourne 3166, Australia

© Cambridge University Press 1987, 1989

First published 1987
Reprinted 1988
Second edition published 1989

Printed in Great Britain at the University Press, Cambridge

British Library cataloguing in publication data

Racism and equal opportunity policies in the 1980s. –
(Comparative ethnic and race relations series). – 2nd ed.
1. Great Britain. Ethnic minorities. Employment.
Equality of opportunity
I. Jenkins, Richard, *1952*– II. Solomos, John
331.6'0941

Library of Congress cataloguing in publication data

Racism and equal opportunity policies in the 1980s / edited by Richard
Jenkins and John Solomos. – 2nd ed.
    p.   cm. – (Comparative ethnic and race relations series)
Bibliography
Includes index.
ISBN 0 521 38968 2
1. Discrimination in employment – Great Britain. 2. Race
discrimination – Great Britain. I. Jenkins, Richard, 1952–
II. Solomos, John.   III. Series.
HD4903.5.G7R33   1989
331.13'3'0941–dc20   89-32977   CIP

ISBN 0 521 38968 2

First edition ISBN 0 521 33013 0

BO

Contents

Introduction to the second edition

Even in the short time since the first edition of this volume was published much has changed in relation to the issues it covers. For this reason we have decided to add a new introduction to bring the coverage of some of its main themes up to date. Obviously we cannot discuss all changes over the past few years, and so we shall concentrate particularly on four of the main variables: the political context; the local politics of anti-racism; equal opportunity in Northern Ireland; and finally on the prospects for the future.

The changing political context of racial equality

After Mrs Thatcher was returned to power for the third time in 1987 she declared that one of her main priorities would be the regeneration of the inner cities. Shortly afterwards she undertook a short tour through Britain's inner cities, with the aim of declaring her government's commitment to regenerating these areas. This tour was supposed to symbolise the high priority given to inner city deprivation during her third administration. On the face of it therefore there are hopeful signs about the prospects for radical changes in policy orientation during Mrs Thatcher's third term of office.

In the years since 1981, when Lord Scarman called for urgent action to tackle racial discrimination and the social conditions which underlay the disorders in Brixton and elsewhere, there has been little evidence of such urgency. Whatever the merit of the particular programme proposed by Lord Scarman – and this has been the subject of some debate (Benyon and Solomos 1987) – the one consistent response that has been evident since 1981 has had little to do with the pursuit of social justice: rather than dealing with the root causes of racial disadvantage and urban unrest the government has chosen to give more resources, more training and more equipment to the police in order to control the symptoms of urban unrest. The government's overall objective has been to decrease public expenditure, for the sake of lower taxation and to encourage an enterprise culture. In this context aid for the inner cities has been dwarfed by the financial cuts applied to inner city local authorities.

Increasingly the most strident political voices are raised in the name of free enterprise and law and order, not for equity and social justice. For the new right and other influential sectors of political opinion the attempt to achieve racial equality through legal and political means is at best naive political folly and at worst a restriction on the workings of the market. The present political climate gives one little cause for optimism that a radical change in governmental priorities in this field is likely (Solomos 1989).

In the aftermath of the 1985 outbreak of urban unrest, central government promised to help those inner city areas particularly hard hit by economic restructuring and urban decay. The impact of such promises in practice has, however, been limited, and there is little evidence that the initiatives which have been set in motion as a result of the urban unrest have had much impact on the socio-economic position of black minorities in the inner cities.

The government's plan of 'Action for Cities' (DoE 1988), issued after Mrs Thatcher's post-election promise, says very little directly about racial inequality. It remains to be seen whether it will suffer the fate of numerous other initiatives on the inner cities and fade into obscurity. But one thing seems clear: since the late 1970s the government has been more intent on reducing the powers of local authorities than on providing for fundamental changes in the social conditions of the inner cities.

In this environment the auguries for equal opportunity and racial equality policies are not good, despite the government's self-proclaimed commitment to the regeneration of the inner cities. Within the present political climate it becomes increasingly unlikely that the government will respond favourably to calls for greater state intervention to combat racism and social injustice. The fate of the CRE's proposals for the reform of the 1976 Race Relations Act is the most clear example of how calls for urgent legal and political reforms have fallen on deaf ears.

Failing a strong lead from central government the CRE has attempted to innovate within the terms of its powers. It has tried to encourage both public and private sector employers to develop and implement equal opportunity programmes. The failure of the government to give it greater legal powers or to support it politically has, however, limited the impact of the CRE's initiatives (McCrudden 1987). A good example is the fate of the Code of Practice for the elimination of discrimination in employment, which came into force in April 1984. First published in draft form in early 1982, the Code went through a number of stages of discussion and redrafting before the government formally laid it before Parliament in April 1983. Since April 1984 the Code has been admissible in evidence to tribunals, and if they think a provision in it is relevant to the proceedings they can take it into account in determining the question. However, the CRE's own survey of employers' responses to the Code showed that many employers were still unaware of its existence, and even fewer had taken any positive measures to put it into practice (CRE 1988: 8).

At a broader level the attempts by the CRE and various local authorities to encourage the development of positive action and contract compliance measures as tools for the promotion of racial equality in employment have met with both legal and administrative resistance. There seems little likelihood that such measures can have a significant impact on the extent of racial discrimination in British society without a broader political commitment to the goal of racial equality.

The relative absence of policy innovation at the national level during the past decade is no indication that the question of racial inequality has been resolved. Rather, the present situation can best be seen as an impasse in the search for means to achieve greater equality for black citizens in British society (Gordon 1989). Unless a way is found to move beyond the present impasse it is likely that racial inequality will remain a volatile and explosive issue in British society for some time to come. If the experience of the past few years is anything to go by it will take sustained political pressure and mobilisation to alter current priorities and establish a radical agenda for action.

Local politics and 'anti-racism'

Perhaps the most notable change in this field over the past few years has been in relation to local politics. Since the early 1980s public attention has been focused on the experiences of a number of local authorities which have introduced radical policies aimed at tackling racial inequality. The most notable cases have been the Greater London Council before it was abolished, the Inner London Education Authority and the London boroughs of Lambeth, Brent, Hackney and Haringey. Nationally, a number of other local authorities have adopted comprehensive policy statements on racial equality and equal opportunity generally.

In all these cases a combination of factors seems to have prompted rapid policy change. First, bolstered by the urban unrest that has been much in evidence during the 1980s, local black politicians and groups have sought to include racial inequality on the local political agenda. Second, a number of left local authorities sought to use the issue of equal opportunity as a mechanism for widening their basis of support among ethnic minorities and other constituencies (Stoker 1988: 207–8). Third, the failure of central

government to respond to calls for radical reform was seen as a sign tha
relatively little change could be expected as a result of the actions o
central government.

The result of these pressures was reflected in three main policy changes
The first addressed the central question of who gets what, and the emphasi
has been on establishing equality of treatment and equality of outcome ii
the allocation process. Ethnic records have been introduced to monito
channels of access and allocation. For example, in relation to housing
authorities such as Hackney and Haringey have sought to monitor mobility
within the local housing stock and the quality of distribution, and to chang
procedures that facilitated discretion and contributed to discriminator
outcomes.

The second policy change has addressed the question of the employmen
of black staff within local authorities. This has resulted in a number o
authorities linking the question of allocative equality with the represen
tation of black and ethnic minority staff in local government departments
Racially discriminatory outcomes, it was argued, were not solely the func
tion of organisational procedures but also related to the under-representatioi
or exclusion of black and ethnic minority staff. Consequently, targets hav
been established to increase the employment of black and ethni
minority staff.

Once again, however, the experience of local authorities seems to mirro
that of central government initiatives, since there has been a gap betweei
the promise embodied in policy statements and the actual achievements o
policies. During the early 1980s authorities such as Lambeth and Hackne
did make some progress in changing their employment practices and servic
delivery to reflect the multi-racial composition of their local populations
Initiatives in specific policy areas such as social services and housing hav
also been put into practice. In Hackney's case the combination of pressur
from the local black communities and a formal investigation by the Com
mission for Racial Equality forced the council to rethink its housing polic
and introduce major changes. During the early 1980s local authorities wer
also the site of important debates about the delivery of social service
and education.

Yet after the flurry of policy activity and change during the early 1980
the last few years have been a period of conflict, negative media publicit
about racial equality policies and in some cases resistance to change by th
local white population. The debates about multi-racial education in Brer
and Bradford, the media coverage of the activities of the 'loony left' in
number of local authorities in London, and the attack on 'anti-racisn
launched by sections of the political right have tended to push even the mo:
radical local authorities on the defensive. Indeed in some cases the publi

attention given to 'anti-racism' has tended to take attention away from the persistence of racial inequality and direct critical attention at those local authorities attempting to allocate resources to minority groups.

Most importantly, perhaps, the increasing fiscal constraints imposed by central government and pressure on the resources available to local authorities have left little room for the maintenance of the initiatives already introduced or for new developments. During 1987 and 1988 there were signs that even previously radical local authorities are now adopting a lower profile on issues concerned with racial equality.

Equal opportunity in Northern Ireland

Reviewers of the original hardback edition of the present collection were united in singling out John Darby's critique of Northern Ireland's Fair Employment Agency (FEA) for particular attention. Robin Oakley, for example, suggested that 'it is to Northern Ireland that we might look if we wish to progress equal opportunity policies further' (*The Times Higher Education Supplement*, 20 November 1987). Robert Cormack, in a similar vein, argued that the province had become the 'lead jurisdiction' in the United Kingdom with respect to equality of opportunity (*International Journal of Urban and Regional Research*, vol. 12, 1988, p. 660). At the end of the chapter in question, however, Darby argues – more pessimistically – that unless the Fair Employment Agency adopts a more aggressive stance in its operations 'by 1990, the issue of equality of opportunity will have gently slipped into the backwater of Ulster politics'.

Since that sentence was written, far from slipping further down the agenda of government in Northern Ireland, questions concerning ethnic equality of opportunity in employment have assumed a greater degree of political importance than hitherto. One reason for this development is the direct pressure exerted by the United States government, in relation to the placing of orders and investment, as described by Darby. In addition, however, there is now the 1985 Anglo-Irish Agreement to take into account, Article 5(a) of which is concerned with the encouragement of measures to prevent economic and social discrimination (Arthur and Jeffery 1988: 103). Finally, the United Kingdom state has probably also been moved to action in part by the need to head off the Irish lobby in the United States, in particular to meet the challenge of the 'MacBride Principles'. These are affirmative action principles which, while they may look routine enough in the American context, are not supported by the US government and have aroused considerable opposition in Northern Ireland, from unionists and constitutional nationalists alike, because of suspicion as to the motives of their proponents and doubts about their legality and appropriateness (Arthur and Jeffery 1988: 29–30; Cormack and Osborne 1987; McCormack 1987; Richmond 1987). The campaign in the United States supporting the MacBride Principles has nonetheless achieved some success in affecting state legislatures and public opinion.

The state has responded to these pressures in a number of ways: *administratively* it has made changes in its own procedures as an employer; *legally*, it has begun the process of altering the legislative framework which defines, promotes and polices equality of opportunity. Less directly, quangos (see chapter 12, note 2) and state-owned companies have also produced responses of one sort or another. We shall discuss each of these in turn, commencing with administrative action.

In 1983, the Fair Employment Agency published the report of one of its most controversial investigations, into the non-industrial Northern Ireland Civil Service (Fair Employment Agency, 1983). The investigation was marked by a series of disputes between external consultants, the FEA and the Civil Service about the findings and their analysis. Depending upon where one stood, the investigation either largely exonerated the Civil Service of persistent charges of discrimination (in its final, published version) or produced strong evidence (in its draft form) of systematic Catholic disadvantage, particularly within Civil Service promotion procedures (Miller, 1986: 227–30; 1988).

Whatever interpretation one adopts – and the circumstances of the investigation's final publication might strongly suggest the latter – the report made a number of recommendations. A direct outcome of these was the establishment of an Equal Opportunities Unit within the Civil Service. As revealed in its Annual Reports (Equal Opportunities Unit, 1986; 1987), the Unit has introduced a personnel monitoring system, concerned with issues such as recruitment, promotion and wastage with respect to religious ethnicity, gender and disability, in addition to a package of measures concerned with such things as recruitment publicity, training, sexual harassment, maternity-related issues and pensions. In short, a comprehensive equal opportunity programme has been introduced, covering both industrial and non-industrial civil servants. While it is too early to see what *difference* all of this activity has made, the Unit's programme represents a major rhetorical and practical step towards enhanced equality of opportunity in Northern Ireland. A further contribution to this has been the Department of Economic Development's *Religious Equality of Opportunity in Employment – Guide to Effective Practice*, issued in 1987.

Legal developments have been even more far-reaching. The Northern Ireland Department of Economic Development published in 1986 a Consultative Paper, *Equality of Opportunity in Employment in Northern Ireland: Future Strategy Options* (Department of Economic Development 1986). Originally commissioned by the Secretary of State in July 1985, the options which the paper offered for comment included an all-embracing regulatory agency covering ethnicity, gender and disability, on the basis of a single anti-discrimination law for all three, and the introduction of a strong form of contract compliance – affecting government tenders and grants – with respect to fair employment practice in the area of ethnicity.

This was followed by a report on fair employment from the Standing Advisory Commission on Human Rights, entitled *Religious and Political Discrimination in Northern Ireland* (Standing Advisory Commission on Human Rights 1987). The Commission draws its statutory authority from section 20 of the Northern Ireland Constitution Act 1973; its role is to advise the Secretary of State on the workings of the law with respect to political or religious discrimination.

The Commission's report is the most comprehensive critical review of the existing legal and administrative measures for preventing discrimination and providing equal opportunities in Northern Ireland and of the available options for improving the situation. It is impossible to do more than summarise briefly some of its major recommendations. Among these are the prohibition of indirect discrimination, the use of the industrial tribunal system to process individual complaints of discrimination (rather than, as at the time of writing, the FEA), the replacement of the FEA by a more powerful agency and the tougher use of contract compliance strategies with respect to government tenders, contracts and grants.

In February 1988, in the wake of the Commission's report and the response to the Consultative Paper, the Department of Economic Development announced a series of proposals. These included the introduction of the legal concept of indirect discrimination as a category of prohibited practice, the introduction of statutory requirements that all organisations with more than twenty-five employees monitor their workforces and that *all* employers provide equality of opportunity and, finally, the foundation of a new regulatory agency to replace the FEA. A White Paper, *Fair Employment in Northern Ireland* (Northern Ireland Office 1988), followed in May; among other changes, the proposed statutory ethnic monitoring was extended to all organisations employing ten or more workers.

The Queen's Speech on the State Opening of Parliament on 22 November 1988 marked the public unveiling of the Fair Employment Legislation (Northern Ireland) Bill. A *Guardian* leader writer (19 December 1988) has summarised the Bill's proposals thus:

> It will require all employers with more than 10 workers regularly to monitor their workforce, submit annual reports to the Government and carry out systematic reviews of their recruitment, training and promotion policies every three years. Any employer who refuses will be committing a criminal offence. A Fair Employment Commission will be given new powers to audit the composition of workforces, issue directives and take recalcitrant employers to a Fair Employment Tribunal, which will have the unique power for a tribunal in the UK of being able to impose fines. Not small fines either. The maximum will be £30,000. Employers which have discriminated in the past, will be encouraged to adopt affirmative action programmes. Employers who refuse to change, will face losing all government subsidies and will be prohibited from tendering for any public authority contract.

This is an impressive package. What it will look like following debate in the House and the Committee process is impossible to predict. Allowing for a reasonably safe passage, however, Northern Ireland will have been given, by UK standards, a uniquely powerful framework of anti-discrimination law (for contrasting views on this, see McCrudden 1989; Miller 1989).

There is more to the situation than the law, of course, although law is at the heart of the matter. The Fair Employment Agency has continued to do its job as well as possible under the circumstances: in March 1988, for example, following an investigation by the FEA, Northern Ireland Railways announced the introduction of a comprehensive 'equality of opportunity charter'. The Standing Advisory Commission on Human Rights, as part of the process of information gathering for its fair employment report, referred to above, commissioned a massive report on *Equality and Inequality in Northern Ireland* from the Policy Studies Institute (Smith and Chambers 1987). Although locally controversial – see the acrimonious exchanges between its authors and Northern Irish academics in *Fortnight*, numbers 258 and 259, January and February 1988 – the report is an unrivalled source of information (for further controversy see Cormack and Osborne 1989; Smith 1988).

Finally, there are state-owned companies to consider. The most obvious case is that of the aerospace company, Short Brothers and Harland, based in Belfast. They have been one of the most obvious targets for United States government pressure, in the context of orders for the C23 Sherpa aircraft. In June 1988, Shorts told the Defence Department in Washington that it planned to increase the Catholic proportion of 'new starts' to 17.5 per cent in 1988, 25 per cent in 1989 and 35 per cent in 1990. The formulation of such explicit quotas implies a form of affirmative action (or 'reverse discrimination') way beyond that which would be permitted in British law. In October 1988, the order was confirmed – for ten aircraft worth £60 million.

This brief resume of recent events in Northern Ireland has done little justice to the complexities of the situation and overlooked much that is of importance. Nor has it attempted a thoroughgoing comparison of the Northern Irish situation with Great Britain (see Jenkins 1988). It is, however, sufficient to allow a number of tentative conclusions to be drawn.

The first conclusion, and perhaps the most obvious, is that despite the strength of the state's administrative and legal response to ethnic disadvantage in Northern Ireland, there is no guarantee that it will actually make much difference. If for no other reason, the depth of recession and economic depression in Northern Ireland places severe limitations upon the possibilities for equality of opportunity (O'Dowd 1986). The interaction of patterns of residential segregation with patterns of industrial location serves to further disadvantage the Catholic community. The equal opportunity situation may be exacerbated by other dimensions of government policy; there is, for example, little gain to be had from greater equality or opportunity in Shorts if the company's operations contract drastically as a consequence of privatisation and the withdrawal of state support. There is, in addition, much opposition to the new package of measures within Northern Ireland, particularly from Unionist and loyalist political constituencies. Inasmuch as the new emphasis on equal opportunity is both less radical than demanded by the MacBride Principles and part of a 'carrot and stick' approach which embraces a tougher line on security and policing, militant republicans are not likely to be impressed either. Finally, there is always a legitimate doubt as to whether the state's commitment to equality of opportunity is genuine or just another exercise in symbolic politics; a serious attempt to produce change or merely window-dressing.

The second conclusion is that, while it is undoubtedly true that the progress which has been made so far in Northern Ireland could have major implications for the rest of the UK, it need not necessarily lead to concomitant changes in Great Britain. Such an outcome is, in fact, unlikely, for a number of reasons. There is, for example – as the use of proportional representation in elections in Northern Ireland illustrates – no reason why radical change in one part of the United Kingdom should 'leak' into another. Northern Ireland is routinely viewed as so utterly different from Great Britain that no necessary political lessons for the mainland are perceived to flow from what happens there (except, of course, when it suits, as in the area of security and anti-terrorism measures). This is all the more so if, as seems likely, the Northern Irish equality of opportunity measures are part of a strategy, commencing with the Anglo-Irish Agreement, which has as its long-term goal the 'solution' of the Northern Ireland problem (and from Westminster's point of view, this probably means divesting itself of responsibility for the province). On top of all of these considerations, the Conservative Party is unlikely to allow any legislative leakage in this area – Tory backbenchers are unhappy about the proposals in their Northern Irish context, let alone in Great Britain.

Finally, the role of the struggle of the Catholic community – a struggle which has embraced a wide range of options, from constitutional politics to non-violent protest to political violence – is worth considering. While this struggle has been significant in re-establishing Ireland as a political problem for the UK, it has only been influential with respect to economic disadvantage and equality of opportunity insofar as it has been able to mobilise the support of powerful external constituencies, particularly in the United States, although the importance of the Republic of Ireland in the European setting should not be underestimated. Similarly, the possibility of an eventual territorial settlement of the problem has also influenced the ability of struggle to make a difference. It should not be forgotten, however, that reform with respect to equal opportunity in Northern Ireland has been accompanied by ever-more repressive security policies.

All of these things have implications for the potential which the struggles of Britain's black communities have for effecting change, as does the fact that Northern Ireland's Catholics are proportionately more numerous than black Britons and, therefore, capable of being more troublesome. To put it quite simply, while the political struggles of Catholics in Northern Ireland have resulted in legislative and administrative reforms designed to promote greater equality of opportunity, they have also resulted in greater legal and administrative repression. In the British context, however, the more limited struggles of black people, while they may be met by repression, are unlikely to generate further reform. The shame is that, in the face of the state's present intransigence with respect to ethnic equality of opportunity in Great Britain, this may be the only avenue open to black people.

Future prospects

Finally, as we move closer to the 1990s, what of the prospects for the future? Certainly the experience of the past decade makes it difficult to be optimistic about the chances of a radical change in public policy on this issue. As the predominant political ideas have shifted to the right, so the probability of the required political action at the national level to tackle the roots of racism and social disadvantage has diminished. At the same time the fundamental changes in the functions of local government which the Thatcher governments have introduced make it more difficult for local authorities to intervene positively to promote racial justice. The situation, however, is by no means static. The frequency of outbreaks of urban unrest during the 1980s indicates that the continued exclusion of black communities and other inner city residents may result in the repudiation of political authority, manifest as civic indifference, as a refusal to comply with laws and directives or as open conflict and violence. While the excluded black and white citizens of urban areas seem set to continue to suffer deprivations and injustice, it cannot be assumed that they will do so in silence.

References

Arthur, P. and Jeffery, K. 1988, *Northern Ireland Since 1968*. Oxford: Basil Blackwell.

Benyon, J. and Solomos, J. 1987, *The Roots of Urban Unrest*, Oxford: Pergamon.

Commission for Racial Equality 1988, *Annual Report 1987*, London: CRE.

Cormack, R. and Osborne, R.D. 1987, 'Fair shares, fair employment: Northern Ireland today', *Studies*, Autumn, 1987: 273–85.

1989, 'Employment and Discrimination in Northern Ireland', *Policy Studies*, 9 no. 3:49–53.

Department of Economic Development 1986, *Equality of Opportunity in Northern Ireland: Future Strategy Options – A Consultative Paper*, Belfast: HMSO.

Department of Environment 1988, *Action for Cities*, London: Department of Environment.

Equal Opportunities Unit 1986, *First Report – Equal Opportunities in the Northern Ireland Civil Service*, Belfast: Department of Finance and Personnel.

1987, *Second Report*, Belfast: Northern Ireland Civil Service Equal Opportunities Unit.

Fair Employment Agency 1983, *Report of an Investigation ... into the Non-Industrial Civil Service for Northern Ireland*, Belfast: FEA.

Gordon, P. 1989, *Citizenship For Some? Race and Government Policy 1979–1989*, Runnymede Trust, London.

House of Commons, *Employment Committee 1987, Discrimination in Employment: Report and Minutes of Evidence*, London: HMSO.

Jenkins, R. 1988, 'Discrimination and equal opportunity in employment: ethnicity and "race" in the United Kingdom', in D. Gallie (ed.), *Employment in Britain*, Oxford, Basil Blackwell.

McCormack, I. 1987, 'The long, long march from '68', *Fortnight*, 257, December 1987: 16–18.

McCrudden, C. 1987, 'The Commission for Racial Equality', in R. Baldwin and C. McCrudden (eds.), *Regulation and Public Law*, London: Weidenfeld and Nicolson.

1989, 'One step forward, two steps back', *Fortnight*, 270, December 1989:14–15.

Miller, R. 1986, 'Social stratification and mobility', in P. Clancy, S. Drudy, K. Lynch and L. O'Dowd (eds.), *Ireland: A Sociological Profile*, Dublin: Institute of Public Administration.

1988, 'Evaluation Research "Ulster Style" ', *Network*, 42, October 1988: 4–7.

1989, 'Legislating for Fair Employment', *Journal of Social Policy*, 18:253–264.

Northern Ireland Office 1988, *Fair Employment in Northern Ireland*, Cmnd 380, London: HMSO.

O'Dowd, L. 1986, 'Beyond Industrial Society', in P. Clancy, S. Drudy, K. Lynch and L. O'Dowd (eds.), *Ireland: A Sociological Profile*, Dublin: Institute of Public Administration.

Richmond, D. 1987, 'Discrimination: the politics', *Fortnight*, 257, December 1987: 15–16.

Smith, D.J., 1988, 'Policy and Research: Employment discrimination in Northern Ireland', *Policy Studies*, 9 no 1:41–59.

Smith, D.J. and Chambers, G. 1987, *Equality and Inequality in Northern Ireland*, London: Policy Studies Institute.

Solomos, J. 1989, *Race and Racism in Contemporary Britain*, London: Macmillan.

Standing Advisory Commission on Human Rights 1987, *Religious and Political Discrimination and Equality of Opportunity in Northern Ireland: Report of Fair Employment*, Cmnd 237, London: HMSO.

Stoker, G. 1988, *The Politics of Local Government*, London: Macmillan.

Contributors

PETER BRAHAM lectures in the Faculty of Social Sciences at The Open University. Author of a number of papers on race relations, migration and discrimination and disadvantage in employment. Co-editor of *Discrimination and Disadvantage in Employment* (Harper & Row 1981).

MALCOLM CROSS is Principal Research Fellow at the Centre for Research in Ethnic Relations, University of Warwick. He has written widely on race relations, migrant labour, unemployment, youth training and economic restructuring in the inner cities. Co-author of a forthcoming book on *Race and the Urban System* and co-editor of a book on *Black Youth and YTS*.

JOHN DARBY is Professor of Social Administration and Policy at the University of Ulster in Coleraine. He is also Director of the Centre for the Study of Conflict, which defines his general research interest. He has written two books – *Conflict in Northern Ireland*, Gill and Macmillan (Dublin) 1976, and *Dressed to Kill: Cartoonists and the Northern Irish Conflict*, Appletree Press (Belfast) 1983 – and edited two books – *Violence and the Social Services in Northern Ireland* (with Arthur Williamson) Heinemann 1978, and *Northern Ireland, the Background to the Conflict*, Appletree and Syracuse University Press 1983.

RICHARD JENKINS is Senior Lecturer in the Department of Sociology and Anthropology, University College, Swansea. Among his publications are *Hightown Rules* (National Youth Bureau, 1982), *Lads, Citizens and Ordinary Kids* (Routledge and Kegan Paul, 1983), *Racism and Recruitment* (Cambridge University Press, 1986), *Taking the Strain* (with Sue Hutson, Open University Press, 1980) and *The Myth of the Hidden Economy* (with Phil Harding, Open University Press, 1989).

NICK JEWSON is a Lecturer in the Department of Sociology, University of Leicester. Recently he has been conducting research, in collaboration with David Mason, into 'racial' and gender inequalities in the labour market. He also has a long standing interest in the sociology of health.

GLORIA LEE is Director of Postgraduate Studies in the Management Centre, Aston University. Author of a number of papers on discrimination in the labour market, the position of young blacks in the labour market, and trade unions and racism. Co-author of *Skill Seekers – black youth, apprenticeships and disadvantage* (National Youth Bureau 1983).

LAURENCE LUSTGARTEN is Senior Lecturer in Law at Warwick University, where he has been teaching a course in Race Relations Law of his own devising for the last decade. He is the author of *Legal Control of Racial Discrimination* (Macmillan 1980), a policy orientated analysis of British anti-discrimination legislation, and of the recently-published *The Governance of Police* (Sweet and Maxwell 1986).

DAVID MASON is a Lecturer in the Department of Sociology, University of Leicester. He has a long standing interest in the sociology of 'race' and recently has been conducting research, in collaboration with Nick Jewson, into 'racial' and gender inequalities in the labour market.

ED RHODES lectures in the Faculty of Technology at The Open University. Has written widely on discrimination and disadvantage in employment, migration and employment, and the impact of the recession on black workers. Co-editor of *Discrimination and Disadvantage in Employment* (Harper & Row 1981).

JOHN SOLOMOS is a Lecturer in Public Policy in the Department of Politics and Sociology at Birkbeck College, University of London. He has edited *The Roots of Urban Unrest* (Pergamon 1987) and has recently published *Black Youth, Racism and the State* (Cambridge University Press 1988).

JOHN WRENCH is a Senior Research Fellow at the Centre for Research in Ethnic Relations, University of Warwick. From 1976 to 1980 he was a lecturer in the Sociology Group, Aston University; from 1980 to 1983, Lecturer in Aston University Management Centre. He has researched and published in the areas of industrial safety, ethnic minorities and the labour market, shiftworking, and trade unions and equal opportunity policies. He is currently working on a study of ethnic minorities and the careers service.

KEN YOUNG is Professor of Local Government Studies and Director of INLOGOV at the University of Birmingham. Author of numerous studies of the politics of local government, inner city policies and race and the local state. Co-author of *Policy and Practice in the Multi-Racial City* (Policy Studies Institute 1981) and co-editor of *Ethnic Pluralism and Public Policy* (Heinemann 1983).

Acknowledgements

This collection is the product of a two-day workshop concerned with the issue of equal opportunity in employment, which the editors organised at the SSRC Research Unit on Ethnic Relations at the University of Aston in Birmingham in July 1983. We are grateful to the Unit, and its then Director, Professor John Rex, for financial support and subsequent encouragement for this venture.

Since the workshop, a number of problems have delayed the final publication of this volume. First, one of us, Jenkins, left the Unit in September 1983 to take up an appointment elsewhere. Second, as a result of the workshop a number of areas which we had neglected were identified; papers specifically concerned with these topics had then to be commissioned. Third, one erstwhile contributor withdrew his contribution immediately before the (then) deadline and a replacement contributor had to be found. Fourth, a couple of contributors delayed their contributions, due to the pressures of their own work. Finally, there were unfortunate delays during the book's production process which were beyond our control. All in all, an editor's task is thankless and fraught with complications. However, despite the time lapse between the initial preparation and final publication of many of the papers, we have made every effort to ensure that, where necessary, information has been updated. As a consequence, we are confident that the usefulness of the collection has not been reduced.

Finally, we owe a heartfelt debt of gratitude to the support staff of the Centre for Research in Ethnic Relations at Warwick, who prepared the manuscripts for publication. Without the unstinting work of Rose Goodwin and Gurbakhsh Hundal, in particular, our task would have been even more difficult.

Richard Jenkins
John Solomos

16 January 1987

PART ONE

The law, politics and equal opportunity

1

Racism, equal opportunity and public policy

JOHN SOLOMOS AND RICHARD JENKINS

In the winter of 1982/3, faced with the possibility of doing research into equal opportunity policy and employment, the editors of this volume began to search the literature relating to the topic. It immediately became apparent that, although much research had been and was continuing to be done, there was a need to co-ordinate the findings and arguments of different researchers and commentators, and to relate them one to the other. With this end in mind a workshop concerned with these issues was organised at the SSRC Research Unit on Ethnic Relations at the University of Aston in Birmingham in July 1983. All the papers included in this volume, with the exception of three, were presented at the workshop and have been revised – in many cases extensively – for publication. The exceptions are the contributions from Malcolm Cross, Nick Jewson and David Mason, and John Wrench, which have since been prepared specifically for this volume.

Defining the issues

Terms such as 'equality of opportunity', 'equality of access', 'anti-discrimination policies' etc., have gained a wide currency over the last few years. So much so, that there is much confusion and unease about what each of these terms means, and, perhaps more fundamentally, what kind of objectives they are supposed to fulfil. Although most investigators agree about many of the 'facts' of racial and ethnic inequality, there seems to be little agreement about what should be done by government and other bodies to help break down racially discriminatory barriers in the main areas of economic and social life. Let us take the present situation in relation to unemployment as an example.

3

According to a wide variety of sources, black workers are more likely t
suffer from unemployment than white workers and, moreover, to fac
greater problems in finding new jobs once they become unemployed (Smit
1981; Rhodes and Braham 1981 and in this volume). In addition, there is b
now a substantial amount of evidence which underlines the parlous employ
ment situation faced by black youngsters (particularly those of West India
origin) in many of the inner city areas in Britain (Brooks 1983; CR
1983a). As the employment situation has deteriorated since the late 1970s
a proliferation of measures by government, race relations agencies an
private and public employers have attempted to increase equality of oppor
tunity for minority workers in the labour market. Although many of thes
initiatives are fairly recent and therefore difficult to analyse at the level c
effectiveness, it is possible to argue that they share the following (ofte
unstated) objectives within the over-arching concept of *equality o
opportunity*:

(a)   To break down direct and indirect barriers of discrimination whos
        outcome is to stop the entry of black workers into certai
        occupational categories, industries, factories, etc.

(b)   To help strengthen the career prospects of black workers wh
        already occupy certain occupational positions at the bottom run
        of the employment ladder.

(c)   To help management to manage workforces which are multi-racia
        in composition but which have no channels of control an
        representation which cover the whole 'multi-racial workforce'.

(d)   To help black workers (particularly the unemployed or those wit
        language difficulties) to obtain training in order to enable them t
        compete for jobs more equally.

(e)   To educate white workers about 'race' and in this way increas
        levels of communication and reduce conflict among black an
        white workers.

A recent document from the Commission for Racial Equality (CRE)
entitled *Implementing Equal Employment Opportunity Policies*
mentions all these possible rationalisations for private and publi
employers developing equal opportunity policies, while arguing that tw
further criteria should be taken into account:

(f)   The need to take into account and satisfy the legal obligation
        which employers face under the 1976 Race Relations Act.

(g)   The need to facilitate the integration of groups in the minority
        community which are especially disadvantaged and ar
        increasingly seen as unemployable (CRE 1983b: 1–2).

Recent studies of employers' attitudes towards equal opportunity initiatives at company level would seem to lend support to the argument that the pursuit of 'equal opportunity' is not reducible to one or other of these factors, and that managerial ideologies use a wide variety of rationalisations for the adoption of 'race' as a strategic issue in personnel management (Hitner *et l.* 1982; Jenkins 1986 and in this volume).

However, as Feuchtwang has pointed out, an inherent difficulty in studying managerial strategies in relation to the pursuit of equality of opportunity is the gap between *formal statements*, which have a symbolic value, and strategies of *implementation*, which are capable of transforming long-established channels of recruitment, channels of promotion and stereotypes of what constitutes a 'good worker' (Feuchtwang 1982: 284). Although policy formulation and implementation are perhaps most accurately conceptualised as different aspects of the same process, to confuse formal statements with practical implementation may mean overlooking the fact that what appears to be a good policy on equal opportunity is in fact nothing more than a paper commitment, which creates an image of success while changing little in terms of discriminatory practices. In his contribution to this volume, Jenkins has made a broadly similar distinction between equal opportunity *statements* and *programmes*, both of which fall within the category *policy*.

The gap between formal policy initiatives and implementation was noted by Kushnick as long ago as 1971, in one of the early studies of the effectiveness of race relations policies. Referring to the need to link policy changes to transformations in political attitudes and action he argued forcefully that:

> To be effective, anti-discrimination legislation cannot operate in a vacuum. It must be accompanied by positive governmental programmes designed to eliminate the social problems which cause and exacerbate racial prejudice, which, in turn, justifies discrimination. This prejudice must also be countered by political leadership from the leaders of the land. (Kushnick 1971: 236)

Yet, over a decade later, one of the recurring themes in discussions of the impact of equal opportunity initiatives is the relative weakness of administrative and political action in support of legal methods of implementation (Bindman 1980; Cross 1982; Little and Robbins 1982). This is not to say that successive governments since 1965 have not committed themselves publicly to the objective of ensuring more equality of opportunity for black workers in employment. Such public pronouncements have not, however, resulted in many actual commitments at central-government level to the enforcement of anti-discrimination legislation. Rather, what has happened is that successive governments have left the task of enforcing legislative measures in the hands of quasi-governmental bodies. This brings us back to the contradiction between strong policy statements and weak policy programmes.

Several difficult and controversial issues arise in this context. Although it seems quite implausible to interpret all government actions in this area as pre-ordained to fail, or as mere symbolic measures which are not meant to succeed, there are a number of awkward questions which confront us in looking at the current state of the art in relation to anti-discrimination policies. What are the assumptions which underlie current policies in relation to racial discrimination in employment? Are such assumptions a realistic assessment of the actual processes through which discrimination takes place? To what extent do legislative measures have an impact on the operation of discriminatory practices in the labour market? If racial inequalities flow, in part, from power disparities in society as a whole, how can policies work without some redistribution of power in favour of the minority communities?

In considering possible alternative responses to these questions, a host of problems have emerged. For example, researchers and practitioners do not concur on what they mean by such terms as 'equality of opportunity' or what they consider to be evidence of a move towards the stated goals of policies. Some writers argue, for example, that it seems unreasonable to see race relations policies as a way of reducing racial inequalities in British society, because the immigration laws passed by successive governments since 1962 actually divide citizens on racial grounds and serve to categorise and stereotype black communities as alien to British society. Others argue that the pursuit of 'equality of opportunity' may do little more than shift public attention away from the ways in which deeper economic and class inequalities are reproduced, which because of discrimination have a specific impact on blacks (Freeman and Spencer 1978; Lea 1980).

What these disputes tell us is that the study of these issues is by no means based on value-free criteria; research in this area is, of necessity perhaps, imbedded in judgements, feelings and reactive responses about what constitutes the 'public good' in the area of race relations. We cannot decide, for instance, whether or not 'equality of opportunity' is being achieved until the assumptions on which this concept is based are clarified and made public. The papers included in this volume have been chosen because they attempt to shed light on the complex issues that have arisen about the success or failure of attempts to secure 'equality of opportunity' in employment. A guiding theme that runs through the papers is the need to strengthen and sharpen the legal and political commitment to the pursuit of greater equality for all, regardless of ethnic or racial background.

Power, equality and anti-discrimination policies

In organising the workshop during which the papers included in this volume were presented, the questions raised above were the main issues that contributors sought to cover and this is reflected in the recurrence of certain themes in all the papers. But our purpose in this volume goes beyond providing substantive material on the dynamics of the legal, political and organisational responses to racial discrimination. Our further intent is to explore a set of issues which commonly go under the broad heading of equality of opportunity, unpack the often contradictory meanings attached to this notion and broaden the terms of debate which dominate current political and policy debate on this question.

Perhaps we can exemplify at least one aspect of this objective in more concrete terms. In a number of recent documents the CRE has called for a strengthening of its powers to implement the 1976 Race Relations Act, as well as a revision of the Act itself; it has done this while accepting that attempts to reduce indirect discrimination since 1977 have not been as successful as may originally have been intended (CRE 1982, 1983c, 1985). Yet even if we accept this demand for more adequate powers for the CRE as one of the conditions for a more forceful pursuit of the fight against indirect forms of institutionalised racism, can it be assumed that such an increase in powers will produce the fundamental changes in employment practices which will allow black workers to participate in the labour market on equal terms with white workers? The assumption that a stronger legal framework may be able to control the prevalent forms of indirect discrimination more efficiently may well turn out to be true, but will such control mean that the actual discriminatory practices will be transformed on a permanent basis?

Another element of current debates which this volume is intended to clarify is the conceptual confusion that underlies the notions used to describe current policy objectives, whether it be 'equality of opportunity', 'equality of access', 'anti-discrimination', 'anti-racism' etc. The very plurality of categories used in current debates would seem to indicate that the objectives being pursued are by no means clear and are in fact essentially contested notions. This gives rise to serious problems in discussing the problems of implementing policies, since the objectives being pursued are necessarily subject to political debate and give rise to strong feelings, either in favour or opposition. In addition, the very vagueness of the objectives being pursued can give rise to quite disparate assessments of how successful particular initiatives have been, since the notion of a 'successful' policy implies that it has achieved, or indeed is capable of achieving, a finite set of objectives.

A good example of the current confusion surrounding issues of this nature can be found in the manner in which the notion of equal opportunity has been applied by the Manpower Services Commission (MSC) in relation to the young black unemployed. The Commission's annual report for 1981–82 accepts that there is a wealth of evidence to show that minority workers have been particularly hard-hit by unemployment. It continues by saying 'In providing services (to ethnic minorities) the Commission's approach has been to maintain and facilitate equality of access by all groups and to establish a number of programmes which deal with particular labour market needs, such as those of ethnic minorities' (MSC 1982: para. 5.25). In practical terms, 'equality of access' (which is used interchangeably with equality of opportunity) has been defined by the MSC as (a) the avoidance of discrimination on its training programmes and (b) the provision of special help to minority youth who have 'special needs' (e.g. language problems or other educational disadvantages). What the outcome of such equality of access might be, however, is nowhere adequately defined. Neither do we have an analysis of how the development of equal access to training schemes can help young blacks get jobs in the labour market. At a minimum, the promise of equal access to all types of training provision – and there is substantial evidence to show that such equality is not being practised – means little unless it is clear to what it actually refers. Does it mean the recruitment of large numbers of young blacks to MSC schemes to 'keep them off the streets', the provision of special or remedial treatment, or an attempt to ensure *equality of outcomes* between white and black participants on training schemes? Systematic confusion between these (potentially contradictory) sets of objectives may actually harm the interests of young blacks rather than advance them.

The chapters in the first part of the book by Lustgarten, Solomos and Darby, are intended to clarify issues of this sort. Taken together, they seek to clarify the inter-connectedness between the assumptions on which policies against discrimination are based, to elucidate the reasons why policies have been so limited in their effectiveness, and to explore the linkages between the legal framework on which they are based and the political context in which they are framed.

Lustgarten argues that, over the last two decades, governments have limited themselves to legislation which aims to provide equal opportunity on the basis of protecting individual rights and imposing proscriptive requirements – rather than positive prescriptions – on private employers. No significant advance towards racial equality has been made or will be forthcoming, Lustgarten contends, as long as a legal approach remains the main plank of governmental action. His own alternative would be an approach largely dependent upon *administrative* interventions by central government. While not ignoring the role of legal sanctions against discrimination, he argues that policy changes must be premised on more positive commitments and initiatives by central-government departments and related agencies.

In the concluding section of his chapter, Lustgarten qualifies his argument by admitting that it is not easy to see how, or by what political mechanisms, his 'administrative approach' could be put into practice. He notes, for example, that governments have so far shown a preference (for immediate political reasons) to be seen to be doing something highly visible rather than undertaking more long-term administrative changes. This argument is central to Solomos's chapter on the politics of anti-discrimination policies, in which he explores more explicitly the limits and possibilities of equal opportunity policies in the context of the unequal distribution of power in advanced capitalist societies. It is important to note here that Solomos is not simply arguing that political power relations impinge upon equal opportunity policies. More fundamentally, he contends that the policies pursued by successive governments have been internally contradictory, combining a normative legal framework with largely symbolic political commitments. This nexus between legal reform and symbolic politics, if true, helps to explain just why governments have felt the need to promise greater racial equality but have been unable to deliver the goods.

Darby adds an extra dimension to the papers in this volume by providing a careful analysis of the attempts by the Northern Ireland Fair Employment Agency to overcome discrimination on the basis of religious ethnicity. He argues that any adequate assessment of the Agency's role must expose the complex nature of the tasks which it is supposed to fulfil, the difficult political environment within which it works and the imbalance between the economic and political power of the ethnic groupings in Northern Ireland. Moreover, he suggests that the Agency by itself cannot be expected to eliminate discrimination or to deliver equality of opportunity. He suggests that this is an objective which is beyond the power of a small, and to some extent marginal, government agency.

If the chapters in Part One lay the groundwork for examining the basic assumptions on which anti-discrimination policies are based and explaining why implementation in practice has been so limited, those in Part Two exemplify the importance and difficulty of analysing the actual development of equal opportunity policies in a number of crucial areas of employment. All the chapters in this part attempt to link the development of policy packages to the specific networks and institutional contexts in which they are situated.

The first chapter, by Cross, provides a critical and timely analysis of equal opportunity initiatives for the young black unemployed. Questioning the traditional wisdom on equal opportunity and presenting detailed empirical data about the training schemes operated by the Manpower Services Commission, Cross argues that there is an inherent confusion in them between the concepts of 'equal opportunity' and 'special needs'. Exploring the rationale of recent initiatives connected with the Youth Training Scheme and the contradictory meanings attached to them, he argues that there is a substantial gap between the stated objectives and the actual outcomes, the policy statements and the programme. In addition, he shows that within the ideology of the Manpower Services Commission there is a tendency to explain high levels of unemployment among young blacks by reference to personal and communal handicaps. This has the effect of marginalising the question of racism, which receives little or no attention, and prioritising those 'disadvantages' which are seen as growing out of minority cultures themselves. It is not accidental therefore, Cross argues, that the reality of 'equal opportunity' does not always live up to the promise.

Young sketches in the complexities of analysing the development of equal opportunity within local authorities, pointing in particular to the intricate web of organisational and professional issues which must be integrated into any coherent policy framework. In Young's view (and here he represents an important and growing strand of thinking) local authorities can become a vital channel for the promotion of equality of opportunity in employment. Drawing upon research carried out over a number of years in a sample of local authorities he shows that there is no single route to equal opportunity at the local level; in fact there is a wide variety of responses from local authorities to the challenge of race as a political issue. After analysing some of the reasons for this variation, Young develops a typology of models of response which attempts to show that the future development of equal opportunity policies at the local level will depend on local circumstances, pressures and decisions as well as the national political context.

Jenkins builds upon the discussion of the manner in which equal opportunity policies work in practice by means of a case study of private sector responses and initiatives. Taking as his starting point the complexity of motives and rationalisations underlying equal opportunity policies in the private sector, he contends that in practice most of these initiatives do not often originate as carefully worked-out managerial strategies, but are the outcome of a variety of internal and external pressures. While not denying that, in some cases, there may be managerial pressure to tackle discrimination on moral grounds, his emphasis is on the organisational, professional and political pressures that have forced equal opportunity onto the management agenda. Drawing upon research relating to a large employer in the

West Midlands and published research about other organisations, he analyses the subtle and often contradictory pressures which help to shape an equal opportunity policy and limit its effectiveness.

Central to the successful implementation of any initiative aimed at equalising the opportunities realistically available to black and white workers – or, indeed, women and men – is the need to monitor and evaluate the effects of the procedural changes which are introduced. This issue is raised in the contribution by Jewson and Mason. They suggest, for example, that the increased formalisation of employment procedures can, in fact, have the opposite effect to that which is intended, by providing a further organisational smokescreen behind which discrimination can operate. In addition, they highlight the differing conceptions of 'equal opportunity' which are mobilised within employing organisations: it is conflict between these different models which is, in part, responsible for some of the difficulties attendant upon the formulation and implementation of equal opportunity policies.

Training is an issue which has received much attention recently. In particular, the role that training can play in the development of equal opportunity strategies has been the subject of debate. Distinguishing between training which caters specifically for black workers and training in race issues for white workers and managerial staff, Lee argues that both forms are likely to play a major role in industry over the coming decade. Drawing attention to the relatively recent development of 'race awareness training', which has gained particular prominence since the Scarman report of 1981, she argues that there are real problems in trying to assess the effectiveness of such training in counteracting racism. Not the least of these problems is the question of how far a greater awareness of racism can actually change institutional and systematic forms of discrimination. While Lee agrees that training by itself cannot eliminate racism, she argues forcefully that it can play a vital role in sensitising public opinion and contributing to wider efforts to combat racism.

While it is generally agreed that trade unions can play a major role in the promotion of equal opportunity, we know little about the actual attitudes and practices of unions on this issue. The importance of Wrench's paper is that he takes up the question of trade union participation in anti-discrimination policies and provides a detailed analysis of why unions have failed to help black workers. Beginning with a summary of official policy pronouncements, Wrench then explores the various reasons why unions have not taken effective action to promote equal opportunity in employment. Citing as examples the tendencies to see racism as somehow peripheral to trade union concerns and to blame black workers for having the 'wrong' attitudes towards union membership, he concludes that it may be too much to expect unions to take action on their own volition. He argues that pressure for change from black workers themselves may provide an important impetus in pushing unions to take an interest in this issue. Part Three consists of two chapters that sharpen the issues posed in the rest of the book. Rhodes and Braham provide a detailed analysis of the impact of the recession and high unemployment on black workers and draw some implications from this broader economic environment for the pursuit of equal opportunity. Advancing a critical analysis of the whole concept of equal opportunity, they argue that, however suited such measures are in a period of economic stability or expansion, in a context of economic recession it is less likely that governments and employers will pursue in a forceful manner measures to help minority workers. While this point is supported in a number of other papers in this volume, the value of this chapter is that it provides solid empirical evidence to substantiate an argument which is often taken for granted. In doing this, Rhodes and Braham are able to highlight a number of questions which will, perhaps, form the focus of future research.

In the concluding chapter the editors attempt to provide a summary of the shared themes to be found in the other papers and to discuss briefly the questions that arose from our discussions during the workshop. Taken together, these themes can be seen as emphasising the need to see equal opportunity as a national political issue of the first importance, and, moreover, as one which requires urgent action if we are to move away from tokenistic measures. In the context of the current recessionary environment, the quest for greater equality regardless of racial and ethnic origins faces many obstacles and must therefore proceed with a heightened awareness of the pitfalls and possibilities that confront it today. This is why, the editors conclude, we need more detailed research about the ways in which the promise of equal opportunity can become more of a reality.

Summary

The principle underlying this collection of papers is simple enough: The rigorous exploration of the assumptions implicit in public policy, the legal framework and the political–administrative channels of implementation, is the most promising route we can take in the search for plausible explanations of the achievements and limits of anti-discrimination policies. Perhaps there are several aspects of the landscape of equal opportunity initiatives which are inadequately analysed in the papers included in this volume. But this cannot be avoided. While there are, no doubt, many more questions which we could have discussed, some details and background issues have been sacrificed to provide an overview of the basic dimensions of equal opportunity policies and initiatives originating from both within and outside government.

In addition we hope that the papers included in this volume will challenge some widely held notions about the possibilities of reform in this area. In this way we hope that they may open up some fundamental questions for further theoretical and empirical debate. Hopefully the chapters which follow will allow some of these questions to be tackled on a firm basis of reliable research and informed analysis.

2

Racial inequality and the limits of law*

LAURENCE LUSTGARTEN

I

In writing the conclusion to *Legal Control of Racial Discrimination* I described the mood of the study as one of qualified pessimism (Lustgarten 1980: 253). I would now, five years on, delete the adjective. It seems fairly clear that the effect of the Race Relations Act 1976 (RRA) in diminishing racial inequality has been minimal, at best. This paper is an attempt to think about why that is so, and what more promising measures might be taken.

Confronted with compelling evidence of widespread racial discrimination and disadvantage, successive British Governments have made use of legal weapons as the primary means of attacking it. They have enacted legislation enabling sanctions to be invoked through the legal process against those found to have committed violations. The legal process can be mobilised either by an individual asserting the right not to be subject to discriminatory treatment or by a specially created administrative body acting either on behalf of an aggrieved individual[1] or exercising its own powers separately defined, by means of the so-called formal investigation. Except in the latter instance, the legislation has proceeded by altering the rights and obligations of private parties and treated discrimination as essentially a matter of private law. Discrimination has, in effect, been made into a specific statutory tort, a point recognised in the remedial provision of the act which explicitly draws the analogy (RRA 1976:s.57(1)).

Measuring the impact of any piece of legislation, or any particular social intervention, is notoriously difficult. None the less, the ineffectiveness of the RRA seems beyond doubt. Whether one looks at studies of the incidence of discrimination undertaken after it came into force (Hubbuck and Carter 1980), the rate of success of individual complaints,[2] the extent and influence of the enforcement efforts of the responsible administrative body, the Commission for Racial Equality (CRE),[3] or seeks evidence of *in terrorem* effects of the law on employers' behaviour,[4] the same conclusion is inescapable.

Several plausible reasons for this ineffectiveness can be suggested: incompetence of the CRE and of those who have represented complainants; unfamiliarity with the legislation in the early years of its existence, or hostility – outright or tacit – to its objectives, on the part of tribunals and judges;[5] and substantive defects, which are many and various, in the Act itself. Numerous specific suggestions for alteration and reform have been made (CRE 1983e).[6] Acting upon them might indeed make marginal improvements in enabling individuals to vindicate their statutory rights, or might enhance the effectiveness of the CRE. But perpetual patching up will not do: the problem goes very much deeper. Ultimately, it is embedded both in the nature of discrimination and in the nature of law, or at any rate of a legal system underpinned and structured at every level by the traditions and presuppositions of the common law.

Of course, the climate within which the law operates has become very much harsher in the past four or five years. There is now a great over-supply of labour and hence much more competition for jobs, which has given employers the whip hand. None the less, this is not the whole story. Promotion and training decisions continue to be made daily and some occupations, such as accountancy and computing, still take on many new entrants. There is less to go round but what does remain is shared out in grossly inequitable fashion. It is obvious that reforming legislation in this or indeed any other area in relation to employment is not on the present government's agenda. We are thus at an hiatus in the terms of reform. We stand at a convenient as well as a very necessary stopping point from which we can reflect upon the effectiveness of attempts in the 1960s and 1970s to protect weak groups in society by means of statute. Lawyers tend instinctively to propose legal changes as a cure for social ills. Yet law is only one form of intervention strategy and one, I believe it is increasingly clear, of limited effectiveness.

Regulation through legal mechanisms is also a process of which our understanding seems to be surprisingly sparse. There is virtually nothing in the voluminous social science literature purporting to address the problem of law and social change[7] which helps the reader understand how legal intervention in social relations actually works at the sharp end. It is imperative that we begin by recognising our ignorance. As a tentative step forward, it may be helpful to identify the various contexts within which legal regulation operates. This exercise may assist in the construction of something we need very badly – a theory of legal change. By 'legal change' I mean the imposition of a rule emanating from some organ of the state, including the judiciary, which requires individuals to act in a manner different from how they would have preferred to act, on pain of some sort of sanction; or, conversely, which enables them to act in a certain way without fear of adverse consequences that otherwise would have existed. A variant, which may be called a public-law type of legal change, involves the creation of some administrative entity with legal powers to do certain things within prescribed limits.

The various contexts within which legal change operates includes the following: First, where the legal system itself is so to speak the primary actor – as with criminal law, procedural rules, or custody and divorce – one would expect the clearest impact of legal change on behaviour, though even here that depends on how deeply the legal system itself penetrates the society. There are examples of colonial societies where the law of the occupying power was just a sort of icing on the cake. There are also instances of countervailing pressures within the legal system, such as judicial or jury resistance or non-co-operation by police or some other enforcing agency.

A second context is where the law seeks to regulate behaviour not directly related to the legal system by adjusting individuals' capacities to act. Legal change may impose or remove penalties for acting in a particular way, or enable certain legal relations to be created. There seem to be two distinct types of legal change here. The first may be called *facilitative*. A powerful group is freed from some imposed restriction or enabled to act in a certain way not previously permissible. Examples include the enclosure acts, creation of limited liability company, validation and recognition of the trust device, removal of equitable notions of contract law that had prohibited certain types of agreements, and changes in tax law to lessen or eliminate liability for some type of transaction. This type of intervention is likely to be relatively effective because the beneficiaries are enabled to carry on the preferred course of action without hindrance. They have the material power, need no assistance and will almost certainly be aware of the change and be capable of taking advantage of it. The second type may be called *protective*. It involves the creation of rights, which the weaker party can assert by means of litigation, in the traditional mode of private law. The protected person must invoke the legal process or the penalties must be so credible that the very existence of the law is a goad or a deterrent itself – the *in terrorem* effect.

For reasons I shall spend much of this paper trying to explain, protective legislation is much less effective. Put broadly, there are problems of mobilisation of the legal process that are severe, indeed debilitating, and do not arise with facilitative law. Three examples of this protective intervention by means of a rights or private-law approach are employment protection legislation generally, such as unfair dismissal and the other provisions of the Employment Protection (Consolidation) Act 1978, the Rent Acts, and anti-discrimination law. There is also public law intervention, which may take two forms. The first is where a state institution itself becomes the primary actor by directly providing a service, as with the creation of the National Health Service or compulsory schooling until a prescribed age. The law here, although occasionally giving rise to litigation, basically provides a structure within which bureaucracies operate. Legal considerations are not prominent in the actors' minds. The second is where the institution regulates, investigates or otherwise may direct or influence the operation of private entities.

I hope these analytical distinctions may prove helpful in exploring some of the problems that have emerged as the complex realities of racial inequality have had to be translated into legal concepts and otherwise wrenched, pressed, squeezed, pounded and torn to fit within the framework of English law.

II

In principle, cases of direct discrimination – adverse treatment on racial grounds – raise no novel issues for the function of legal adjudication. Facts must be found – or inferred – about specific past events involving a limited number of individuals, and in cases where the information is not directly available, the courts are accustomed to constructing presumptions or other devices so as not unduly to hinder the plaintiff's proving his case.[8] Indeed, they have done this in discrimination cases.[9] The formal burden of proof is not an insuperable obstacle. The real problem is the unsympathetic response of tribunals[10] – their unwillingness to draw inferences supporting complainants' claims. In the face of the ambiguity inevitable in such cases, they have tended to credit the respondents' explanations. This is a matter of political or personal predilection, not of legal incapacity.

Indirect discrimination, however is a very different matter. It makes unlawful those policies or practices which are not racist in intent but which have a disproportionate adverse effect upon a racial minority. In its present form it is a somewhat narrow and awkwardly phrased expression of the idea of institutional discrimination (Lustgarten 1980: 8–14; McCrudden 1982b: 303). As such it requires the courts to find 'social facts' about broader societal relationships – the socio-economic condition of ethnic *groups*, the working of labour markets, the employment practices of firms and industries, and the like. Courts in the United States, from which the concept of indirect discrimination was borrowed, have long experience with evaluating data of this type in the form of the so-called 'Brandeis brief', but this is an activity alien to the English courts and one with which, to judge from the reported cases, they feel profoundly uncomfortable. Racial disadvantage in the fullest sense is outside the law entirely. By 'racial disadvantage' I mean material, psychological or social inequalities, bearing disproportionately upon racial minorities. Examples are under-achievement in schooling, higher rates of unemployment, or residential concentration in decaying neighbourhoods. Discrimination is both a major element and a continuing long-term cause of disadvantage, but the latter has a self-perpetuating dynamic of its own and extends much wider and is the product of several additional and even less tangible influences.

The reason the law cannot extend to racial disadvantage is that no one is formally responsible. In law one needs an identifiable defendant who has done something, or to whom a decision can be imputed. There are therefore tight limits to what legal regulation can reach; at the least, some formally articulated or reasonably clear policy is required. This can be seen even in the much narrower area of litigation under the present statute: a significantly disproportionate number of reported cases[11] have involved public sector employers, who far more commonly than those in the private sector use published criteria, clearly enunciated rules and formal procedures in deciding upon hiring and promotion. Their decisions can thus be more readily subject to critical examination than idiosyncratic judgments made without reference to articulated standards or review of extensive personal documentation.

By definition, discrimination is the antithesis of individualised decision. A person is ill-treated, or shares some social circumstances, because of his involuntary membership of a group. There is, therefore, a collective dimen-sion to every discrimination case which is difficult to fit within the traditional processes of law. Adjudication in English law has conven-tionally proceeded by *individuation*: the realm of relevant evidence is marked with narrow boundaries, and the courts, whilst permitting represen-tative actions, have restricted the number of parties by the narrowness of the 'common interest' test of *Markt & Co. Ltd* v. *Knight Steamship Co. Ltd.*[12]

This individuation may be partly explicable in terms of managerial rationality – the need to keep litigation manageable in a judicial system that has minimal support services for judges and relies exclusively upon oral presentation of evidence and legal argument. But there is also an ideology at work – the exaltation of individualism by the common law. This underpins even quite technical rules of procedure, as in the rule that a third party cannot adduce evidence of even a central finding of fact in an action between the other parties with whom he is not privy,[13] or in the refusal to admit as evidence, let alone accord *res judicata* effect, to judgments against defendant facing a virtually identical claim from a different plaintiff (as in roduct liability cases); or even to enter judgment automatically in favour of ll plaintiffs in a successful representative action (Miller 1983). Discrimination law is hampered in several ways by individuation, but in one so important as the restrictions on the scope of remedies. These may e backward-looking (compensatory) or forward-looking (changes in iscriminatory policies and practices). Because all members of a minority roup will have been identically affected by the discrimination, it is reasonble that all such persons adequately qualified and shown to be affected be ccorded the same remedy as the individual who has won his particular ase. In the United States, this is accomplished by means of the class ction, but there is nothing magical about this particular procedural device; is quite conceivable that the representative action could be adapted to chieve the same result. The practical consequence is that an American mployer adjudged to have discriminated will face a large bill for compenation to all those within the class. It therefore often becomes cheaper and asier to obey the law: the employer is forced to bear the true cost of his legality because its effect is fully taken into account rather than measured nly in relation to the individual who has had the courage, persistence and atience to bring an action. This cost-maximising deterrence is not possible nder English law and its absence, by making discrimination cheap, irtually ensures the ineffectiveness of the rights approach.

An analogous point applies to forward-looking remedies. Although the tatute permits a so-called 'action recommendaton', it is merely a recmmendation, not an order. Moreover, it cannot extend to a matter that oes not affect the complainant personally. This is explicitly provided in the tatute,[14] with the consequence that if the evidence reveals that disriminatory policies have excluded black applicants, tribunals are not mpowered to order the employment of those who can be shown to have een victimised, let alone impose any sort of hiring targets based upon abour-market percentages. This again follows from the fact that legislation Britain accepts the assumptions and practices of common law, in this istance its long-standing refusal to order specific performance of the ontract of employment. The late Professor Kahn-Freund explained this ance as an application of the doctrine of mutuality: since the common law ould not recognise servitude, nor order any person to work for a given mployer, it followed that no employer could be compelled to engage any idividual (Kahn-Freund 1974). Interestingly, though a partial statutory cursion has been made into this principle by the reinstatement and rengagement provisions for those unfairly dismissed, these remedies – which re supposed to be primary – are hardly ever used (Dickens *et al.* 981).

The deadening influence of the common law is brought into sharp focus by a comparison with American civil rights law – federal legislation creating causes of action heard in federal courts. Apart from constitutional litigation, those courts concern themselves almost exclusively with interpretation of statute. They do not see that task as one of subtle linguistic analysis, nor do they locate statutes in relation to pre-existing *legal* rules. Rather they treat major statutes as blueprints of *social* policy. Hence they attempt to inform themselves fully about the social reality of the 'mischief', interpret substantive provisions broadly in light of that understanding – not in relation to the pre-existing common law – and even create new remedies in a purposive effort to effectuate the legislative aim. The legislation created a muscular skeleton, but the courts at all levels have put on the substantial flesh.

Moreover, the American Congress, unlike Parliament, has long since abandoned its subservience to the assumptions, values and doctrinal constraints of common law. The breakaway can be traced back as early as the creation of the remedy of treble damages in the anti-trust (restrictive practices) legislation of 1890, and has proceeded apace. In the present context, the most relevant example is the labour legislation in the 1930s, in which the Congress began using re-instatement as a protective remedy for those engaged in trade union activities. It consciously drew upon this precedent when fashioning the much broader remedies involving hiring members of the victimised class in the employment discrimination legislation of 1964.[15]

Another problem that has befallen anti-discrimination efforts in this country arises from the peculiar nature of English administrative law – again a reflection of the common law tradition. The CRE has been given virtually unique powers of enforcement, which combine investigation with the imposition of a sanction – the non-discrimination notice (RRA 1976: ss.58–9). It is not a very potent sanction, but its novelty lies in the fact that it is imposed by the investigative body itself, subject to challenge in the courts. The judiciary have ensnared the Commission in a spider's web of technicality only partly commanded by the language of the Act. They have taken a much more restrictive approach in comparison with, for example, the latitude they have permitted Department of Trade Inspectors under the Companies Act.[16] I think their attitude reflects a hostility to what they see as an unacceptable amalgamation of executive and judicial functions – the body conducting the fact-finding also issues the notice. In this instance they are not evincing hostility to discrimination legislation as such, but giving effect to an ingrained pattern of thinking about administrative powers. One can see a similar process at work in their attitude to the Civil Aviation Authority (CAA) as constituted in the 1970s. In a persuasive critique of the

Skytrain decision,[17] G. R. Baldwin pointed out that the CAA was a constitutional innovation deliberately designed as a body with considerable discretionary powers which would remain subordinate to central-government policies (Baldwin 1978). It was meant to combine what were traditionally understood as executive and judicial methods in a delicately balanced legal framework which the court simply failed to understand. An independent regulatory agency possessing the quasi-judicial power to issue injunctive-type orders and make rules at the same time is something readily familiar to lawyers in the United States and Canada but quite alien to the English courts, which are therefore unwilling to allow a body given such power by Parliament to exercise them in the way that was intended. Thus, both protective intervention to enhance rights of individuals, modifying private law, and the public-law creation of a novel mechanism of control have foundered badly on the conservatism of the common law.

I have examined features of discrimination and disadvantage which make it particularly difficult to use a private-law approach to combat them effectively, or indeed to fit comfortably within the traditional pattern of litigation. Additionally, however, there are several distinctive characteristics of legal expression and adjudication, independent of any particular legal culture, which lawyers tend to take for granted but which cumulatively present serious impediments to the effective use of law to implement social policy. I shall use illustrations drawn from discrimination litigation, but equally appropriate examples could be taken from any complex area, such as housing, industrial relations or planning.

Law demands specificity. It is not sufficient to argue that the defendant is within the spirit or broad policy canvas of the legislation. Unforeseen or marginal cases may fall out with the precise statutory language, as in the decisions holding that rent officers, JPs, and Youth Opportunity Programmes' (YOP) trainees, are not covered by the discrimination statutes,[18] or that language may be read in a wooden, literal way, as in the reading given the prohibition of victimisation.[19] Conversely, it may be argued that the plaintiff is not technically within the protected class even though he has undoubtedly suffered discrimination, as in the controversy over whether Sikhs are an 'ethnic group'.[20]

Legal process involves technical rules of procedure specified by statute or rule of court and, equally important, judicial notions of appropriate procedure grafted onto these. Each particular rule may be 'twisted' by the defendant, that is used to his advantage. This has been one of the main things plaguing the CRE in its formal investigations. 'Terms of reference' are required for each formal investigation and the House of Lords has held that these must be based on some specific evidence and that without such evidence the investigation is without statutory authority.[21] The practical import is to narrow the range of discriminatory practices into which, at least initially, the Commission may enquire. More seriously, the Court of Appeal has read the statute to permit the recipient of a non-discrimination notice to contest the findings of fact upon which the notice is based, notwithstanding Lord Denning's recognition that this might make the whole process so cumbersome that formal investigations would grind to a halt.[22] Use of the law involves skills which large-scale employers may be expected to command far more readily than complainants. Mark Galanter's well-known article, 'Why the "haves" come out ahead' (1974), which demonstrates the inherent advantages enjoyed by 'repeat players' over 'one-shot players' in litigation, goes a long way towards explaining both the relative ease with which discrimination claims have been defeated, and also the fact that individual complainants are more likely to be successful if they obtain aid from the CRE – itself a repeat player on the other side. The element of skill also means that each potential loophole will be explored in depth – or is it breadth? – delaying tactics adopted, and the like. This, as the saying goes, is standard operating procedure for good lawyers and partly accounts for the long delays in formal investigations which so exercised the House of Commons Select Committee in its heavily critical report on the CRE (Home Affairs Committee, Sub-Committee on Race Relations and Immigration 1981b). Yet short of forbidding alleged discriminators to defend themselves in a legal forum, these tactics cannot be curbed.

Legal decision and reasoning proceed by attempting, so far as seems possible, to draw clear lines and to resolve questions with finality by applications of an abstract rule or principle. Institutional discrimination and racial disadvantage require more subtle, long-term policies which must be capable of alteration as experience replaces conjecture and demographic and economic change alter the condition of ethnic minorities. In this area, primary reliance upon legal tools is like trying to etch figures in glass with a pickaxe.

Law merely imposes minimum standards. Compliance is satisfied by strict adherence to the letter; it is perfectly legal to do nothing more. If great areas of concern are outside the effective reach of the law – as I have argued is inevitably true of racial disadvantage – no one is under any legal responsibility to do anything about them. Moreover, emphasis upon defining minimal compliance may discourage developing and implementing more imaginative and innovative measures directed at the ultimate problem – racial inequality – and certainly channels attention to the narrow issues of achieving the least that is required.

Running in tandem with the previous point, legal regulation ultimately works in negative fashion; it imposes constraints, backed by penalties for non-compliance. Yet as a general principle of human psychology, it is anything but obvious that punishment, or its threat, is the most effective means of moulding behaviour. Carrots rather than sticks – or, perhaps, a judicious combination – are likely to prove more persuasive. In particular, financial inducements to profit-conscious employers are far more likely to overcome resistance and even stimulate voluntary innovation than the rather remote possibility of mild sanctions. A few strategically placed OBEs for managing directors of firms which take the lead in implementation of equal opportunities policies, or even Queen's Awards for Race Relations, would be worth their weight in gold-plated victorious tribunal decisions.

There is a final point to be made about the rights approach, particularly in the context of discrimination: from the government's point of view, it is cheap. It simply ignores the realities of racial disadvantage. It does nothing to assist in the development of human capital; thus for the most disadvantaged it is simply irrelevant. And the costs of enforcement are laid upon the victim. It is an expression of classical liberalism, albeit in an enlightened form, and its inadequacies expose the severe limitations of that tradition as the basis of social justice.

To conclude, an approach to discrimination that relies upon the use of negative legal sanctions for violation of rights created by statute can at best have modest impact as a means of eradicating discrimination, and virtually none upon the more pervasive and subtle manifestations of racial disadvantage. An invigorated administrative enforcement body would certainly be welcome. But to rely on law enforcement as the primary approach[23] seems to me an advance commitment to fighting the battle with one hand firmly tied behind one's back. This is not to deny the need for legislation, which remains essential as a pressure upon those activated by racial *animus*, or those who will not act without compulsion to remove unnecessary barriers to the fair evaluation of the competence of black workers. Legislation is also required to provide enabling legal support for the implementation of remedial policies discussed below. But it cannot by itself bring about any significant reduction of racial inequality.

III

It may be interesting to attempt a thought experiment, one which I fear will remain in the realm of pure thought for some time to come. It is to imagine a government genuinely and forcefully committed to equalising the conditions of ethnic minorities.[24] What would be its priorities and its methods?

For reasons already suggested, whilst strengthening the Race Relations Act would be one element in its strategy – especially since the damage done by judicial interpretation needs to be repaired – it would constitute only a secondary and supportive measure. The emphasis of such a government would be on an *administrative* approach – on the use of discretionary policies, rather than legal rules.[25] What follows is a schematic outline of what the critical elements of such a strategy would be.

First, every major policy decision would be vetted in advance for its impact on ethnic minorities. Key economic decisions, such as incentives for the establishment of new industries in particular areas or the level of construction of public sector housing to take but two, are of disproportionate importance to ethnic minorities, who are concentrated in declining inner areas, suffer high rates of unemployment and, in the case of West Indians and Bangladeshis, are disproportionately reliant on council accommodation. To take one important example, much recent growth has occurred in places where blacks are notably absent, like Milton Keynes, at the expense of inner city areas. This exacerbation of racial inequality might have been prevented by consideration of whether the area was likely to attract black settlers and, if not, what measures could be taken to encourage and assist reasonable numbers to venture there.

The fundamental point is that the ethnic dimension be considered an essential aspect of all such decisions. Creation of a race-specific administrative body is a recipe for marginalisation – a deflection of the responsibility that should be shouldered by those taking the critical decisions, which in present conditions are economic. If ethnic matters are the domain of a specialist body, even inside government, it will follow inevitably that the ethnic factor will become part of the decision process only at a later, reactive stage, and not at the critical point of initial policy formulation, when the issues are defined and the parameters drawn. Hence all government departments should impose upon designated high-level officials responsibility for this aspect of policy formulation and for monitoring the ethnic impact of policies at the stage of implementation. More broadly, a cabinet committee chaired by a senior minister should be established for the same purposes.

One consequence of this enhanced role of government is alteration of the role of the Commission for Racial Equality. It need no longer be an all-purpose body purportedly representing the interests of ethnic minorities. It would be freed to direct its energies primarily to law enforcement and to training others, workers in citizens advice bureaux and law centres, trade union officials and social workers, in the intricacies of representing individual complainants. It might also assume the role of a watchdog overseeing the effectiveness of remedial action policies adopted by central government, which no other organisation presently on the horizon is as well positioned to fill.

Another critical area is use of government's economic power, notably as a purchaser of goods and services. This has become known as contract compliance and has had measurable impact on achieving widening of employment opportunities for blacks in the United States (Freeman 1983). It has been little used in Britain, although some efforts have been made recently by the Greater London Council and West Midlands County Council to use this power. In order to be accepted and remain on the approved list for doing business with government, the supplier must adopt a remedial-action policy which works toward employment of black people at all levels of his workforce in proportion to their presence in the local labour market. Periodic reports detailing efforts made and progress recorded must be filed and employment records must be open to inspection by officials of the relevant department. If good-faith efforts are not undertaken, a term is included in the contract permitting cancellation by the government purchaser; if extra cost is thereby incurred, this must be paid by the contractor who has failed to comply with the contractual term. A similar though less rigorous device was an important element in the counter-inflation strategy of the mid-1970s. Whilst it raises hackles among lawyers raised in the spirit of Dicey (Daintith 1979; Elliott 1978; Ganz 1978), that can hardly be the measuring rod of the validity of social policy.

Finally, there is the role of central government as employer. In this category I include the nationalised industries and the National Health Service (the nation's largest single employer) which can be effectively controlled by government through formal or 'nod-and-wink' directions and by financial measures. Here, again, I can only sketch the outline of an effective remedial-action policy in employment that could be implemented by central government forthwith. New legislation is not required; what has been missing for years in successive governments is the political will to use what already rests in the statute book. This inaction has undermined the credibility of all public pronouncements about racial equality. Central government is an employer on a massive scale. It is the one area where politicians proclaiming commitment to equal opportunities for racial minorities can have an immediate impact on employment practices. If political leaders can demonstrate the practicability of remedial-action policies and commitment to carrying them through, they can both provide a model for the private sector and local authorities and stand on firm moral and political ground when exhorting – or if eventually necessary, requiring – them to take similar steps. Impact, resources and strategic implications combine to make the performance of government in this sphere of paramount importance.

Two little-used sections of the Race Relations Act are central to remedial-action programmes. They are both exceptions or derogations from the moral principle and legal rule that is otherwise paramount in the Act: that race may not be used as a criterion of selection.[26] Section 38 permits employers to 'encourage' members of ethnic minority groups, and they alone, to apply for work. More important, it empowers employers to offer special training limited to some or all of their black employees for work in which racial minorities are disproportionately absent, relative either to their presence in that employer's work force or to the labour market from which he normally recruits. Blacks cannot be given a job on the basis of race, but whites may be excluded from the training programme, which may be run by the employer or on the basis of secondment. Section 37 is virtually identical, but applies to training bodies, notably the Manpower Services Commission and industrial training boards. They may establish courses restricted to minority groups where they are under-represented in a particular type of work throughout the whole of Great Britain or in any particular area; if the latter, preference is limited to blacks 'who appear likely to take up that work in that area'.

Within this permissive framework, the strategy of remedial action would seem to involve six major elements. None of them applies distinctively to central government; indeed, they apply identically to all large employers.[27]

Acknowledgement
The point of departure is the crashingly obvious one that explicit attention to the condition of racial minorities is a valid policy consideration. Yet the only study to investigate practice in this area found that very few local authorities had actually got this far by the end of 1980, and indeed that some had explicitly rejected doing so (Young and Connelly 1981). This was the position notwithstanding that local authorities have been singled out for special responsibility by Section 71, which places upon them a duty to 'make appropriate arrangements' to ensure that their various operations are carried out with a view to eliminating unlawful discrimination and promoting equality of opportunity. This attitude is now changing in many places, but remains influential, particularly in institutions less directly open to overt political pressure. A great deal remains to be done simply to ensure that those taking employment decisions accept that they have a responsibility in this area. Here the action of central government as being seen to take the lead is essential, but whilst the Department of the Environment has begun to speak sympathetically about ethnic monitoring in housing, the Civil Service as employer has done little more than a pilot ethnic headcount.

Information
It is obvious that policy formulation, implementation and evaluation cannot be conducted in the dark. An employer needs to know the ethnic dis-

tribution of his work force in relation to concentration in particular tasks, levels of skill and responsibility, evaluations by superiors, rates of rejection for upgrading and promotion, and the like. He also needs analogous information on rejected applicants. The best means by which to acquire this information without unnecessarily raising hackles and/or fears is open to debate, but the need for it is not.

Active recruitment

This involves tapping hitherto unexplored sources that are particularly likely to produce black candidates capable of meeting present standards. Examples would be adverts in the ethnic press; use of Job Centres; notification of vacancies to black organisations – e.g. the Indian Workers' Association, mosques, social clubs – even though they are not normally concerned with employment; and recruiting visits to particular schools with a high proportion of black pupils. In relation to the internal labour market, able blacks should be identified and encouraged to apply for promotion, secondment and other avenues of progress. In the long term pressures of the latter kind will be critical to real black advancement.

Dismantling barriers

Here action of two kinds is required: The first, perhaps simplest, is for the employer to make absolutely clear to all employees that direct discrimination or racial abuse is not to be tolerated and that verifiable instances of such behaviour will result in discipline and/or dismissal. So long as this position is stated clearly and consistently enforced and fair fact-finding procedures followed, there is no doubt that a dismissal under such circumstances would be held to be fair.

More difficult is the alteration of employment practices that effectively disadvantage racial minorities. Here one must decide, either on the basis of information gathered (as suggested above) or on more impressionistic evidence, which of the existing selection criteria and formal or informal arrangements that structure decisions about employment are working to the disadvantage of minorities.

Even more important in a time when employers have their pick of a crowded field of applications, is sceptical evaluation of hiring and promotions criteria. Requirements such as experience, maximum age and examination passes or other academic credentials are often not at all necessary for their possessors to do a particular job adequately. They may save the employer time by enabling him to weed out some of the surplus of candidates, but they are often not at all job-related and demonstrably work to the disadvantage of at least some minority groups. That they are unnecessary can be seen by the fact that in the past couple of years employers have begun to raise the stakes, particularly with respect to educational credentials for initial entrants. This is not because the nature of the job has changed, but because it is a simple rationing device to screen out some of the excess of candidates – people who years before in a buoyant labour market would have been quite acceptable. Indeed, someone who learned a trade 20 years ago may well be less suited to carry out a particular job than someone who has learned it more recently but informally; one reason to be sceptical of the necessity of many apprenticeship qualifications. Similarly with experience requirements, which can be devastating where direct discrimination has in the past made acquisition of experience impossible for blacks.[28] Yet, more often than not, the employer would be hard pressed to demonstrate the necessity of such a requirement to ensure that the job was done properly, particularly if the employee works as part of a group and can learn quickly. Elimination of such unnecessary barriers may well not be required by law, but is both essential and open to management to achieve voluntarily.

A general point, applicable to all measures under this heading, is that trade unions must be drawn into the implementation of remedial action, to maximise its effectiveness, minimise resistance and conflict, and prevent employers from invoking their opposition, real or purported, as an excuse for inaction.

Changes in personnel selection
Those making key decisions about personnel – interviewers, selectors and supervisors – must be trained to be aware of and sensitive to the differences in culture and experience that may affect the behaviour of ethnic minorities at work, or merely their ability to present themselves to best advantage. Designating or hiring personnel officers with specific responsibility for remedial action and monitoring will also be required.

Training initiatives
Perhaps most important of all, active efforts will be necessary to produce sufficient ethnic minority workers who can meet genuine qualifications. Several measures devoted to developing human capital can be envisaged: formal on-the-job training; cadetships wherein blacks are taken on as supernumeraries and, having proved their abilities, become strong contenders for permanent posts as vacancies arise; or grooming people with good potential but inadequate qualifications by singling them out for secondment to courses enabling them to acquire those qualifications. More systematically, a specialist Equal Opportunities Unit within the Government will need to identify types of work for which few qualified blacks appear to be available. It would then either create its own training courses, or arrange and if necessary provide the funds for the Manpower Services Commission to do

o. Particularly for higher and more responsible levels of employment, special training programmes will be essential, for ethnic minorities have found very little room at the top.

Conclusion

The conclusion may be stated briefly. For 20 years, governments have contented themselves with enacting legislation creating individual rights and imposing limited negative requirements on private employers. They have done very little to put their own house in order, although, at least until the onslaught of privatisation, Britain had the largest public-sector labour force in Western Europe. They have done even less to assist and encourage the private sector, or to offer a credible model of successful practice. It is impossible to say whether the preference for a legal approach was based upon an exaggerated faith in the efficacy of law; on the need, for political reasons, to be seen to do something highly visible, such as enacting a statute; or was a conscious alternative to taking on a wider long-term expensive and controversial commitment. It does seem tolerably clear, however, that continued reliance on the legal approach in the future will signal a decision that racial equality has been accorded low priority, and perhaps also that greater importance has been accorded to being seen to be doing something rather than actually doing it.

3

The politics of anti-discrimination legislation: planned social reform or symbolic politics?

JOHN SOLOMOS

Introduction

The current state of political conflict and argument over the future of race relations in Britain has brought into sharper focus the question of how adequate the measures which successive governments have taken to overcome direct and indirect forms of racial discrimination actually are. After all, critics argue, there have been measures against discrimination on the statute book since 1965 and there seems to be pitifully little evidence to show that black minorities have benefited greatly from such measures in terms of equality of opportunity, let alone equality of outcomes. Moreover, it is argued, while anti-discrimination measures may have served specific ideological and political functions, such as defusing protest and co-opting some sections of the black middle class within the state institutions (particularly after 1981), they seem to have produced little improvement for minorities in terms of employment, housing, and social welfare provisions.[1]

Another criticism which has surfaced in the current period is encapsulated in the Home Affairs Committee's much discussed report on the functioning of the Commission for Racial Equality (CRE), which was published in 1981 (Home Affairs Committee 1981b; Cross 1982). In a rather controversial overview of the Commission's work since its formation under the 1976 Race Relations Act, the Committee's report pinpointed weaknesses in objectives, organisation and implementation procedures which, it argued, hampered adequate action against discrimination. In a particularly controversial section on the operation of the CRE from 1977 onwards the Committee stated:

> The Commission's gravest defect is incoherence. The Commission operates without any obvious sense of priorities or any clearly

defined objectives. There are few subjects on which they prove unwilling to pronounce and few projects upon which they are unwilling to embark. Where specific policy objectives have been established, they are rarely translated into concrete activity. Commission staff respond to this policy vacuum by setting their own objectives and taking independent initiatives, which not surprisingly peter out or go off at half-cock. A distressing amount of energy which should be channelled into a coherent and integrated programme leading to clearly defined objectives is thus frittered away. (1981:x)

Although the validity of this judgement on the work of the Commission has been challenged from a number of angles,[2] it seems fair to say that it serves to highlight a common line of attack on the work of the CRE and one which has gained some popularity over the last few years. In particular, the criticism that 'where specific policy objectives have been established, they are rarely translated into concrete activity', although perhaps something of an over-generalisation, has achieved a kind of popular acceptance across a number of ideological perspectives.

Over the last eight years the work of the CRE has been a central focus for criticisms of anti-discrimination policies,[3] but this should not blind us to the broader political issues, which must also be considered in any critical analysis of the possibilities and limits of reform being brought about by measures aimed at achieving more equality of opportunity in employment and other areas where blacks suffer from discrimination in British society. The role of central and local government, the judicial system, political leadership, political organisations and pressure groups must be taken into account in any analysis of the broader political economy of what are sometimes euphemistically called 'race relations policies'.

The main objectives of this paper are therefore somewhat broader than those chosen by a number of critics of current measures, which seem to focus unduly on the strengths and weaknesses of the CRE and the industrial tribunal system, but somewhat narrower than those approaches which seem to argue that political interventions to remedy discrimination must always fail because of the systemic limits of the capitalist system (Bourne and Sivanandan 1980; Lea 1980; Mullard 1982). It seems to me more useful to approach this question from the angle of explaining how and why policies have been limited in practice and by what constraints, rather than by assuming that such interventions are structurally pre-ordained to fail. In this way it may be possible to unpack and question the language and meanings within which policy assumptions have been formulated, the contradictions and limits of implementation processes, and suggest ways of broadening the existing political debate to take account of objectives and issues which have been systematically ignored or under-played. In addition, it then becomes possible to explain past failures in a way which opens up avenues for further debate and analysis.

The state and policy formation: some analytical problems

Before proceeding to the specific discussion of the objectives and limitations of anti-discrimination policies in employment, I want to take a small theoretical detour and discuss the problems involved in analysing the origins, formation and implementation of policies. This seems to be necessary since much of the discussion of race relations policies over the last decade or so has been rather ghettoised, and has made little use of the theoretical and conceptual debates that have taken place in relation to the state and processes of policy formation. In this section of the paper I shall introduce those aspects of these debates which are of particular relevance to an analysis of the political context of anti-discrimination policies.

Analytical models of the state have flourished over the last few years, deriving inspiration from both neo-Weberian ideas and Marxist ideas about the role of state power in advanced capitalist societies.[4] Part of this theoretical interest in the role of the state can be explained as the outcome of the increasingly complex linkages between the state and various aspects of modern society, particularly through social welfare agencies and economic policies. Numerous authors have noted this development and attempted to articulate theories of the state and political power which aim to explain the reasons why such a development has taken place (Poulantzas 1978; Jessop 1982; Held *et al.* 1983; Miliband 1983). In particular, such theories have aimed to push the frontiers of debate about politics beyond the narrow concern with electoral and parliamentary processes, looking more broadly at the complex interface between the institutions of political power, the economy, social relations and ideological relations.

Building upon recent developments in a number of branches of political science and sociology a number of authors have begun to talk about the *political economy* of contemporary capitalism, a term which encapsulates all the elements of this broader objective (Leys 1983; Held *et al.* 1983). Although much of this debate has been carried out at a high theoretical level of abstraction, the value of this new approach for the study of interventions in the areas of race relations seems to me to be two-fold. Firstly, it serves to highlight the interconnectedness of political power with other social relations. For example, recent studies of welfare politics have shown how the cutbacks in welfare services during the seventies were the outcome of pressures emanating from the deeper crisis faced by British society during this period (Gough 1979; Golding and Middleton 1982). Secondly, it

erves to direct attention to the limits of reform strategies in societies
dominated by market relations. A good example of this approach is represented by the work of Claus
Offe. Counterposing his approach to the mainstream of 'policy sciences',
Offe (1984) makes the interesting point that while there are numerous
studies which attempt to improve implementation through the improvement
of legal, organisational and planning techniques, few writers seem to ask the
question of why reform strategies have had only limited success even after
numerous attempts at rationalisation. Drawing upon recent Weberian and
neo-Marxist debates about the contradictions of welfare politics, Offe has
argued that the history of state interventions in relation to welfare provisions, unemployment and training policies and economic management
cannot be seen as the realisation of some valuable human goal but rather as
the contradictory outcome of the pressures on the state to manage both the
demands of class and other social interests, and the exigencies of structural
pressures arising from accumulation processes. Because the state is always
subject to such contradictory pressures 'social policy development can
never deal with these problems consistently' and 'the solution to one set of
problems in no way connects with the solution to the other' (Offe 1984:
103–4). Thus, Offe sees the emergence of a 'social problem' as involving
both the development of processes of policy formation, programme design
and implementation, and the definition of what issues are in need of political
resolution (Offe 1975, 1984). He argues, therefore, that any analysis of
specific policy initiatives must involve the comprehension of the claims and
definitions of 'problems' upon which they are based, and the mechanisms
proposed for their resolution. In addition, however, he agrees with Habermas
that the political and ideological symbols used to mobilise support for
programmes of action must be based on statements which cannot
necessarily be seen as serving the interests of one sectional interest in
society (Habermas 1976).

According to this analytical model the state is by no means a neutral vehicle
with pre-ordained political goals, since the apparatuses directly or indirectly
linked to it play an important role in defining what 'policy problems' are and
how they are to be tackled. For example, the idea that a specific issue is
resolvable through short-term ameliorative actions would tend to favour
goals which are seen to work in the aftermath of particular statements
emanating from the government, while the notion that 'planned social
change' is required would favour sets of measures which promise results at
some unspecified date (Edelman, 1977, also argues this point).

In short, then, recent debates on the role of the state in contemporary
capitalist societies have served to highlight a set of questions and tentative
hypotheses about the emerging linkages between the state and society.

While it may be unwise to attempt to fit the complex and contradictor interventions which have shaped race policies in Britain into any narrov analytic framework, there does seem to be some merit in setting out som questions arising from the state debate which may be applicable to the cas of anti-discrimination policies in employment. If, as Offe and others con tend, the state faces contradictory imperatives, can we expect it to resolv issues of race discrimination successfully? To what extent can politica mediation remedy inequalities which may arise in part from the operation o market forces? If these inequalities have not been significantly remedied i the past by state policies, to what extent can better techniques of implemen tation be expected to succeed? What measures would be necessary to ensure that the enforcement of 'equality of opportunity' for minorities is no cut back like other 'social policies'?

Responses to these questions may of course vary, giving rise to severa other difficult and controversial issues. For example, is the success of policy initiative to be measured in terms of publicly stated objectives an criteria? Or do we look for the hidden agenda of problem definition on whicl formal policy pronouncements are based and pay attention to symbolic an other related outcomes? Answers to these two questions are difficult, sinc there is usually very little information available about the background fears, pressures and values which are the context that help to shape policies And judgments about the 'success' or otherwise of a policy are by no mean a simple exercise in statistics, since they may in large part depend upon th definition of the objectives to be attained, e.g. 'equality of opportunity' ma not be accepted as a valid measure of success in overcoming discriminatiol (Lea 1980; Feuchtwang 1982).

What these questions and problems point to is the inherent difficulty o analysing responses to 'policy problems' without some understanding of th assumptions, values, claims and struggles that shape the perception of th problems which policies are supposed to ameliorate or remedy. As number of critical studies have shown, it is quite mistaken to assume tha public pronouncements about the objectives of policies are an adequat reflection of the actual outcomes (Habermas 1976; Edelman 1977).

An additional problem may be that initiatives which receive much publi attention and promise to reform existing inequalities are in fact unable to change basic structural relations based on fundamental economic an social inequalities. A number of American studies which have analysec responses to the crisis of welfare, the housing crisis and the racial crisis o the sixties, have pointed out that there seems to be a tendency for such pro grammes to have limited resources, power and access to mainstrean governmental institutions (Haveman 1977, Friedland 1982). This is partl because governments tend to respond to demands for change emanating from relatively powerless groups with publicly announced and widely broadcast promises of fundamental change in the short term, by setting up quasi-governmental mediating institutions and by emphasising their responsiveness to the demands of powerless groups. But it may also be the result of an awareness among policy-makers that initiatives which are popularly seen as helping minority groups (such as 'anti-poverty' and 'anti-discrimination' programmes) help absorb and limit the scope of change, while being popularly seen as 'helping' the poor, the blacks, or whichever group demands to which they are responding.

To return to the basic objective of this paper, and bearing in mind the analytical distinctions discussed above, the question to be addressed about anti-discrimination policies in employment is: why have attempts to regulate and outlaw racial discrimination and disadvantage in employment been so limited in their effectiveness? This is of course a huge question and it would be impossible to address all its dimensions in a paper of this size. Indeed, it is doubtful if all the dimensions of this question are fully addressed in this book as a whole. The main focus of this paper will therefore be on the political context within which policies against discrimination have developed, and the limits imposed by the absences, contradictions and biases of the current political commitments to equal opportunity policies. In addition, some reference will be made to the proposals to strengthen the legislative and administrative mechanisms set up after the 1976 Race Relations Act. It is to these issues that we now turn.

Anti-discrimination policies: the social and political context 1965–75

The history of anti-discrimination policies in Britain dates back to the early sixties, when first the Conservative governments of 1958–64 and then the Labour governments of 1964–70, developed a view of race and immigration which combined acceptance of the demands for controls on immigration with the proclamation that those migrants already resident should be protected from discrimination and benefit from government action to give them 'equality of opportunity' with their white counterparts.[5] This consensual view of the 'dialectic of immigration controls and race relations legislation' was first clearly articulated during the early stages of the Wilson administration and played a major role in the influential White Paper on *Immigration from the Commonwealth*, which was published in August 1965, and subsequent government reports and legislative measures (Freeman and Spencer 1978).

The White Paper is an interesting example of the logic that underlay both the 1965 and 1968 Race Relations Acts and which exerted some influence on the drafting of the 1976 Race Relations Act. Asserting that race questions within British society were intimately tied to immigration, Harold Wilson introduced the White Paper by arguing that strict immigration controls had to be combined with measures 'to promote integration in the widest sense of the word, in terms of housing, health, education and everything that needs to be done to minimise the possible social disturbance arising from this social problem' (quoted in Deakin 1969: 5). The linking of *immigration controls* with *integration measures* was a significant development, since it signalled the first official move towards institutional measures to manage domestic race relations as well as controlling immigration at the point of entry (Freeman and Spencer 1979; Miles and Phizacklea 1984).

The White Paper was, of course, not published in a vacuum. In the same year, the Labour Government passed the 1965 Race Relations Act, which represented the first legislative measure against discrimination. Significantly, the Act consisted of little more than an enunciation of general principles against discrimination and it did not cover employment and other important areas of discrimination (Hindell 1965). During 1965–68 a number of developments in the Labour Government's thinking of 'race' took place, which helped to further institutionalise the ideology of *integration* as the basic principle of official thinking and policy-making. There was, for example, a concerted attempt within the Labour Party, which was partly fostered by the Home Secretary of the time, to 'take race out of politics' and to establish it as a policy issue of the same order as housing and educational provision for disadvantaged groups in society (Deakin 1969; Freeman and Spencer 1979). In addition, the Labour government showed a particular interest in the race riots taking place at the time in America, and it saw integration as an ideology that could help bring about the kind of reforms that could prevent violent explosions of street disorder and urban revolt (Rose *et al.* 1969; Halsey 1970).

With this broader political and ideological climate it is not surprising that both the 1965 and 1968 Acts were primarily concerned with visible and symbolic gestures, which promised reform but which actually paid little attention as to exactly how this promise was to be implemented in practice. The 1968 Act, for example, while it extended the provisions of the 1965 Act to the main arenas in which discrimination took place, namely housing and employment, did not develop enforcement powers to the same degree (Kushnick 1971; Bindman 1980). This led to the 'gap between policy and practice' which was pointed out by numerous government and academic studies during the period 1968–75.[6] It also seemed, on the surface at least, to lend support to the claims emanating from within the black communities and radical circles that race relations legislation was merely a symbolic gesture, which was, in effect, programmed to fail (Sivanandan 1982).

The emphasis in the White Paper on *Immigration from the Commonwealth* on minimising the 'social disturbance arising from the racial problem' was consistent with the broader political climate during the late sixties which tended to (a) locate the black communities (or, more narrowly, immigration) as a social problem and (b) look to highly visible quasi-governmental agencies as the institutions for managing the consequences of the 'problem' and ultimately 'integrating' the minority communities into the wider society. Part of the purpose of the 1965 and 1968 Acts was therefore to help establish conditions for the inclusion of race within the policy agenda, but only in the context of a prior definition of 'immigration' and 'race' as either causal or conditioning factors in the development of social problems.

The climate of opinion dominant through the late sixties was one in which the objective of 'racial equality' was firmly linked to a perception of immigration as a problem. This was encapsulated in Roy Hattersley's famous aphorism that 'without integration, limitation is inexcusable; without limitation, integration is impossible'. From this perspective the twin objectives of government policy were to limit immigration and facilitate the integration of immigrants through a 'strategy of equal opportunity, accompanied by cultural diversity, in an atmosphere of mutual tolerance' (Jenkins 1967: 216).

In addition to the perception of immigration as an immediate 'problem', to which government had to be seen to be responding, another dominant influence on official thinking at the time was the fear that without 'integration' the new generations of blacks would become a danger to social order and political stability. Roy Jenkins, as Home Secretary, expressed these fears throughout the period 1965–68 and thus helped create a climate of opinion in which the need for race relations legislation was intimately linked to the perceived dangers which would arise if no action was taken. An example of his approach can be gathered from a speech made in 1967 about the future of race relations. Arguing, firstly that many of the first generation immigrants would assume 'that they would tend to do only the more menial of jobs here, because these are better than no jobs at home',[7] he then went on to warn:

> The next generation however – who will not be immigrants but coloured Britons – will make no such assumption, and will expect full opportunities to display their skills. If we frustrate these expectations we shall not only be subjecting our own economy to the most grievous self-inflicted wound, but we shall irreparably damage the quality of life in our society by creating an American type situation in which an indigenous minority which is no longer an immigrant group feels itself discriminated against on the

grounds of colour alone. One of the most striking lessons we can draw from experience in the United States is that once this has been allowed to happen even the most enlightened and determined Government and voluntary action cannot avert outbreaks of racial violence. . . What we must ask ourselves, therefore, is whether the action we have so far taken is sufficient to avoid these possible dangers. (Jenkins 1967: 216)

This fear of an 'American type situation' came back to haunt policy makers later on, particularly during 1980–81, but its immediate impact on government actions during the late sixties and early seventies was not very marked. Official discourses on race were still too preoccupied by immigration issues to take more seriously the more difficult question of how to tackle institutionalised racialism in British society and how to develop the promise of 'equality of opportunity' regardless of colour from the level of symbolic politics to effective action.

It was not surprising, therefore, that apart from the minimal legal injunctions prohibiting direct forms of discrimination, which formed the core of both the 1965 and 1968 Race Relations Acts, governments took little or no firm action to support their own stated objectives of making discrimination illegal and ensuring equal access for blacks in areas such as housing, employment, and social welfare. An early study of the implementation of the 1965 and 1968 Acts reached the conclusion that their impact was severely limited because of:

(a)   the limited nature of the definition of discrimination as the outcome of individual action;
(b)   the weakness of the powers given to bodies such as the Race Relations Board to implement the law or to develop equal opportunity strategies;
(c)   the lack of support from both central and local government for anti-discrimination initiatives, and a failure to use their powers and resources to influence employers and other bodies not to discriminate (Kushnick 1971).

From this perspective the reasons why there developed a noticeable gap during the period 1965 to 1975 between the promise of 'racial equality' and the reality of minimal change in levels of discrimination (Smith 1977), was due more to the lack of adequate powers and political support than any inherent problems in implementing a strategy aimed at equality of opportunity. This same study made this point very clearly when it argued that:

To be effective, anti-discrimination legislation cannot operate in a vacuum. It must be accompanied by positive Governmental programmes designed to eliminate the social problems which cause and exacerbate racial prejudice, which, in turn, justifies discrimination. This prejudice must also be countered by vigorous leadership from the political leaders of the land. Without these activities, the coloured population will continue to be a ready scapegoat for whatever social and economic pressures, inadequacies and frustrations are felt by the host population. If this happens, or is allowed to continue, then the assumed willingness to obey anti-discrimination laws upon which the Government has been counting, will not be present; and the law will not be able to control and eliminate discrimination effectively. (Kushnick 1971: 236)

This passage captures quite well the processes by which the effectiveness of legislation against discrimination has been limited since 1965, since in many ways the assumption on which successive governments have based their actions has been precisely the one Kushnick criticised over a decade ago: that is, governments have assumed that legislation to counter discrimination could somehow be implemented by quasi-governmental agencies charged with special responsibility for race relations without direct support from mainstream government departments.[8]

While the period since 1976 will be analysed in more detail in the next section, it is important to note here that the first decade of anti-discrimination legislation cannot be seen as completely distinct from the more recent developments. It was during the post-1965 period that a number of assumptions about the 'race problem' took shape and exercised an enduring influence on subsequent events. Apart from the ideology of equal opportunity, which has been discussed above, the most important of these was the notion that the enforcement aspect of the legislation was in a sense less important than the symbolic aspect. The following assessment by James Callaghan (who replaced Jenkins as Home Secretary) serves to illustrate this argument:[9]

> The race problem is as much a question of education as of legislation. I think the law can give comfort and protection to a lot of people who do not wish to discriminate but who might otherwise be forced by the intolerant opinions of their neighbours to discriminate. Any legislation introduced, I think will have less emphasis on the enforcement side than on the declaratory nature of the Act itself, which must show where we stand as a nation on this issue of principle. (Quoted in Kushnick 1971: 235)

This viewpoint exercised a direct influence on the 1968 Race Relations Act and helped assuage the fears expressed by racists that the government was acting in favour of blacks. In addition it combined a declaration of principle with little or no positive enforcement procedures, and this helped give the Labour Government an image of being a party of liberal conscience on race while it actually achieved little in practice.

It may be, as the Dummetts pointed out, in a forceful critique of the role of government in race relations during the sixties, that the 'declaratory nature' of race relations legislation during 1965–75 was not a principled stand against discrimination, but a half-hearted attempt by an embattled administration to be seen to be doing something about the 'race problem' – both from the viewpoint of the white majority and the black minority (Dummett and Dummett 1969). This interpretation has much to recommend it, since it fits in with the mass of evidence which shows that during the decade after 1965 both the Labour and Conservative parties operated on the principle of *depoliticising race* or *taking race out of politics* (Freeman and Spencer 1979; Reeves 1983). The question of anti-discrimination policies thus came to be seen as an element of this broader strategy of the political management of race and race-related issues, and governments made little effort to grapple with the root causes of the discrimination which their policies were supposed to overcome, or even to implement fully the limited objectives of the first two Race Relations Acts.

Implementing anti-discrimination policies 1976–85

As a number of studies have shown, however, the 'declaratory' emphasis of the 1960s race relations legislation was internally contradictory in that it was premised on bringing about changes which were outside of its immediate control or its limited resources.[10] While this gap between policy and practice could be explained at first as one of newness or lack of time, by the early seventies these arguments were being criticised as excuses for the failure of the state to tackle racial discrimination in employment (and other areas) seriously (Abbott 1971; Lester and Bindman 1972; Select Committee 1975). At the same time the empirical research of bodies such as Political and Economic Planning showed that high levels of discrimination persisted and this was taken to imply that the efforts of the Race Relations Board from 1968 onwards had produced little or no change (Smith 1977). More critical studies took their cue from this evidence to argue that race relations legislation, particularly when linked to racialist immigration controls, could be no more than a gesture or symbolic political act which gave the impression that something was being done about discrimination (Moore 1975; Sivanandan 1982).

The debate about the effectiveness of the 1965 and 1968 Acts raged throughout the early seventies,[11] and began to have a certain impact on the very organisations charged with implementing the legislation. The Race Relations Board, for example, produced a critical analysis of the operation of race relations legislation which argued, among other things, that the 1968 Act was very limited in its effectiveness because of the concentration on individual forms of discrimination and the lack of resources for implementing the law fully. It also argued that racial discrimination was less a matter of 'active discrimination against individuals' than the reproduction of 'situations in which equality of opportunity is consciously or unconsciously denied' (Race Relations Board 1973). In 1974 the Central Policy Review Staff produced a report on race relations, which, although never published, exercised an influence on policy makers through its emphasis on the need for a strong government role in this field in order to forestall future disorder (CPRS 1974). At the same time the Select Committee on Race Relations and Immigration launched a major investigation of the administration of race relations, which produced a major report on *The Organisation of Race Relations Administration* in 1975, which exercised a major influence on government thinking.

Though all of these reports looked at the situation from a specific administrative angle, they all showed a number of assumptions which eventually helped to shape the 1976 Race Relations Act. The most important of these assumptions were:

(a) The need to go beyond the narrow definition of discrimination used in the 1965 and 1968 Acts, in order to include institutionalised or unintended forms of discrimination.

(b) The need to strengthen the administrative structures and legal powers of the Race Relations Board in order to allow for a more effective implementation of anti-discrimination policies, including penalties for those found guilty of discrimination.

(c) The need for a more interventionist stance from central government departments, particularly the Home Office, to buttress the role of race relations institutions.

Taken together these assumptions were seen to support the need for stronger action by government because 'there is a growing lack of confidence in the effectiveness of Government action and, in the case of some groups such as young West Indians, this lack of confidence can turn into hostile resentment' (Select Committee 1975: vii). In addition, they were seen as supporting the need for more efficient social policies on race in order to achieve the original aim of Roy Jenkins of achieving a 'genuinely integrated society' where there was 'equal opportunity, accompanied by cultural diversity in an atmosphere of mutual tolerance' (Race Relations Board 1973: 18).

These reports also signalled a move away from the *declaratory* stance favoured by Callaghan, which shaped the 1968 Act, towards a combination of *educational* and *legal* measures aimed at counteracting racial discrimination. The rationale for this shift, interestingly enough, was seen largely in terms of the relative failure of legislation to stabilise the situation or to gain the confidence of black groups.

More fundamentally, perhaps, the weight of evidence that went into these reports had a major impact on the White Paper on *Racial Discrimination*, which was published in September 1975. This accepted the relative failure of past policies to achieve fundamental changes, the need for stronger legislation, and the need for a 'coherent and co-ordinated policy over a large field of influence involving many Government Departments, local authorities, the existing and future statutory bodies concerned with the subject and, indeed, many individuals in positions of responsibility and influence' (Home Office 1975: 5). It also accepted the need for a broader governmental role to tackle those 'more complex situations of accumulated disadvantages and of the effects of past discrimination' (6). The rationale for this emphasis was the recognition by the government that the majority of the black population were 'here to stay' and that policies had to be based on recognition of this fundamental principle.[12]

While the broader 'co-ordinated strategy' called for in the White Paper was not implemented fully, the following extract provides a clear example of the links it made between the role of the law and the role of the government:

> Legislation is capable of dealing not only with discriminatory acts but with patterns of discrimination, particularly with patterns which, because of the effects of past discrimination, may not any longer involve explicit acts of discrimination. Legislation, however, is not, and can never be, a sufficient condition for effective progress towards equality of opportunity. A wide range of administrative and voluntary measures are needed to give practical effect to the objectives of the law. But the legislative framework must be right. It must be comprehensive in its scope, and its enforcement provisions must not only be capable of providing redress for the victim of individual injustice but also of detecting and eliminating unfair discriminatory practices. The Government's first priority in the field of race relations must be to provide such a legislative framework. What is more, it is uniquely a responsibility which only the Government can discharge. At the same time the Government fully recognises that this is only part of the subject;

that the policies and attitudes of central and local government are of critical importance in themselves and in their potential influence on the country as a whole. (Home Office 1975: 6).

Many questions could be asked about this definition of the issues, in particular about the distinction between 'explicit' and 'inexplicit' forms of discrimination. What is important to note, however, is that although the role of government is prioritised there is no detailed analysis of how to link the legal strategy with a broader administrative support structure working towards equality of opportunity. More fundamentally, while this strategy was recognised as involving major expenditure implications, as well as a reassessment of priorities in existing programmes, no attempt was made at this stage to assess what these were, or to examine how the government's own contribution to the new strategy was going to be implemented. Rather the emphasis was placed on changing the legislative framework, while the wider changes promised in the Select Committee report and the White Paper were not implemented.

Against this background the 1976 Race Relations Act 'represented a strengthening and extension of existing anti-discrimination policy rather than a new and unfamiliar policy' (Nixon 1982: 366). The most important innovations were (a) an extension of the objectives of the law to cover not only intentional discrimination but racial disadvantage brought about by systemic racism; (b) a re-organisation of the Race Relations Board and the Community Relations Commission into a joint agency, the Commission for Racial Equality (CRE); and (c) a different procedure for the handling of individual complaints of discrimination, which in the case of employment cases were to be handled directly by the industrial tribunals rather than processed through some body like the Race Relations Board.

The first innovation was intended to overcome the problems of proving the existence of institutional filter processes that were biased against minority workers. While *direct discrimination* was defined by the 1976 Act quite straightforwardly as arising 'where a person treats another person less favourably on racial grounds than he treats, or would treat, someone else', it also put on the statute book the category of *indirect discrimination*. This was defined as consisting of 'treatment which may be described as equal in a formal sense as between different racial groups but discriminatory in its effect on one particular racial group'. An example of what could be defined as *indirect discrimination* is the application of conditions and requirements for jobs which may mean that:

(a)   the proportion of persons of a racial group who can comply with them is considerably smaller than the proportion of persons not of that racial group who can comply with them;

(b)   they are to the detriment of the persons who cannot comply with them;

(c)   that they are not justifiable irrespective of the colour, race, nationality or ethnic or national origins of the person to whom it is applied (Home Office 1977: 4–5).

The introduction of the concept of *indirect discrimination* into race relations legislation was partly based on the American experience of affirmative action against institutionalised forms of racism, which was widely commented upon during the immediate period leading up to the 1976 Act (Abbott 1971; Lester and Bindman 1972). Indeed, according to one account both the American programmes based on the Civil Rights Act of 1964 and the post-1976 British concern with indirect discrimination are attempts 'to circumvent the problems of proof of intentional discrimination, to go beyond its individualised nature, and to provide a basis for intervening against the present effects of past and other types of institutional discrimination' (McCrudden 1983a: 56).

The second innovation, the setting up of the CRE, resulted from the experience of the organisational management of educational and legal measures against discrimination during the period 1965–75. The setting up of an agency that combined roles previously held by the Community Relations Commission and the Race Relations Board was seen as paving the way for a more coherent implementation of the law and the promotion of equality of opportunity and 'good race relations'. The Commission was seen as having three main duties:

(a)   to work toward the elimination of discrimination;

(b)   to promote equality of opportunity and good race relations; and

(c)   to keep under review the working of the Act and draw up proposals for amending it (Home Office 1977: 45).

Under the first two headings the Commission was empowered to carry out formal investigations into organisations where it believed unlawful discrimination was taking place, to help individual complainants in cases of discrimination, and to issue codes of practice which contain guidance about the elimination of discrimination in the field of employment or for the promotion of equality of opportunity. In addition the Commission was to carry out promotional work aimed at bringing about changes in both the attitudes and behaviour of employers toward minorities (Ollerearnshaw 1983).

As mentioned above, the third major innovation introduced by the 1976 Act allowed individuals direct access to courts or industrial tribunals for redress in respect of complaints under the Act. Although the CRE could offer individuals assistance in carrying through their complaint, direct access to industrial tribunals was seen as providing a stronger basis for a *legal strategy* against discrimination in employment to complement the work of the Commission. This viewpoint was also supported by reference to the need to treat cases of race discrimination in the same manner as cases of sex discrimination or complaints of unfair dismissal.

Given these stated objectives, and the government's promise of an 'effective race relations policy', it may seem surprising at first sight that by 1981 the view of the Home Affairs Committee was that the record of the CRE was 'a very disappointing one' and that it lacked 'any obvious sense of priorities or any clearly defined objectives' (Home Affairs Committee 1981b). However, almost all the academic research that has been done on the effectiveness of the 1976 Act in bringing about fundamental changes, has questioned both the impact of the CRE and the individual complaints procedure.[13] Peter Sanders, who has been involved in the work of the Commission since its formation, has concluded that 'patterns of discriminatory behaviour are still deeply entrenched' (Sanders 1983: 75). From a more critical perspective a number of authors have questioned the priorities and methods which have characterised the work of the Commission since 1977, with the objective of suggesting that it take a more radical stance and use more positive methods of implementation (Feuchtwang 1981; Gordon 1982).

While it is important to acknowledge the relative absence of detailed evidence about the workings of the 1976 Act, it does seem by now to be clear that both the formal investigations and the individual complaints procedures have (a) not worked out as planned, and (b) produced little or no impact on discriminatory practices in employment. In addition there is clear evidence that the penalties and compensation available in cases where discrimination has been found are by no means sufficient.

From 1977 to 1983[14] the CRE started twenty-four formal investigations in employment, although three were eventually discontinued. Although the fieldwork on all these investigations is now complete, only eleven have been published, including ones on BL Cars, Massey Ferguson and West Yorkshire Passenger Transport Executive (CRE 1984). Apart from the delays in completing the investigations, it is also clear that most of them have been of small employers and the CRE has made little effort to analyse patterns of discrimination in large employers. While the slowness of the formal investigations procedure was blamed by the Home Affairs Committee on the inadequacies of the CRE, there is also clear evidence that the ambiguous nature of the law has acted as a brake on its ability to carry out investigations successfully or speedily. By 1983 the formal investigation procedure was so unworkable that the CRE itself proposed a sharpening of its investigation powers in order to reduce delays (CRE 1983e). Whatever the impact of these proposals in the longer term, the current reality is that the 'Commission's formal investigations have made little impact on levels of discrimination' (Sanders 1983: 79).

The picture in relation to individual complaints is by no means clear, due to the lack of a critical analysis of the various stages of the complaints process, but the existing evidence suggests that there is a very low level of success in proving discrimination. Since 1978 a large percentage of complaints of discrimination have been concerned with employment as Table 3.1 shows:

Table 3.1 *Complaints of discrimination*

Year	Employment	Non-employment	Total
1978	699	334	1,033
1979	619	367	986
1980	458	321	779
1981	547	317	864
1982	595	361	956
1983	567	427	994
	3,485	2,127	5,612

Source: CRE Annual Report 1983e: 11.

Of these totals, however, not all complaints actually reached an industrial tribunal for adjudication. A large number, approximately half each year are settled without a hearing. Other cases are dropped before they reach this stage. During 1982 there were 200 tribunal cases heard, of which 30 were successful. In 1983 there were 124 tribunal cases, of which 30 were successful. All in all, between 1978 and 1983 there were 136 successful tribunal cases, or about 10 per cent of the total (CRE Annual Reports 1978–83).

The CRE can claim a certain amount of success in that 97 of the 136 successful cases between 1978 and 1983 were supported by the Commission. But these successful cases can only amount to a small amount of reported cases of discrimination, let alone those cases that go unreported. Against this larger background the number of successful cases does not amount to anything more than a symbolic gesture which has done little to challenge the entrenched roots of institutionalised racialism in employment. This has been acknowledged in some respects by the CRE, which has, during 1983–84, taken two significant steps, in its own eyes at least, to strengthen the enforcement of the 1976 Act.

The first step was the approval of the Secretary of State for Employment of the *Code of Practice* for the elimination of discrimination in employment, which came into force in April 1984. First published in draft form in early 1982 the Code went through a number of stages of discussion and redrafting before the government formally laid it before Parliament in April 1983. Since April 1984 the Code has been admissible in evidence to tribunals, and if they think a provision in it is relevant to the proceedings they can take it into account in determining the question (Home Office 1977: 39). The Commission itself considers that it 'will do much to advance the cause of racial equality at work' (CRE 1984: 15).

The second step was the publication in July 1983 of the CRE's proposals for the reform of the 1976 Act. This document recommended a number of basic changes to strengthen the implementation process, including:

(a) A clarification of the meaning of both direct and indirect discrimination, to take account of the complex situation on the ground.

(b) The setting up of specialist tribunals to deal with discrimination cases, which had the power to order changes to prevent a recurrence of discrimination.

(c) A clarification of the procedures for formal investigations in order to cut out delaying tactics by employers or other bodies.

(d) A redefinition of the law to allow for more effective positive actions to redress the effects of past and present discrimination.

(e) A strengthening of the sanctions against those found to be unlawfully discriminating (CRE 1983b).

Peter Newsam, the CRE's Chairman, introduced this document by pointing out the gap between the stated intentions of the law and its actual practice between 1977–83:

> The intentions behind the 1976 Act are generous. They reflect Parliament's commitment to legislate for the elimination of racial discrimination . . . Unfortunately, the Commission's experience over the past six years shows that in some important respects, the law as it is now interpreted in the Courts is either unclear or ineffective. This makes it hard for individuals to obtain justice. Furthermore, it leads to prolonged and, the Commission believes, often avoidable litigation in Courts and Tribunals. (CRE Press Release, 9 July 1983)

The logic of these proposals, the future of which is as yet unclear, is that they will (a) make the law easier to implement through both legal and administrative channels, and (b) ensure that the development of equal opportunity policies is backed up by a stronger push from the CRE to deal with institutionalised patterns of discrimination.

The proposals contained in this document, along with the Code of Practice, may represent an important initiative in the development of equal opportunity policies over the last two decades. In particular the emphasis on combining more action by central government with an integrated strategy of challenging racist practices, goes beyond the symbolic promises made by successive governments. There are grounds, however, for thinking that the experience of the post-1976 period shows up a number of limits which work against the implementation of anti-discrimination policies.

The limits of political interventions and racial inequality

The arguments developed in the previous two sections have analysed in some detail the types of policies that exist at central government level to counter and remedy racial discrimination. Although some criticisms of the presuppositions and implementation strategies of these policies have been made already, it may be useful to establish in more detail the basic limits which have prevented the adequate implementation of existing policies. This will lead in turn to some questions about alternative approaches which go beyond current strategies.

The limits of existing policies against discrimination are threefold. First, legislation against discrimination has been passed on the basis of a taken-for-granted assumption that the enactment of legal measures outlawing discriminatory acts can produce changes in everyday discriminatory practices in employment. Recognition of the limits of the law in this field, as expressed for example in the CRE's *The Race Relations Act–Time for a Change?* (1983e) and *Review of the Race Relations Act 1976: Proposals for Change* (1985), has usually been seen as evidence of the need to strengthen and make more efficient the legal channels of implementation. Little attention has been paid to the need for wider administrative and political strategies against discrimination (see Lustgarten 1978, and his paper in this volume), or to the development of positive action programmed by central government. This has meant that anti-discrimination policies have operated in a vacuum and an environment which has been generally negative, if not hostile (Freeman and Spencer 1979; Gordon 1982).

Second, successive governments have promised reform of racial inequality while actually doing very little to break down the structural separation and relative powerlessness of organisations such as the CRE to bring about fundamental changes. Thus there has been no cohesive plan linking the various elements of state intervention, even when this has been called for in various government reports since the mid-seventies. Referring

o the situation since 1976, Bindman has argued that at best what has been
chieved is 'the perpetuation of existing inequalities', and that this is
unlikely to change short of a radical policy package covering the major
policy areas:

> The most pressing need . . . is not for changes in the law but for a
> substantial strengthening of the legal and economic powers and
> inducements to apply effective equal opportunity policies. This
> will only come about if there is greater readiness by the courts and
> the law to enforce the law, if more resources are provided for law
> enforcement, and if the Government demonstrates its commitment
> to racial equality by using its executive powers. (Bindman
> 1980: 258)

This analysis is remarkably similar to the CRE's own estimate of the
problems it faces (CRE 1983b), and has also been supported by a number
of other studies of the operation of the 1976 Act (Layton-Henry 1980;
Cross 1982). What it makes clear is the inherent difficulty of bringing about
undamental reform through piecemeal actions.

Third, there is also a broader structural limit on the operation of the 1976
Act, namely the impact of the economic recession and the deflationary
political goals pursued by the Conservative government since 1979.
Although, as argued above, the broader economic environment cannot be
seen as determining the limits of government policies in a deterministic
fashion, there is a linkage between what is happening within the state and
the demands on resources placed by wider pressures, e.g. economic
downturn, high levels of unemployment. It is interesting to note that, in this
regard at least, the CRE's perception of the government's response to the
Scarman Report on the 1981 disturbances in Brixton singles out this limit
as crucial:

> So far the response (to the Scarman Report) by the Government
> and others has been disappointingly inadequate. It lacks the sense
> of urgency that runs through Lord Scarman's report in particular.
> Of course, it is more difficult in a time of recession, when unem-
> ployment is high and resources are scarce, for a massively expen-
> sive effort to be made. But it is precisely at such a time that the
> vulnerable sections of society suffer most, and even steps that
> require only a comparatively modest outlay are not being taken by
> the Government. (CRE 1983a: 3)

The lack of progress on this front seems to be confirmed in the 1984 Annual
Report of the CRE, where it makes a similar complaint about the lack of
centralised planning of the state responses to counter the impact of the

recession on ethnic minorities (CRE 1984). The impact of the recession or the effectiveness of anti-discrimination policies will be analysed more fully later on in this volume (see chapter below by Rhodes and Braham), but it seems quite clear that the pursuit of 'equality of opportunity' as a goal of governmental policy cannot be made sense of outside of the pressure placed on this stated objective by the economic and political forces of society as a whole (Offe 1984).

Given these three basic limits, and I hope this chapter has demonstrated their impact has been vital in limiting the effectiveness of anti discrimination policies since 1965, there are still a number of questions that need to be asked. Are these limits an inherent aspect of social policie within a capitalist society, such that reform policies will always be symbolic in character? Or are there counteracting measures which can be used to change these limits and allow for a more radical package of social policie on race and other issues to be implemented?

There is a need for much more detailed research before these question can be answered satisfactorily,[15] but the weight of existing evidence would seem to support the thesis that race relations policies have functioned largely at the symbolic level since 1965, although slightly less so since 197((see e.g. Brown and Gay 1985). While much was promised in the aftermath of the 1980–81 riots and some policy changes were implemented,[16] it is still uncertain whether this period marked another major turning point in rac policies. What is not supported by the evidence, however, is a purely conspiratorial analysis of race policies which sees them either as buying of protest or as gestural measures which are bound to fail. Such an analysi cannot explain why policies have failed, since it is based on the assumptio that they are bound to fail. At the same time it is also wrong to see a strengthening of legal powers and a stronger political commitment as a panacea that will resolve all problems.

What is needed at the present time are detailed studies of the role of the state and government institutions in the development of 'race relations policies', the reasons why certain definitions of the 'problem' have gaine currency, and the reasons why a major gap has developed between th promise of equality and the reality of high levels of discrimination and systemic racism. Such accounts will allow us to go beyond the limits of existing discourses and provide a basis for a more reasoned development of alternative strategies for change.

Conclusions

In his study of the contradictions of social reform and welfare state policie Offe has argued that 'the increasingly visible conflict between the promis and experience, form and content of state policies can lead . . . to a growing difficulty for state policies to win acceptance for the legitimating roles on which political power is based' (1984: 144). This contradiction between promise and experience, Offe argues, can lead to a seemingly endless series of short-term and at times self-defeating, strategies aimed at securing immediate requirements for legitimacy from one interest or the other. Thus he characterises the contemporary state institutions in welfare state capitalist societies as caught in a situation of crisis management rather than producing planned social reform. From a rather different theoretical perspective Edelman talks of 'words that succeed and policies that fail' (1977: chapters 1, 2).

The preceding account of the politics of anti-discrimination policies in employment would seem to fit into Offe's account of 'crisis management' in at least two ways. First, the various initiatives pursued by successive governments since 1965 have operated in a political environment where the pursuit of racial equality has been less of a clear political commitment than a series of knee-jerk reactions to real or imagined dangers resulting from non-action. Examples of this kind of reactive pursuit of anti-discrimination policies have become quite common since the 'riots' of 1980–81 (Glazer and Young 1983). This in turn has helped create the image that something is being done to close the gap between the 'promise and experience' of measures against discrimination and mobilise a new consensus in favour of the pursuit of broadly defined aims such as 'equality of opportunity' and 'anti-racism'. The second way in which the political pursuit of equality of opportunity fits into Offe's crisis management model is through the promise it holds, symbolically at least, that it can resolve the contradictions in existing policies through organisational changes, better record-keeping, more open information channels and more legal reform. By explaining past inadequacies through the weakness of existing implementation channels, governments have been able to legitimate the need for constant changes and the promise to do better in future.

Debates over the reform of existing measures against discrimination will undoubtedly continue over the next few years, given the mass of evidence which questions their effectiveness in promoting their stated goals. No doubt if the proposed changes outlined in the CRE's 1983 document on *The Race Relations Act 1976 – Time for a Change?* and the 1985 document on *Review of the Race Relations Act 1976: Proposals for Change* are actually adopted there will be a greater likelihood that effective help will be given to individual black workers and even to whole groups of black workers. More effective measures by central and local government to promote equal opportunity in employment will also help, as a number of recent studies have persuasively argued (Young and Connelly 1981; Ouseley 1981; Glazer and Young 1983).

Some doubt must remain, however, as to the possibilities for implementing extensive reforms in the context of what is sometimes called 'recessionary politics', and the increasingly virulent forms of racism which are beginning to surface (see e.g. Lacey 1984; Applebey and Ellis 1984) For example, the euphoria over the Scarman Report led to a flurry of reports, pronouncements and research studies as to how best to develop more positive measures for racial equality. Such measures were seen as the best insurance against a recurrence of the violent confrontations that took place in areas such as Brixton and Liverpool 8 during 1980 and 1981 Although such actions as were taken during 1981 and 1982 did produce some immediate results, recent research on Liverpool would seem to cast doubt as to whether the reforms have produced longer-term improvements (Parkinson and Duffy 1984). Indeed the 1985 urban protests in Handsworth, Brixton, Toxteth and Tottenham have pointed once again to the limits of what has been achieved since 1981. There have been numerous promises of reform, but little has been achieved at the level of structural changes in employment and social conditions.

Will changes in administrative and legal procedures, the pronouncement of equal opportunity policies and ethnic record-keeping produce more permanent structural changes than the riots seem to have achieved? Can we expect a stronger legal framework to produce the results which have been promised before but not actually achieved? These are of course major questions and it may be unwise to give hypothetical answers on such complex issues. What can be said, perhaps, is that it seems implausible to expect the mere strengthening of the 1976 Act to produce the kind of changes which would be necessary to transform the operation of racialist practices at an institutional level. The possibility for such radical changes may be more in those attempts which are being made to reshape the actual exercise of political power to take account of racial issues, whether it be at central or local government level.

While there is no doubt that some important changes have been brought about by successive attempts to promote equality of opportunity in employment through the law, the dominant question on the political landscape of race relations remains: why has so little change been achieved since 1965? This paper has suggested, from an analysis of the political dimension, some of the reasons why. The quest for more adequate explanations of past and present limits on reform represents one of the ways through which we can achieve a more clear awareness of what needs to be done to make anti-discrimination policies more than an exercise in symbolic politics or reactive measures to deal with specific crises. It is in this sense that we need to go beyond a critique of existing policies and look at the actual possibilities and limits on change at all levels of employment, and the role of central and local government in bringing about necessary changes.

The need to develop alternative approaches for overcoming racial dis-
rimination remains an important task, since there can be no rational
ssessment of current policies without an attempt to show what is possible
utside of the dominant official approaches. The present period resembles
n many ways the early seventies, with seemingly intractable debates about
he effectiveness of existing policies on race and the need for new ones. The
lifference between then and now, however, is that the black communities
re beginning to flex their political muscle and to articulate their own
lemands for change. Any new package of policies will have to take account
f these demands if it is not to merely impose another solution from the top.
The costs of not doing so may be that black communities will begin to look
utside of traditional political channels to achieve their demands, and thus
uestion the whole basis of the policies pursued since 1965.

4

Religious discrimination and differentiation in Northern Ireland: the case of the Fair Employment Agency

JOHN DARBY

Before the troubles

The relationship between perceived discrimination and violence in Northern Ireland has a long pedigree. The first official report into a riot in Belfast pointed to the fact that only six or seven Roman Catholics were employed in the municipal police force of 150 was a major cause of the disturbance (Belfast Riots Report 1857: 4). The official report into the causes of the most recent rioting in the city also suggested that their origin lay in discrimination rather than in constitutional differences: 'Jobs and houses are things that matter and touch the life of the ordinary man more than issues of "one man, one vote" and "the gerrymandering of ward boundaries" ' (Cameron Commission 1969: 56).

Although it is notoriously difficult to find reliable statistics about Northern Ireland's work forces, evidence has been available for some time of significant economic imbalances between Protestants and Catholics. In the Civil Service, for example, the Northern Ireland Office has admitted that only 15% of senior posts were held by Catholics, a figure considered to be a considerable over-estimation by some academic researchers (see Donnison 1973; Northern Ireland Office 1973; McKeown 1973); a 1971 study of employees in Belfast Corporation Electricity Department found 61 Catholics in a force of 1,346 (*Irish News* 11 March 1971); in Fermanagh, a county with a majority of Catholic residents, only 32 Catholics worked among the 370 employees of the county council in April 1969. Within the private sector levels of denominational imbalance were even higher in some industries; in the engineering industry, for example, it has been claimed that the proportion of Catholics employed by Harland and Wolff, Mackies and the Sirocco Engineering Works varied from 6% to less than 1% (Boehringer 1971).

The picture of imbalance in employment has not been disputed in general, at least by academic critics. There has been dispute, however, about its causes. Religious discrimination has been certainly the paramount explanation, and there is no shortage of evidence that direct discrimination was widely practised in Northern Ireland. Indeed, during the franker days of the Unionist administration at Stormont, members of the government were willing to admit their own practice of discrimination and to encourage others to do the same. Among the numerous examples, perhaps the best known was the speech in 1933 by Sir Basil Brooke (later Lord Brookborough and Premier):

> There are a great number of Protestants and Orangemen who employ Roman Catholics. I feel I can speak freely on this subject as I have not an R C about my own place . . . I would appeal to loyalists, therefore, whenever possible, to employ good Protestant lads and lasses. (*Fermanagh Times* 13 July 1933)

That the intention to discriminate was more widespread was confirmed in the Cameron Commission's report on the employment practices of some local councils. The Commission was satisfied that discrimination against Catholics was practised by local councils in Londonderry, Dungannon, Armagh and Omagh urban districts, and by Fermanagh and Tyrone county councils. Cameron also pointed out that 'Newry urban district council, which was controlled by non-unionists, employed very few Protestants' (Cameron Commission 1969: 60).

Explanations other than discrimination have also been proposed to explain these imbalances.[1] It has been suggested, for example, that the predominance of Catholics in the western parts of the province, which are less attractive to industrialists, provides part of the reason (Simpson 1983), an explanation which cannot explain satisfactorily the relatively higher Catholic unemployment in West Belfast. More recently, Paul Compton has argued that 'the structure of the Roman Catholic community itself', and in particular its high fertility rate, provided a better explanation than discrimination for Catholic disadvantage (Compton 1980); it is difficult to evaluate this claim since he provides no evidence on the relative employment experiences of large Protestant and Catholic families.

Whatever the individual merits of these suggestions there has been a move away from the view that Catholic disadvantage is a result of an accumulation of individual acts of discrimination. Two recent research papers, for example, have argued that, while the origins of imbalance were certainly to be found in systematic discrimination, the patterns of employment and the structure of Northern Ireland's industry maintained the religious disparities without the need for discrimination (Cormack,

Osborne and Thompson 1980; Murray and Darby 1980). But whether or not discrimination is an historical or current problem, there is little doubt that Catholics and Protestants hold profoundly different views about it. In Richard Rose's 1969 survey, 74% of Catholics believed that they were treated unfairly and 74% of Protestants denied this. Of greater relevance to the Fair Employment Agency, which was established seven years later 69% of the Protestant respondents in the survey said that they would disapprove 'if the government passed a law making it illegal to refuse a job o rent a house to a Catholic because of his religion' (Rose 1971: 483).

Reforms 1969–75

While Nationalist members of the Northern Ireland parliament recorded a persistent record of protest against religious discrimination, their ability to improve matters was hampered both by Unionist intransigence and the ambivalence of the Nationalists themselves towards reform. Until the 1960s most Nationalists regarded the abolition of the Northern Ireland state as a prerequisite for any change. From 1967 the emergence of the Northern Ireland Civil Rights Association (NICRA), which publicised very successfully the level and forms of Catholic disadvantage and which was prepared to work for reforms within Northern Ireland, removed the initiative from the Nationalists. Between 1969 and 1973 a number of the NICRA demands were forced through. Some of these related either implicitly or directly to discrimination in employment and were the antecedents of the Fair Employment Act of 1976.

The most significant reforms which indirectly affected discrimination were the reorganisation of local government in 1972 and the removal of housing, health, social services and educational administration to centralised boards. In effect, the local councils were deprived of considerable patronage in housing allocation and employment. The reforms which set out to tackle discrimination more directly were the creation in 1969 of the Parliamentary Commissioner for Administration (Ombudsman) and the Commissioner for Complaints to investigate cases of maladministration against, respectively, government departments and local councils/public bodies. In both cases the Commissioners were restricted to investigating individual complaints and could not initiate general enquiries. Between 1969 and 1977 the Parliamentary Commissioner received 277 complaints, investigating 125; there were no findings of religious discrimination. In the case of the Commissioner for Complaints, whose office was established to deal with religious discrimination, only 6% of the 3,892 complaints received between 1970 and 1977 alleged religious discrimination, and in only three cases were the findings positive (Birrell and Murie 1980: 147,

185). Although it has been suggested that the existence of the Office has improved standards of impartial recruitment, the history of the Commissioner for Complaints' Office throws doubt on the effectiveness of individual investigation as a means of reducing either religious discrimination or imbalances.

None of these reforms tackled the difficult issue of discrimination in the private sector until the then Secretary of State for Northern Ireland, William Whitelaw, established the Van Straubenzee working party in 1972. The committee, representing both sides of industry in the province, reported in 1973 that it was agreed on the need for legislation to make religious and political discrimination in private employment illegal, and on the need for a body to police the legislation. These recommendations were the basis for the 1976 Fair Employment Act and the Fair Employment Agency, with the important addition that the legislation and Agency covered public as well as private employment.

The Fair Employment Agency: legal bases

The Fair Employment (Northern Ireland) Act made discrimination in employment on the grounds of religious belief or political opinion illegal. It also created the Fair Employment Agency and gave it two main duties. The 'less important' of these (Cooper 1981: 7) was the elimination of discrimination and the Agency was provided with powers to receive and investigate complaints and with procedures for enforcing its decisions. It was obliged to seek a settlement by conciliation if possible but, if this was not successful, it had the power to issue recommendations to the employer and to take action in the county court on behalf of the complainant; the respondent also had the right of appeal.

The Agency's 'principal duty' (FEA Fifth Annual Report 1981: 5) was to encourage equality of opportunity, and the Act again detailed certain requirements and powers. As a result of these, a *Guide to Manpower Policy and Practice* was issued and employers and others were to subscribe to a voluntary *Declaration of Principle and Intent* to promote equality of opportunity. Section 12 of the Act empowered the Agency to initiate general investigations; if its findings supported the view that an employer was not providing equality of opportunity, it was again required to seek a solution through conciliation. If this failed, the Agency could serve a notice requiring changes in recruitment and promotion patterns, to make an application to the county court.

It has been argued by McCrudden (1982a) that the absence of an antidiscrimination law tradition in Northern Ireland, in contrast to that in North America, has loaded the Agency with a number of problems. These might be summarised as:

(a)   uncertainty among the victims of unfair employment practices about the likely effectiveness of the Agency;
(b)   lack of experience among those entrusted with enforcing the law;
(c)   confusion about the Agency's relationship with the courts and with government departments; and
(d)   difficulty in the internal relationships between Chairman, Agency members and staff.

One result of these initial problems has been the Agency's enforced preoccupation with procedural rather than substantial issues. Another is to emphasise that the Agency's success must be measured not only in its progress towards achieving the general objectives specified in the act but in its ability to develop strategies and relationships which countered the absence of an anti-discrimination law tradition.

The record

The activities of the FEA have been assessed at different stages in its development by Osborne (1980), Schmitt (1981) and McCrudden (1982a). Rather than repeat the substance of these evaluations, the aim of this paper is to update them and to concentrate on a consideration of the Agency's strategy. The FEA's record on research, individual complaints and general investigations will be considered in turn.

Research

Research occupied an unfashionably high profile during the first five years of the Agency's operations. This arose from the lack of data on the precise extent and nature of religious imbalance in employment, and the reasons for it. If information was scarce, however, there was no shortage of theories: the Protestant work ethic; relative differences in the educational qualifications of Protestants and Catholics; the concentration of Catholics in industrially unattractive locations; different vocational expectations of Protestant and Catholic young people; the perpetuation of past practices – all of these hypotheses, and more, were presented as explanations of lower Catholic employment, but none had been systematically examined. The Agency initiated a programme of research which was designed to investigate the extent and variation of occupational imbalances (based on the 1971 census), and then to test in turn each of the major hypotheses.

The net result of the research programme has been to discount such general theories as different work ethics and to suggest that educational disparities were small and diminishing. It now seems clear from the evidence that the key explanatory factors are not so much related to current discrimination against Catholics as to the perpetuation of historical patterns of discrimination. Whatever the initial reasons for these, and prejudice played at least a part, the current problem is the inertia factor which sustains them. FEA research projects into the expectations and aspirations of young school leavers in Belfast, Londonderry and Strabane have stressed the importance of Catholic expectations of discrimination and the inherent advantage to Protestants of controlling access to jobs through employment practices and family contacts. Thus the FEA research programme provided information to instruct the Agency's strategy and policies.

Apart from some technical criticisms and accusations by one academic that the Agency has neglected to consider larger Catholic family size as an explanatory factor in religious imbalance (Compton 1980) – a charge which has sparked off some academic debate in Northern Ireland – the Agency's research programme is generally regarded as one of its more successful enterprises (see Osborne and Miller 1980; Cooper 1981; Rolston 1983).

Individual complaints

The obstacles to tackling discrimination in employment by means of investigating individual complaints are well known and all have applied in Northern Ireland to the disadvantage of the FEA: an unsuccessful applicant may never discover who was given the job and thus would be unaware of discrimination; he or she may be ignorant of the Agency's powers and procedures, or even of its existence; for some Catholics in Northern Ireland there is little confidence in the legal system; fear of publicity is another deterring factor, especially for white-collar workers. Even when cases are considered by the Agency, the inevitable shortage of hard evidence and the difficulty of establishing whether rejection was due to lack of experience, personality factors or religious background, has produced very few positive findings of discrimination – only 18 between 1977 and 1983. This in itself may deter further complainants from approaching the Agency. The effect of these hurdles was neatly summarised by the Agency's chairman: 'It requires the purest coincidence of one person having both a cast iron case and being willing to make a complaint for a case to be sustained' (Cooper 1981: 9). This is borne out by the individual complaints considered by the Agency between 1977 and 1983, which themselves have survived the early hurdles including that of satisfying the Agency's terms of reference (see Table 4.1).

Three factors predominate in the FEA's experience of individual investigations. The first is the very small number of complaints between 1977 and 1985, from a peak of 130 in 1978–79 (only 42 of which could be investigated) to 25 in 1983–84. The second feature is the small number of posi-

Table 4.1. *Complaints on which the FEA took decisions, 1 April 1977 – 30 November 1985*

	Discrimination	No discrimination
Public sector	19	131
Private sector	18	122
Total	37	253

Source: Fair Employment Agency, *Annual Reports* 1976–83.

tive findings of unlawful discrimination; of the 253 cases which the Agency had examined by March 1983 only 37 were positive, suggesting either that the level of actual discrimination was low, or that the barriers to a successful complaint were too formidable. The third feature is the subsequent record of the cases in which the Agency found that discrimination had taken place. By June 1983 the number of these had risen to 18. Of these, seven were appealed in the county courts: three of these appeals were successful, two were rejected and two are proceeding. There are some signs that employers who have been found guilty of discrimination have become less prepared to appeal the FEA's decisions. Of the Agency's first eight positive findings, six were appealed, although not all of them appealed to the county courts; but only two of the four findings of discrimination during 1981–82 were appealed, and all the earlier settlements had been honoured.

McCrudden has suggested ways in which some of these deficiencies might be remedied, including 'an increased reliance on making inferences of discrimination on the basis of "harder" evidence of this (statistical) type' (McCrudden 1982a: 627). There is little reason to suppose that this would increase significantly the number of people who survive the complicated process from actual discrimination to settlement. The main lesson underlined by the FEA experience in individual investigation is that it can rarely have more than a marginal influence on the problem, especially in legal settings like that in Northern Ireland where, for reasons of tradition or lack of inclination, the courts are unlikely vanguards for a reforming crusade. More productive results may come from other strategies.

Equality of opportunity

The other main responsibility of the Fair Employment Agency is to promote equality of opportunity in employment between people of different faiths. This has been universally conceded by every major commentator as its main and most difficult job. The FEA describes it as 'the principal duty of the Agency' (FEA fourth annual report) and Osborne has described powers associated with this responsibility as 'the backbone of the fair employment legislation' (Osborne 1980: 132).

The Agency inherited or adopted a battery of strategies in the pursuit of this duty, ranging from soft persuasive approaches to quite substantial powers of legal enforcement. Its first annual report demonstrates a considerable amount of time spent on what might be described as educational or evangelical activities – seminars, lectures, television appearances and liaising with employers and trade unionists – designed to publicise the aims of the agency and encourage a general debate on equality of opportunity. The drafting of a *Code of Manpower Policy and Practice* was another early priority required by the Act; its importance to the Agency was the need for an agreed code of practice which, it was hoped, could be accepted voluntarily by many employers and establish a norm against which they could be measured. A third, allied, strategy, also required under Section 6 of the Act, was to invite representatives of organisations, employers and workers to sign a voluntary *Declaration of Principle and Intent*, and to publish a Register of those organisations which had signed it; by 1983 there were 5,067 organisations on the Register, but this excluded twenty of the twenty-six district councils. It has been suggested by Osborne that the large number of signatories had little significance, as only 17% of the firms who had signed the declaration had reviewed their employment practices (Osborne 1980: 137).

The most powerful tool available to the Agency in encouraging equality of opportunity is its right, under Section 12 of the Act, to initiate investigations into firms, industries or professions. By 1983 twenty-one such investigations had been completed or were at different stages of research or negotiation. These ranged from investigations of individual manufacturers to general investigations of Belfast's engineering industry, employment patterns in Londonderry and the Northern Ireland Electricity Service. It is in the field of general investigations that the most serious criticisms have been levelled at the Agency. There have been three major charges:

The Agency's espousal of investigations had been reluctant and tardy:
The FEA's first completed investigation was mentioned in its Fourth Annual Report in 1981, five years after the Agency's formation. According to the FEA itself this caution arose both from a preference for conciliatory approaches and because of difficulties claimed by employers in providing details of the religious composition of their workforces. In retrospect, Bob Cooper accepts that the Agency may have exaggerated the efficacy of persuasion and the 1982 Annual Report adopted a more impatient tone

towards employers: 'The Agency remains unimpressed by those employers who persist in the attitude that the composition of their workforce is not actually known' (Sixth Annual Report 1982: 10). The publication of the completed investigations has been equally slow. This also was rooted in the FEA's adoption of a soft approach: 'The Agency does not use its investigative procedure to pillory those who fail to afford equality of opportunity' (Fifth Annual Report 1981: 8). While the publication of more reports would certainly add to the FEA's political unpopularity, the failure to publish has been interpreted as failure to confront the issues and lend substance to the debate about equality of opportunity (Rolston 1983). Three investigations were published in summarised form in the Agency's 1982 Annual Report, and two in the 1983 Report. In 1984 the Agency published separately its Report into the Fire Authority.

The Agency lacks a strategy for its investigations, proceeding too much on an ad hoc basis:
Commenting on the Agency's approach to general investigations, McCrudden charged that they 'have seldom been part of a coherent plan thought out in advance and followed consistently' (McCrudden 1982a: 629). It is difficult to disagree, from a study of the FEA's investigations then and subsequently, with this diagnosis of '*ad hoc*ery': some were prefaced with the phrase, 'following the investigation of a complaint . . .' indicating that they were prompted by an individual complaint; some, like the Civil Service investigation, arose from commonsense based on *prima facie* evidence; one, at least, emerged from the regional interests of one member of the Agency. Apart from their haphazard provenances, the investigations give cause for concern because the willingness to move from individual complaints to general investigations calls so heavily on the Agency's small budget as virtually to rule out forward planning. It was for this reason that McCrudden advocated the adoption of a 'strategic enforcement plan' (McCrudden 1982a: 636) which concentrated the Agency's resources on planned and realisable objectives.

The FEA's dependency on government funding has reduced its effectiveness:
Tension between quangos[2] and the governments which established them is scarcely novel, as the experience and the eventual closure of the Northern Ireland Community Relations Commission demonstrated in the early 1970s (for discussions of this, see Griffiths 1974; Rolston 1978). Finance is often the instrument of control. In 1975 the FEA envisaged that the staff would expand to 40; in March 1983 the total staff, including clerical

workers, came to 12. More important than government's ability to restrict the Agency's activities by limiting its staff is the charge that it has also been able to frustrate or delay investigations into sensitive issues. The most dramatic of these was the Agency's proposed investigation of employment patterns in the Northern Ireland Civil Service – a controversial area. The Agency announced that the study had commenced in 1979 (Fourth Annual Report 1980: 11), and subsequent references reflect a series of frustrating skirmishes with the appropriate authorities. The report for 1980–1 announced that 'rather more problems were experienced with the analysis of the available data than had been first envisaged . . . It is hoped to produce in late 1981 or early 1982 a preliminary report.' In the following year major progress was announced and the completion was envisaged 'by the Autumn of 1982' (Sixth Annual Report 1982: 6). The seventh report revealed that further delay had been caused by the failure of the Civil Service to respond to the draft report. That such delays gave rise to suspicion of government pressure, or at least effective delaying tactics, should cause no surprise and do not make the Agency's task easier or its independence evident.

The Agency's critics: offence and defence

The critics of the Fair Employment Agency amount almost to a Who's Who of the Ulster establishment. The Church of Ireland and the Northern Ireland Chamber of Commerce are among its milder critics, the latter suggesting that the Agency has 'not had a useful effect on industrial relations' (Rolston 1983: 218). More vituperative criticisms have come from political parties. The Democratic Unionist Party, in particular, with the Official Unionists in close attendance, has urged a strong campaign in local council meetings for the Agency's abolition, notably in Craigavon and Cookstown, and the *Declaration of Principle and Intent* has been ceremoniously torn up in Larne. The DUP deputy leader, Peter Robinson, described the Agency as 'neither fair nor needed' (*Sunday News* 23 January 1983). In the Northern Ireland Assembly a motion calling for its abolition was passed by 21 votes to 9, with the Independent Unionist, Frank Millar, proposing it in these terms:

> The mistakes it makes are clearly to its own advantage. It is making a case for it to stay in existence. The time has come to tell the Government that in the interests of community peace the Fair Employment Agency should be done away with, and its functions as a tribunal transferred to another body. (*Belfast Telegraph* 8 March 1983)

The Alliance Party, which provided the opposition votes to the motion, has itself expressed misgivings about the Agency's attempts to persuade employers that they should record the religious affiliations of their workers. To complete the circle, a motion at the 1983 Annual Conference of the Social Democratic and Labour Party called for the scrapping of the Agency; its proposer, Dr Brian Feeney, described the Agency as 'ineffective, spineless, and window-dressing', going on to say that, 'after ten years of the FEA the Catholic population is still marginal to the Northern Ireland economy in employment terms' (*Sunday News* 23 January 1983). Although the motion did not find a seconder the Agency's apparent failure to satisfy any political grouping in the province does not provide it with much political muscle to flex.

Among academic commentators, there is some level of accord on the FEA. The extent of its task and the difficulties in tackling it are widely acknowledged; there has been general approval, with some exceptions, of the Agency's research programme; there has been criticism about the Agency's poor success rate in investigating individual complaints, some finding their explanation in the Agency itself, others sceptical about the likelihood of tackling discrimination by the investigation of individual complaints. The main division among academic commentators has been about the FEA's brief: Does the Fair Employment Act provide it with sufficient powers? Has the Agency failed to make full use of the powers provided under the Act? Has the Agency's emphasis on assimilation strategies been used as an excuse for avoiding the necessary confrontation with the Ulster political and economic establishment?

McCrudden, the most thorough external researcher on the Agency, had no doubt about where the fault lay:

> The experience of the legal enforcement of the Fair Employment Act is, therefore, a depressing picture of a massive task, of the possibility of change, but of an Agency which has failed to meet that challenge. A complete overhauling of the FEA is necessary. Agency procedures, structures and policy must all be re-thought. (McCrudden 1982a: 636)

This places the blame squarely on the Agency's cautious and ineffectual interpretation of the Act rather than on restraints imposed by its clauses. Rolston shares this view and advocates a 'full frontal attack on the structures within Northern Ireland'; he goes on to argue that such an attack, in the unlikely event of its being launched, would certainly fail because it would 'call into question the whole logic at the basis of British management of Northern Ireland in the past decade' (Rolston 1983: 223).

In other words, Rolston suggests that sectarianism is at the basis of government in Northern Ireland, so government is unlikely to engineer the dismantling of its own foundations. Even commentators like Schmitt and Osborne, who have a generally benign view of the Agency, are critical of its reluctance to dirty its hands. In 1980, for example, Osborne pointed out that the legal requirement for the Agency to carry out the expensive and time-consuming investigation of individual complaints carried with it 'a danger that the main thrust of the legislation providing for wide investigatory and advisory activity, will be neglected' (Osborne 1980: 136). During the intervening five years, however, Osborne believes that the record of the Agency has substantially improved, as evidenced by the adoption of monitoring and affirmative action by the Northern Ireland Electricity Service, and by its work with the Northern Ireland Housing Executive.

Underlying many of these criticisms is the suggestion that the FEA has been, at best, ineffectual or, at worst, a token sop to minority grievances. Members of the Agency have argued, however, that what has been criticised as ultra-caution was in fact a careful strategy based on a gradual process along a number of different fronts. The argument goes along these lines:

> The early confusion in the public mind about discrimination, equality of opportunity and the role of the FEA made an early emphasis on publicity and educational activities inevitable. More precisely the almost total absence of useful research data was a severe constraint on the Agency and forced it to initiate its essential, but low-profile, research programme between 1977 and 1981. At the same time the completion of the *Guide to Employment Practices* and the Register were necessary preliminaries to more interventionist strategies, as well as being required from the FEA under the Act. Add to these the need to employ and train a staff in essentially new skills, within a budget which came to less than £120,000 in 1978–79, and the construction of a firm bridgehead was a clear priority in the early years.

> Since then, the argument proceeds, there has been steady progress towards a stronger presence. In particular the emphasis had shifted from individual complaints to the more radical Section 12 investigations, but not before the former had performed a useful function in initiating the judiciary and legal profession into the intricacies of the new legislation – most notably in the Duffy -v- Craigavon Borough Council case, which established that a prima facie case of religious discrimination existed if, when a 'better' candidate failed to get a job, the successful candidate was of a different religion

(Cooper 1981, 8). Most important, the Agency had clarified its view that inherited hiring procedures were much more significant than individual acts of discrimination in frustrating equality of opportunity. Bob Cooper's summary of the Agency's record in 1981 expresses a considerable level of satisfaction: 'In the public sector a considerable improvement has taken place and there are areas of employment where Catholics have significant representation at very senior levels where there was little or no representation in the past ... As far as the private sector is concerned I believe that the process of direct individual discrimination has substantially diminished, but I believe that the problems of inequality of opportunity are still enormous.' (Cooper 1981: 11–12)

Given this defence to the criticism, by what criteria can the performance of the FEA be assessed? For Rolston, as already mentioned, the political and administrative framework within which the Agency functions ensure that it cannot achieve real reform. Even if such radical criticisms are disregarded, assessment remains a problem. Clearly the Agency's duties under the Act – the elimination of discrimination and the promotion of equality of opportunity – are too general to be useful. It is the FEA's success or failure in translating these aspirations into strategies which provides the ultimate criterion for assessing it.

The FEA's first two annual reports are dominated by two different emphases: educational activities such as lectures, seminars and media appearances; and the preparation of a beachhead for future interventions, like the drafting of the *Guide to Manpower Policy and Practices*, the establishment of the Register of Equal Opportunity Employers and the research programme. In retrospect these educational activities may have been over-emphasised and did little to instruct the public about the Agency or its objectives. Although the initial research programme achieved its own expressed objectives it did not generate follow-up research projects. Although two research projects have subsequently been funded, the Agency's research role has clearly diminished.

After the first spurt of individual complaints against discrimination, the annual rate has settled at under 50 investigations a year. It may be that the real value of the complaints' watchdog is its deterring presence rather than its sharp teeth, but it is difficult to argue that the amount of time and resources required to produce 18 positive findings of discrimination in seven years is too expensive a drain. The advances in the courts' recognition of the problem is useful, but marginal.

It is accepted by both the FEA and its main critics that the key measure for the Agency's success or failure is less the elimination of discrimination than the ability to promote equality of opportunity, mainly by means of

Section 12 investigations. This occupied less than a half page in the Agency's second annual report in 1979, but contained the following promise: 'It is the intention of the Agency that the main thrust of the work of the Agency during the next two years shall be conducted under this section of the Act.' This at least can be measured in terms of investigations initiated by the Agency, and by the publication of findings. In 1979–80 the year following this declaration, four new investigations were started, compared to a total of six in the previous two years, and in 1980–81 a further four began. The momentum was not sustained. In 1981–82 only two new Section 12 investigations began, and 1982–83 saw the start of two more. The slow progress in conducting some of these projects, particularly the extensive Civil Service investigation, and in publishing others, also stand as challenges to the good intentions of 1979. The Agency's sixth annual report also included the first three reports of investigations in any detail, perhaps in response to criticism from outside. More to the point, it is not easy to detect a more careful selection and control over the selection of investigations, and McCrudden's earlier criticisms of the Agency's reactive rather than pioneering approach still stand as the most serious challenge to the FEA's record.

A more selective future?

Of course there can be no objective evaluation of the Agency's successes and failures – it depends on the observer's expectations of what a body like the FEA can achieve. This then must be the starting point – that the Agency cannot eliminate discrimination, nor can it deliver equality of opportunity. To expect that it can is to expect too much. This is not to say that it cannot perform a useful, even essential, function. It is to argue that the Agency must identify more specific targets for itself, and recognise that some deserve more energy than others. These targets may be identified from its record and from its powers. In ascending order, three broad objectives might be suggested.

The investigation of individual complaints should be a continuing but limited, function:
The low level of positive findings – 18 in seven years – suggests either that direct individual discrimination occurs infrequently in Northern Ireland, or that legal process has a limited value in detecting it. Nevertheless two reasons apart from the actual cases themselves justify its retention: the first is the need to continue the education of the legal system in Northern Ireland in case-law on discrimination; and the other is the possible, if untestable, thesis that the Agency's activities may act as a deterrent.

This should be recognised as the limited function which it inevitably will become.

The general investigations under Section 12 of the Act are the most promising strategy available to the Agency:
Both for raising consciousness on the essential issue of equality of opportunity and for providing a basis for Agency policy. In its early years the research programme, possibly the Agency's most successful enterprise, performed this function. Its future value is likely to diminish. But the recent retreat from Section 12 investigations, and the failure to implement McCrudden's sensible suggestion of the establishment of strategic targets for investigation which take into account the FEA's limited resources, are matters for concern. They are clearly the most potentially effective overt direct weapon in the Agency's arsenal, but the time for confining their use to field tests is over.

The economy, rather than the courtroom, is the only arena where large-scale improvement in equality of opportunity can be won:
Certainly the decline in the economy since 1973, when serious discussion about Fair Employment legislation began, is seen by the FEA as a major obstacle to its success. At that time the Northern Ireland unemployment rate stood at 6% and a major problem for some employers was finding suitable workers. According to Bob Cooper 'there were powerful economic reasons why companies should promote equality of opportunity' (Cooper 1981: 12). Ten years later the unemployment rate had risen to over 20%. Even if companies wished to alter their patterns of employment to satisfy FEA requirements, few were in a position to take on new employees. In the Agency's view 'the deterioration in the employment situation in Northern Ireland has had a major adverse impact on the creation of equal opportunity' (Fourth Annual Report 1980: 4).

There are two flaws in this argument. The first is that, even by the FEA's own assessment, the advances towards equality of opportunity were scarcely remarkable even in the Agency's early years. The other is that, while the rise in unemployment has certainly not helped to remedy imbalances – not least because the principle of 'first in, first out' has eroded some of the recent gains in such sectors as banking – the accompanying changes in Northern Ireland's economic structure also provide openings for significant improvements in equality of opportunity.

One of these gains – the increasing insistence on proper employment practices from employers and customers outside Northern Ireland – was well illustrated in 1983. Short Brothers and Harland in Belfast, bidding for a £33 million contract from the United States Air Force, was challenged by

Irish–American groups to explain why only about 5% of its 6,000 labour force was Catholic. While denying discriminatory practices, Shorts drew up, with union and work force approval, a seven-point Affirmative Action Programme. This programme, started in April 1983, included the introduction of 'all practical means to encourage job application from Catholics' (*Sunday News* 19 June 1983) and regular reports to the FEA on the religious breakdown of all applications and appointments. Since then individual Catholics have been encouraged to apply for jobs, and career teachers in Catholic schools have been surprised to be contacted by Shorts for the first time, informed of forthcoming appointments and assured by the Employment Manager that 'we are anxious to ensure that all young people have the opportunity to apply for those positions' (letter from Shorts to schools, 28 February 1984). More substantially, Shorts announced their interest in expanding into the vacant De Lorean factory in West Belfast; to the sensitive antennae of local politicians this was really expression of an intention to employ more Catholics.

Regardless of the precise details of the Shorts' case, it provides the FEA with a model for pressurising employers to alter discriminatory employment pressure; there is no sign that Shorts would have introduced its programme without the American prod. It remains to be seen if the Agency will exploit this new opportunity in other areas of employment. The changing economic circumstances also present opportunities for the Agency on the domestic front. One of these arises from Northern Ireland's unusually high dependence on public-sector employment. A third of all employees in Northern Ireland work in the public sector. In addition, private industry depends heavily on public support through grants, rebates, salary support schemes etc., and this dependence has risen considerably since 1970 as a result of Northern Ireland's economic decline and civil strife. For example, in the construction industry, which employs about 7% of the labour force, 'some two-thirds of the industry's output was directly for the public sector and much of the remainder was either partially or indirectly financed from public funds' (Northern Ireland Economic Council 1981).

How does this relate to the FEA? In 1981 the government announced that, from March 1982, 'tenders for Government contracts would not normally be accepted from firms ... unless they held an Equal Opportunities Certificate' (FEA, sixth annual report 1982: 4). The Fair Employment Agency has the power to remove this certificate from employers. It is therefore in a position to remove from firms a source of income which has increased in importance each year. In 1980 Osborne believed that 'the potential for linking government contracts to the Declaration is superficially attractive, but its voluntary nature does not lend itself easily to this possibility' (Osborne 1980: 131). The growing dependence on government funding, however, makes the link between contracts and the Equal Opportunities Certificate a more powerful sanction. Nevertheless, further strengthening of this power, including the provision of resources for monitoring actual employment practices by firms, must be recognised as a major priority by the FEA.

The issue is not merely one of substance, but of approach. No strategy will succeed unless the FEA accepts that there are limits to what can be achieved by conciliation. Negotiation has produced some useful results for the Agency, notably the agreement by the Northern Ireland Electricity Service to review their employment procedures, and should certainly be applied when appropriate. It must be recognised also that there are areas of unequal opportunity, especially some with political connotations, which have been and may continue to be unyielding. In those cases it must be accepted without prevarication that the Agency is involved less with an issue of persuasion than with an issue of enforcement of rights.

It is true that the adoption of a confrontational role, even on a selective basis, would attract more opposition and intransigence than the gradualist approach adopted so far. The alternative may be that, by 1990, the issue of equality of opportunity will have gently slipped into the backwater of Ulster politics. On balance, the Fair Employment Agency needs to worry less about having a hostile image than about having no image at all.

PART TWO

Dimensions of equal opportunity

5

'Equality of opportunity' and inequality of outcome: the MSC, ethnic minorities and training policy[1]

MALCOLM CROSS

In the short history of the Manpower Services Commission (MSC) it has emerged as one of the most powerful influences on the labour market. But it is also itself influenced by labour-market pressures. In the first part of this chapter I want to argue that real and perceived changes in the demand for labour, both qualitative and quantitative, have brought about a major transformation in the Commission's role, such that it has now adopted a much more interventionist stance. I will comment on the nature of this development, before passing on to consider how the Commission has come to define the needs of ethnic minorities. In the last part of this section I will consider the Commission's equal opportunity policy in the light of the previous argument. The second part of the chapter is more empirical; I will look firstly at what appears to be happening to ethnic minority participants in MSC sponsored schemes, particularly the Youth Training Scheme (YTS), before finally arguing that far from breaking the bonds of labour-market inequality, the 'equal opportunity' policy so far adopted is likely to exacerbate labour-market inequalities. Some survey and other evidence is adduced to substantiate this claim.

The early years of the MSC

From its inception in 1974 until 1980 or 1981, the MSC pursued a relatively non-interventionist training strategy. Leaving aside its role in sustaining employment services, the first few years were largely devoted to supervising and co-ordinating the Industrial Training Boards (ITBs). These Boards, established originally under the 1964 Industrial Training Act, had the power to levy employers and make grants for suitable industrial training in their respective fields. In the 1973 Employment and Training Act, which brought the MSC into being, this provision was softened as firms were able to gain exemption from levy on the grounds of already providing adequate training facilities. By 1975–76, for example, two-thirds of the three million workers in engineering were in firms exempt from training levy. However, the ITBs had the task of monitoring their respective sectors, reporting on training needs and suggesting ways by which industry itself could redress imbalances or provide for skilled deficiencies.

Following a Ministerial instruction in November 1980, the MSC undertook a review of the twenty-four ITBs, sector by sector, and subsequently two-thirds of them were abolished. Hitherto their existence had received considerable support from industry on the grounds that they enabled the content of vocational training to be determined by industrialists themselves (Richardson and Stringer 1981). However, by 1981 the picture had changed and the MSC was under intense political pressure to assume direct control of industrial training. What accounts for this change? The three major factors were: first, that skill shortages had been affected by the recession, so that the earlier assumption that unless the company trained its new recruits it would lose its competitive advantage no longer applied as recruitment all but ceased. Second, there began to be grave doubts about the wisdom of traditional skill-training at all as the labour process itself changed, so that what had once been skilled jobs became de-skilled as a result of technological change. This is not to say that the need for skills diminished – far from it – but the need became increasingly for individuals with generic skills that they could hawk to the highest bidder. This fact, together with increasing pressure on profits in the early phase of the recession, led to a dramatic downturn in industry-led training and a developing insistence that *public* funds ought to be applied to vocational training at all levels, rather than the diminishing resources of the private firm.

The other major pressure in the mid-1970s was the gradual rise in unemployment. The response to this was three-fold. First, at the adult level those who were unemployed or in jobs which provided no training opportunities could apply for a place at a skill centre for re-training or initial training under the Training Opportunity Scheme (TOPS). By 1977 TOPS was taking more than two-thirds of the MSC training expenditure (CEDEFOP 1980). Second, there was a move to create jobs, most clearly characterised by the Special Temporary Employment Programme (STEP) which provided modest-income employment to the long-term unemployed. Finally, and perhaps most significant, the disproportionate impact of rising unemployment on young people produced a new determination to counter the corrosive impact of idleness. As the introduction to the Holland Report, which led to the founding of the Youth Opportunities Programme (YOP), put it: 'Unless some constructive alternative can be found, the motivation and abilities of a substantial proportion of the working population may be prejudiced for years to come' (MSC 1977: 7). It is important to remember that the schemes envisaged in the Holland Report were seen as temporary and restricted to the unemployed. In fact, the particular gaps in provision that YOP was meant to fill were for the '. . . least able boys and girls'. The new schemes were never intended for all unemployed young people but only those with 'special needs': 'To make an opportunity available for every unemployed young person would be absurd and undesirable even if it were feasible which, in our view, it is not' (MSC 1977: 43).

Accordingly, the Youth Opportunities Programme and the Special Temporary Employment Programme were administered by a new division of MSC entitled 'Special Programmes'. Although the schemes remained voluntary for their duration, the MSC extended the provision so that even in the first year of YOP, a commitment was given to offer all unemployed school leavers in 1978 a place on YOP by Easter 1979. This was repeated in 1980 and from January of that year those under 24 years of age who had been unemployed for twelve months or more were offered a place on STEP (MSC 1980: 7).

As unemployment rose in 1980–81, a 'special' programme for the young unemployed began to look increasingly irrelevant. What was needed was a broader intervention to prepare all of Britain's young people for the new era of a post-industrial society. What this was seen to involve was training in new skills for a minority and some kind of useful, character forming and discipline inducing experience for those who were unlikely to participate directly in the new employment. The urban disturbances of April and July 1981 gave a new impetus to this development and to the New Training Initiative, which was published in the lull between these two months of inner-city storm. It is to that period that we now turn; a period of emergent dualism.

Emergent dualism

The New Training Initiative of May 1981 marked a watershed in MSC policy. Major training initiatives before had lain with the Training Opportunities Scheme for adults and the Youth Opportunity Scheme for unemployed youngsters. However each had experienced dramatic declines in job placement as general unemployment rose. Thus, even in the year 1980–81 the proportion of white adults on TOPS courses in employment three months after completion of their retraining course fell from 69% to 53%. For ethnic minorities the fall was similar, from 48% to 36%. In fact, by the close of that year less than a half of whites (46%) and under a third of blacks (30%) were working in the trade for which they had been trained (MSC

1981b). Similarly, the fall in placement under YOP was as great, although not quite as dramatically sudden. In 1978, when YOP started, 68% of youngsters left to enter employment; by 1981, the figure was 35% (H.C. *Debs*, 10 November 1983: col. 219). Although the ethnic minority work-placement rate varied from region to region, it was unlikely to have exceeded 20% overall by 1981.

The initial response of MSC was to emphasise the need for a thorough-going reform of skill training, on the grounds that structural changes in the economy were the root cause of the problem. Thus the New Training Initiative summarised the issue in the following terms:

> The new markets and technologies require a more highly skilled, better educated and more mobile workforce in which a much larger number of professional and technical staff are supported by a range of more or less highly trained workers who perform a range of tasks and who are involved in a process rather than the repetitive assembly or manufacture of a part of a specific product. (MSC 1981a: 2)

In other words, new skills had to be taught to an upper echelon of the work force while the others became more flexible and adaptable to technological change. On this basis the document proposed its famous three objectives: to develop skill training overall; to provide for a comprehensive pre-vocational experience for young people; and to extend parallel provision for adults.

Of course these objectives overlap; one is concerned with *what* people know, the other two with *who* is to be trained. The important point is that from this time onwards the problem is seen in largely dualistic terms. There is a need to up-grade the skills of those who will lead the technological revolution *and* to adapt the ideas and assumptions of those remaining to a new pattern of working or non-working life.

This dualism is present in both the subsequent documents that carried the policy forward after the central ideas had been subject to public debate and governmental scrutiny (MSC 1981c; HMSO 1981). Thus the Youth Task Group Report (MSC 1982a), which laid the ground work for the current Youth Training Scheme (YTS), makes it clear that while most of what is on offer is vocational *preparation*, for a minority it is intended that YTS should be the first year of vocational *training* analogous to the first year of an apprenticeship. The programme incorporates the previous apprenticeship support package (the Training for Skills Programme) although this only accounts for approximately 10% of places. These places are with private employers, most of whom will provide their own 'off-the-job' training facilities or will have long-established relationships with further education colleges.

The old YOP programme was itself highly complex and diverse, incorporating courses of work experience on employers' premises as well as lower-level courses and assessment periods of an introductory or remedial kind. Although YTS is now a twelve-month course, and although it always incorporates a three-month period of 'off-the-job' education, these elements of work experience on employers' premises have been retained. The only difference is that rather than hand this component over to (often small) employers, with all the problems of substitution for existing labour and the dangers of cheap labour exploitation that this entails, the MSC has chosen to allocate these places to private training agencies whose sole function is to organise and design the training element, pay the trainees their allowance and find the employer for a work experience period. Of course, some of the old problems may remain but the private training agency acts as a useful buffer between the MSC and employers.

Finally, where responsibility for directly sponsoring schemes has been maintained, YTS incorporates those parts of YOP which were more remedial and introductory in focus. These are themselves divided into the so-called Mode B1, which consists of training workshops and community projects run largely by charitable bodies and local authorities, and Mode B2 where the MSC sub-contracts the course to further education colleges or similar bodies.

Thus, there are three distinct elements to the YTS. The first two are rather confusingly grouped together as 'Mode A' because they are administratively handled in a similar way. Mode B1 and Mode B2 are very similar and, in any case, the latter was never intended to account for many places. Overall, the Task Group Report makes it clear that approximately two-thirds of places will be organised under the Mode A category. The dualistic element is not, as first appears, the distinction between Modes A and B; it is the separation of a small group to be trained separately with large or medium size private employers from the remainder who will receive a pre-vocational package which at best will do little more than provide a relevant introduction to a skilled career.

Looking back three years later, one member of the Task Group, David Stanley (Deputy Director, Education and Training, CBI) clearly recognised the twin tasks that they faced: 'We all felt that there were two objectives. One was an economic objective . . . the preparation for work. The other was to tackle a social need because of the high level of youth unemployment' (H.C. 209 – ii 1984–85: para 102). YTS was seen to be making a contribution to new skill needs by helping to provide a stratum of technicians and skilled personnel, while at the same time providing those without qualifications the discipline they would have previously received at work.

The same assumptions are present in the document prepared in response to the third training initiative: the provision of better opportunities for adults (MSC 1983a). An identical argument is put, namely that '. . . a new pattern of skills is needed rapidly' (MSC 1983a: 5). The only difference is that adults who are unemployed are more likely to have benefited from the discipline of work so that the second argument, in defence of work preparation and work experience, is less apposite. For this reason the plan, entitled *Towards an Adult Education Strategy*, concentrates on the argument of using skill development for economic ends: 'This suggests that more effort should be put into training and re-training those already in employment or about to start a new job, rather than into purely speculative training or training for stock' (MSC 1983a: 7). As a result the document questions the wisdom of the TOPS scheme, catering as it does largely for the unemployed, in favour of 'occupational training' with particular reference to the 'new technologies and newly emergent skills'. The only exception to this is the adult version of most YTS provision which is pre-vocational. The paper argues for the retention of 'basic (non-occupational) education and training opportunities' for those suffering disadvantage in the labour market.

There are those who have argued that the training for young people and adults is based on contradictory assumptions (Ryan 1984). On the one hand, YTS is moving towards an apparently comprehensive strategy, while for adults the cutback in TOPS appears to be restrictive and highly selective. In fact, viewed in the way suggested here, the two schemes are highly compatible. With ever increasing rates of unemployment, the MSC has developed a clear dual strategy: to use high level training for a minority to assist economic restructuring and to employ work experience, temporary work and work preparation as a *substitute* for employment. The MSC *Corporate Plan* for 1983–87 makes this entirely clear when it says: '. . . this year's Plan must embody two distinct strands to reflect the two major labour market influences on the Commission's strategy . . . namely the continuing considerable levels of activity within the labour market and high unemployment' (MSC 1983b: 9). The fact that unemployment is so high amongst young people is bound to tilt provision on these assumptions towards the young. Unlike adults, the provision for the young unemployed cannot be minimal because they have not benefitted from work discipline. The result is an expanding expenditure profile with a greater and greater concentration of resources on the young unemployed. Table 5.1 shows this pattern for estimated expenditure between 1981 and 1986.

It also shows, however, that pre-vocational and non-vocational expenditure on adults will rise, although most of these are the young unemployed too old for YTS. Expenditure in response to unemployment will rise by an average of 103%, while actual training expenditure at constant prices is due

Table 5.1 *MSC estimated expenditure by type, 1981–6 (1981/2 prices)*

Distribution by training area			
	1981/2	1985/6	Per cent change on 1981/2 expenditure 1981/6
Pre-Vocational training and temporary employment			
Young people[a]	45.8	65.9	+116
Adults[b]	11.7	12.1	+54
Vocational Training			
Young people[c]	4.7	2.4	−23
Adults[d]	37.4	18.8	−24
Other R and D etc.	0.4	0.8	+251
Total	100.0 (£911.5m)	100.0 (£1368.6m)	+50

a YOP/YTS and Unified Vocational Preparation (UVP).
b Community Enterprise/Community Projects and Community Industry.
c Apprentice Support (TSPA).
d TOPS ITB grants and other direct training.

Source: MSC *Corporate Plan* 1982–6.

to fall in real terms by an average of 24% over the period. It must be emphasised, however, that this table is rather crude. As I have already shown, the top 10% or so of YTS places ought really to be regarded as vocational *training*, while under TOPS provision there is a substantial pre-vocational preparatory expenditure. Unfortunately, it is not possible to break expenditure down more accurately in unpublished data and as the MSC itself has written: 'It may be difficult to categorise programmes according to whether they serve labour market recovery or the unemployed' (MSC 1983b: 9).

What we can see is the clear development of this dual strategy coupled with the rising curve of public expenditure. Although some cuts have since occurred, the general pattern is for the social and political objective of coping with the unemployed to figure more prominently in expenditure. The task of providing for new skills is seen as clearly separate, and so far it is making less impression on expenditure plans. Indeed, the White Paper published in January 1984 on the first of the National Training Initiative objectives – developing skill training in general – makes it quite clear why this is so (HMSO 1984). The responsibility for providing skill training is still regarded as the employers'. 'It is for them (employers) to make the investment in training people to do the work they require . . .' HMSO 1984: para. 10).

Training in occupational skills is the responsibility of employers and trainees, not the government. The government's role, through the MSC, is to press for the modernisation of skill training to reflect new technological needs in response to industrial and commercial pressures. The existing Skillcentre network, for example, will be rejigged to '. . . adopt a commercial approach in identifying and supplying the training that the Commission and employers want' (HMSO 1984: para 37). Meanwhile, the second strand in the dual strategy – coping with the needs of the unemployable – is supported and sustained, both through the acceptance of the YTS programme and through an endorsement of the proposed adult education strategy.

The major changes described here have, of course, to be viewed in a political context. The particular meaning attached to the term 'vocational' has itself changed; we are a long way from traditional usage as a preparation for a trade or calling. There has been a dramatic increase in expenditure by central government in training from £10 million in 1960 to £580 million in 1980 to nearly £1 billion in 1983–84 (at 1983 prices), and it is based on two parallel arguments. One is that training tailored closely to industrial and commercial needs will aid economic recovery; the other is that the discipline of work experience is necessary to maintain the work ethic in the unemployed. In another political environment these theories might be less important; there is no sound empirical reason for concluding that a trained work force is even a necessary, let alone a sufficient, condition for economic recovery. Similarly, while it may well be that mass unemployment is a stimulus to social unrest, it is not at all evident that the unemployed are in any meaningful sense 'unemployable' or lacking in the capacity to work effectively. These topics deserve serious academic attention, but that is not the main purpose here. What are the implications of these developments for ethnic minority workers? How does this emergent dualism affect them?

The ideology of special need

To introduce the concept of 'ideology' is to enter a contested terrain. I am not interested here in arguments about the relationship of 'ideology' to particular social and economic formations, nor in debates over the status of 'ideology' when compared with 'science'. However, the term is useful in connoting, at the most general level, the capacity of historically powerful interests to legitimate their position. As Anthony Giddens has written, we can usefully identify three principal forms of ideological representation (Giddens 1979: 193–6). These are evident in the universalising of sectional interests, the denial of conflict and contradiction and in the 'naturalisation' of the present or 'reification'. It is this last sense which is pertinent here, not simply as used by Lukács (1971) to connote a quality of capitalist social relations, but to refer to a taken-for-granted assumption of the natural order which in fact 'explains', and thereby legitimates, a pre-existing structure of domination.

The MSC has consistently assumed that black minorities in British society have 'special needs'. In the early period when YOP for the 'least able' and least employable was developed, its whole administration was subsumed under a 'Special Programmes' Division. This Division commissioned five reports under the rubric 'Special Programmes: Special Needs', one of which was on ethnic minority young people (MSC 1979). This document, which was prepared in collaboration with the Commission for Racial Equality, recounted the evidence on discrimination and argued a case for targeted vocational training (under Sections 35 and 37 of the Race Relations Act, 1976). It also recommended more consultation with minority communities and greater efforts at attracting young blacks onto training programmes. In fact, the Report did not receive a response in these terms. The overriding view prevailed – that ethnic minorities were more in need of remedial provision and 'preparatory courses' which were designed to overcome their putative deficiencies in employability. The bracketing of black youngsters with the other 'problem' groups makes this clear. 'Special needs' were also felt to exist for young offenders, the educationally subnormal and the physically and mentally handicapped.

The evidence of YOP follow-up studies and independent inquiries show that black youngsters were, unsurprisingly, more likely to be located on those parts of YOP provision which catered for the least employable, i.e. those with the highest level of remedial provision (Cross et al. 1983). For example, in a study carried out for the MSC itself, Courtenay found that 'non-whites' were almost three times as likely as whites to be on preparatory and remedial courses (Courtenay 1983). As far as MSC was concerned, this was not to be seen as a reflection on labour-market inequalities, but could be accounted for in terms of the geographical distribution of schemes and cultural preferences:

> The MSC's policy of catering for special groups has been to encourage their integration into the mainstream of YOP, while recognising their special needs; and one measure of the success of

this policy is that such groups are represented on the Programme at least in proportion to their numbers among young unemployed people. Their representation on particular schemes within the Programme may be more uneven because of factors like the local availability of schemes and general cultural norms. (MSC 1981c: 6)

Thus the over-representation of ethnic minority youngsters on short preparatory courses or on basic remedial training is presented as a function of where they are and what they prefer. The same assumptions pervade the documentation describing the structure of YTS. By 1982 the dualistic theory of labour-market needs had become more developed and ethnic minorities are mentioned only in the context of the second major need; that is how to cope with those whose capabilities do not match current requirements. Where the modernisation of skill training is mentioned (the first of the NTI objectives) there is no mention of ethnic minorities. The assumption is made that black applicants will gain unhindered access to YTS but that special provision is required to enable them to take advantage of this facility. In 1982, following the reorganisation of MSC and the reintegration of training under a new Training Division, one section was specifically charged with 'policy on work preparation, race relations and industrial language training'. The Annual Report for that year makes it abundantly clear that ethnic minorities are particularly in need of preparatory courses (MSC 1982b). For example, these courses are only discussed in a section entitled 'ethnic minorities' and are therefore not perceived as suitable for others. The Commission's policy is described as one of 'concentrating special training provision (e.g. preparatory courses) in those areas where disadvantaged groups predominate . . .' (MSC 1982b: 34). It then goes on to mention special training facilities in Charlton, Lambeth, Birmingham and Merseyside. As far as adults are concerned, preparatory courses are again mentioned as specifically suitable for blacks and mention is made of literacy and numeracy training and the provision of language training courses (MSC 1982b: 34). Again, in the later discussion paper on adult training, in pursuit of the third NTI objective, ethnic minorities are only mentioned in the context of the second task of 'non-vocational' training for the unemployed. Thus:

> basic (non-occupational) education and training opportunities must be preserved and improved for those who have been out of employment for some time or who, like the disabled, ethnic minorities and women returning to work, may suffer disadvantage, which can be remedied by training, in getting a job. (MSC 1983a: 11)

The black unemployed are therefore perceived as suffering a 'disadvantage' which can be remedied by 'non-occupational' training. There is little doubt, therefore, as to what the 'needs' of ethnic minorities are seen as being. They are regarded as 'disadvantaged' in the labour market and therefore particularly suited to pre-training interventions designed to enhance employability. With the coming of two-year YTS from April 1986 there appears at first sight to be a move away from this position. The new proposals follow from a significant shift in government policy towards greater emphasis on skill training itself and away from merely a containment strategy on unemployment. Moreover, the White Paper announcing these developments emphasises the need for '. . . employers to make a substantial contribution towards the costs of the new scheme' (HMSO 1985: 8). The old Mode A/Mode B distinction has been abandoned and schemes can now be run only by designated 'Approved Training Organisations' (ATOs). The MSC itself has responded to criticisms of the previous arrangements by confirming: 'it will be essential to eradicate the false perception of first and second class trainees within the scheme which is closely identified with the existing mode structure' (MSC 1985a: 9). Under the new proposals the funding procedure is for an ATO to receive £110 per contracted place per year, plus £160 for each filled place per month.

Despite this apparently significant shift in emphasis and design, the underlying pattern of the new scheme is very similar. The system is entirely voluntary on the part of employers and since only one in five companies participate at all this means that places cannot be guaranteed. There must be a subsidiary arrangement to provide places where a shortfall exists. As the Director of the MSC's Youth Training Directorate put it 'we need Mode B provision just to make good things like the Christmas undertaking for unemployed school leavers' (H.C. 209 – i 1984–5: para. 12). Because ATOs are responsible for recruitment, it also follows that some young people are going to be regarded as less desirable so that, again, the MSC has to provide a secondary system for those who will 'respond better to the sort of initial treatment they get within the Mode B scheme where the staffing ratios are slightly higher and (where) it is possible to devote perhaps a little more time to individuals than some employers are prepared to give within the Mode A scheme' (H.C. 209 – i 1984–5: para. 12).

Under the new arrangements the residual Mode B schemes will be run by ATOs who receive an additional payment of £110 per place filled. Because of this extra payment, these places will be known as 'premium' places. The Under Secretary of State for Employment has summarised the reasons for the introduction of premium places in these terms: 'Premium places have been introduced in recognition of the extra costs faced by providers of training programmes for young people with special training needs and to ensure provision in areas where sufficient employer based places may not be available' (H.C. *Written Answers* 18 February 1986: col. 135). Those who are regarded as 'disadvantaged' and who live in areas of high unemployment cannot expect a place with an employer. Rather they will occupy a place in a new secondary sector which is more focused than before on catering for 'special needs'.

Equal opportunity policy

Following the public disorder in 1981 a new interest emerged in Section 71 of the 1976 Race Relations Act, which imposes a duty on local authorities to administer their services and respond to needs on the basis of 'equal opportunity'. The MSC has itself responded to this trend, particularly as far as young people are concerned. The Youth Training Board, for example (the body which oversees the YTS), has adopted an 'equal opportunities' policy and has declared that it 'will look to all parties involved in the preparation and delivery of individual programmes, and in the recruitment of young people, to avoid discrimination and to accept the principle of equality of opportuity for all' (YTB 1982: unpublished statement).

Moreover, the *Task Group Report* of 1982 had spoken of 'positive opportunities for disadvantaged groups' (MSC 1982a: para. 3.12). Also a paper by the Special Groups section of Training Division declared that YTS should not 'replicate inequality' (unpublished paper, April 1983). However, this same paper specifically rejects 'positive action' as the way forward and defines 'equal opportunity' as 'meeting the needs of young people from ethnic minorities'. Subsequently the proposals enshrined in this policy paper appeared in a leaflet for managing agents, sponsors and providers (YTS L26, September 1983) and MSC has gone some way towards promoting the CRE's *Code of Practice* in employment by reprinting a revised version of it as a pull-out section of its *Youth Training News* (January 1984: no.8), which is available, although only on request, to managing agents and scheme sponsors. Moreover, under the new scheme arrangements an even stronger commitment to 'equal opportunities' is evident. Following a report to the YTB in February 1985 training organisations will have to demonstrate a 'positive commitment to equal opportunities' before they attain approved status.

The essential point, however, is that 'equal opportunity' is a phrase with a multitude of meanings. It may refer to equality in access, or experience or even of outcome. More important, as a policy objective it assumes that we already know the answer to the prior question of 'opportunities equal to whom or what?'. In this case, the answer is unambiguous: ethnic minorities must be provided with avenues to training and possible employment that are equal *with those who are like them*. Those who are like them are those who have special needs for training in employability and the discipline of work because of their 'disadvantage'. This is quite unlike the alternative meaning of 'equal opportunity' which stresses the necessity of treating everyone *in the same way* regardless of their apparently different needs. The latter meaning is much more common in discussions of gender inequality. Where a history of racial and ethnic stereotypes exists, the former meaning can confirm rather than confound inequity. It can be employed to defend differences that do not exist.

Ethnic minorities in the labour market

The empirical evidence on the experience of blacks in the labour market is as familiar as it is clear. The arguments do not need rehearsal here: suffice it to say that, notwithstanding the operation of the 1976 Race Relations Act, there is a clear tendency for labour-market inequalities, originally derived from the incorporation of migrant labour from the New Commonwealth, to become sustained by the operation of direct or indirect discriminatory practices. These problems appear to have become compounded in the recession and subsequent restructuring with the run-down in manufacturing and the tendency for employment to relocate outside so-called 'inner-city' areas (Massey and Meegan 1982; Fothergill and Gudgin 1982). As previous research has shown, industrial distributions are still dissimilar between black and white, particularly if the comparison is made with those of Caribbean origin, nearly half of whom are in engineering, vehicle repair industries and transport. Equally striking is the division by socio-economic group. In the case of those of West Indian or Guyanese origin, three-quarters of men in employment are in skilled or semi-skilled work compared with slightly over half the 'whites' (*Labour Force Survey 1981*: Table 4.25).

One result of this situation is the higher incidence of unemployment amongst ethnic minorities. For example, the national *Labour Force Survey* (HMSO 1982) has shown that in 1981 15.7% of white males in the 16–29 age group born in the UK were unemployed, compared with 36.7% of the non-white males in the same age group (*Labour Force Survey* 1981: Table 4.23). There is also evidence to suggest that as the recession has deepened, the relative position of non-whites in relation to employment has worsened (Cross 1985a).

A natural corollary of these data, in the context of an understanding of how discrimination has worked in Britain over the last generation, would be the prediction that those from ethnic minority origins who might be in a position to benefit from skill training would be more qualified by education and aptitude than those with whom they could be sensibly compared.

Indeed, the MSC's own data support this proposition. Thus YOP follow-up studies consistently showed black trainees to be as well qualified as whites, even though they were more likely to be on less desirable schemes. For example, even in a survey of 3,000 YOP trainees in 1980–81, which compared whites in all locations with blacks in all locations (that is, it did not take account of the fact that blacks would be more likely to attend inner-city schools and come from households with a higher incidence of poverty and unemployment), found that non-whites were similarly qualified to whites, with about a third having no qualifications and more than a half of each group possessing a qualification in English (Courtenay 1983).

As an interim conclusion then, we can say that the MSC has firmly located ethnic minorities in the second of its two categories of the labour force. This has happened notwithstanding an equal opportunity policy because this policy has itself come to rest on a mistaken assumption of 'special need'. The outcome may be that in the new, more interventionist stance currently being adopted, ethnic minorities are disproportionately located in schemes with a tenuous or non-existent connection with the labour market. New data on the YTS, themselves the product of the equal opportunity initiative, allow us to explore this proposition.

Ethnic minorities and YTS

In the early part of the chapter, the point was made that, like YOP before it, YTS is a complex, heterogeneous package. Part of the heterogeneity is built in by design and is reflected in the system of financing. Thus, as the *Task Group Report* stated: 'It should . . . be the aim that private sector and public sector employers should provide the majority of opportunities' (MSC 1982a: 4.13). These receive the block grant, with its in-built subsidy for employee training on a 3:2 ratio, while in other cases the managerial responsibility is assumed directly by the MSC, even though a voluntary organisation or local college may itself provide the 'training' experience. Mode B broadly follows the pattern established under YOP and is clearly thought of as a residual or secondary sector within YTS. Thus the White Paper on implementing the NTI initiative says of YTS in general: 'Large numbers of sponsors will be needed for the different elements within the scheme, which must be carried out within industry and commerce *if it is to be truly effective*' (HMSO 1981: 8; my emphasis). Mode B schemes have either a tenuous or non-existent connection with industry and therefore must be thought of as 'less effective'. Certainly, there is evidence that fewer Mode B trainees enter employment after training than Mode A trainees (Cross and Smith 1986).

The first question to ask, therefore, is whether ethnic minority youngsters are equally represented on Mode A provision for if they are not it means that their contact with the real world of work diminishes. Table 5.2 provides a partial answer to this question using national data provided by the MSC. Although the racial or ethnic categories are based on visual assessments by sponsors or scheme staff, there is no reason to suppose that they are totally unreliable at this level of aggregation, although clearly they provide only a crude classification. What the data show is that both gender and race appear to make a difference. At the extreme a majority of black males attend Mode B schemes while less than one in five white girls do so. White boys and white girls appear therefore to have a head-start in getting into those parts of YTS which are said by the Department of Employment to offer 'the most realistic workplace experience and training' (H.C. *Debs* 1 May 1984: col. 93).

Of course, national data such as these take no account of the regional distribution of schemes or of the ethnic minority population. Moreover, Table 5.2 does not provide a breakdown of Mode A schemes, even though they account for such a clear majority of places. Perhaps the most important distinction within Mode A is between those schemes run by private or public employers, where a complete programme of training is provided by the managing agent, often on their own premises, and those run by local education authorities or private training agencies which then place individuals for a six-month period with an employer for work experience. The former operate selective recruitment while the latter tend not to, partly because their income, and for those that are privately run their profitability, derives from the number of places filled. Following the division contained in the *Task Group Report* (1982) we can call these Mode A1 and Mode A2. This division is really very important for, as was argued earlier, the MSC now sees its role as helping industry to modernise skill training on the one hand and instilling work discipline for those who are not going to work in the near future on the other. This is a crude oversimplification and, of course, between those two will come those who may work, although probably only at lower levels of skill. From the perspective of this chapter, it becomes crucial to ask: What are the chances of ethnic minority young people getting on to Mode A1 schemes – that is, those actually run by industry itself and from which we can suppose that those who will really receive a *vocational* training will be recruited? Mode A1 places are approved by the MSC through two routes, either locally through an area office or centrally through MSC headquarters in Sheffield. The latter places are those organised by the Large Companies Unit (LCU) which in 1983 provided 3% of schemes in Mode A but 24% of places (MSC 1984a). This difference is accounted for by the fact that the average number of places on a locally organised Mode A scheme is 58 but on an LCU scheme it is 556. Nationally, only 8% of all schemes and places in Mode A are run by non-employers but this rises very dramatically in some parts of the country, as we shall see.

To look in more detail at what happens within Mode A, I will select one part of the country, that covered by the Birmingham and Solihull Area Office. This office handles approximately 26% of all West Midlands YTS starters or 3.3% of the national total. More important, it covers 49% of the ethnic minority (Afro-Caribbean and Asian) starters in the West Midlands or 14% of the national figure. Using the division contained in the *Task Group Report*, Table 5.3 gives the overall picture for the Birmingham and Solihull area office in October 1984. The same over-representation of ethnic minority entrants in Mode B places is evident although the overall concentration in this Mode is less than for the national picture. This is because of the very large Mode A2 sector which is the result of the degree to which private training agencies have come to dominate YTS schemes in the Midlands. Representation by minorities on these schemes is roughly the same as for whites. The crucial difference lies in Mode A1 where Afro-Caribbean and Asian youngsters are dramatically under-represented. Even Mode A1 is, of course, far from homogeneous. It contains different types of employers, some large, some small and, of course, those operating in different sectors of the industrial world. Table 5.4 breaks down Mode A1 still further, separating the manufacturing employers (including engineering and vehicle repair etc.) from services (including transport) and public employers (defined here as local authorities or local offices of central government departments etc.). Table 5.4 shows that minorities, particularly Afro-Caribbean youngsters, are under-represented in the secondary sector and that they are nearly three times less likely to get into private industrial schemes as are their white peers.

Looked at another way (Table 5.5), the recruits to private industrial schemes are predominantly white with only between 6% and 7% coming from ethnic minorities. This compares with an estimated proportion of 15% of potential recruits in this age-range for the Birmingham area as a whole (MSC 1984b). Considered from the point of view of openings into higher level skilled employment, some of the individual instances are very striking. Thus in 1983–84 Hardy Spicer Limited offered 24 places, all but one to boys, and 23 of these were white. In the same year, Jaguar Cars took on 7 trainees, all of them white. Land Rover took 34 youngsters in 1983–84 while Joseph Lucas took 11 girls into clerical and administrative work and 9 boys into engineering; all these trainees were white. Similarly, Austin Rover took 176 recruits in that year, 95% of them white. In the service industries, the position was little different; even British Rail and the Post Office (both considered here as 'private' employers), who between them took 97 youngsters, did not manage to recruit more than 3 from either West Indian or Asian origins.

Table 5.2 *YTS starters by mode and race, 1984ᵃ (GB)*
(per cent)

Mode	Race									
	White		Afro-Caribbean		Asian		Other		All	
	Male	Female	Male	Female	Male	Female	Male	Female	Male	Female
Mode A	69.9	81.4	47.9	65.5	57.0	69.5	58.4	71.8	69.1	80.7
Mode B1										
Community Projects	15.9	10.8	23.5	17.4	11.7	13.5	22.6	17.8	16.1	11.1
Training Workshops	7.3	4.0	16.9	7.8	10.1	7.9	9.5	4.4	7.6	4.2
ITEC	2.1	0.9	3.4	1.6	4.5	2.0	3.7	2.0	2.2	1.0
Mode B2	4.8	2.9	8.3	7.7	16.7	7.1	5.7	4.0	5.0	3.0
All schemes (N)	100.0 (154762)	100.0 (123713)	100.0 (3454)	100.0 (2827)	100.0 (2288)	100.0 (1850)	100.0 (2616)	100.0 (1947)	100.0 (163120)	100.0 (130337)

ᵃ First ten months.
Source: MSC unpublished statistics.

Table 5.3 *YTS trainees in Birmingham by Mode and race 1983–5*

Mode					
			Race		
	White	Afro-Caribbean	Asian	Other	All
A1	30.1	13.5	14.1	(23.5)	27.7
A2	49.4	53.2	52.0	(35.3)	49.9
B1	19.1	29.6	27.7	(38.2)	20.5
B2	1.4	3.4	6.2	(2.9)	1.9
Total	100.0	100.0	100.0	100.0	100.0
(N)	(6940)	(723)	(448)	(34)	(8145)[a]

[a] This table exceeds the annual figure because it amalgamates data over the two-year period 1983–4 and 1984–5, where available.
Source: MSC Training Division (Birmingham and Solihull Area Office) October 1984.

Table 5.4 *YTS trainees in Birmingham by Mode and race, 1983–4 (%)*

Mode					
			Race		
	White	Afro-Caribbean	Asian	Other	All
Mode A1					
Private employers (manufacturing)	8.9	2.6	4.5	(2.9)	8.0
Private employers (services)	19.1	8.8	8.0	(20.6)	17.6
Public employers	2.1	2.1	1.6	0	2.1
Mode A2					
Private training agency	45.6	49.9	44.4	(14.7)	45.8
Other[a]	3.8	3.3	7.6	(20.6)	4.1
Mode B1	19.1	29.6	27.7	(38.2)	20.5
Mode B2	1.4	3.4	6.2	(2.9)	1.9
All	100.0	100.0	100.0	100.0	100.0
(N)	(6940)	(723)	(448)	(34)	(8145)

[a] Includes otherwise unclassified.

A crucial problem is to try to explain this phenomenon. It may be said that applicants for these positions are not qualified but this is an unconvincing explanation for reasons which were discussed earlier (see Cross 1985b, which explores this question). It may be that Careers Office staff do not send ethnic minority youngsters to private employers for fear that they will be discriminated against. This last point is probably valid, but the fac

Table 5.5 YTS Mode A allocations in Birmingham by race and type, 1983–5 (%)

Race	Mode A1				Mode A2		
	Private employer (manufacturing)	Private employer (services)	Public employer	All	Private training agency	Other[a]	All
White	93.9	92.5	87.1	92.6	84.8	80.3	84.5
Afro-Caribbean	2.8	4.5	8.8	4.3	9.7	7.3	9.5
Asian	3.1	2.6	4.1	2.8	5.3	10.3	5.7
Other	0.2	0.4	0	0.4	0.2	2.1	0.3
Total	100.0	100.0	100.0	100.0	100.0	100.0	100.0
(N)	(656)	(1435)	(171)	(2262)	(3729)	(330)	(4059)

[a] Includes otherwise unclassified.
Source: MSC Training Division (Birmingham and Solihull Area Office) October 1984.

remains that notwithstanding a commitment to equal opportunity, the crucial upper section of YTS, which is the only part that could be truly called *pre-vocational*, as opposed to non-vocational, is not providing even chances for black youngsters to gain a toe-hold in the ladder to a secure, well-paid future.

Conclusion

It is not the purpose of this chapter to argue that MSC officials, or the Careers Offices or even private employers operate systematically and in concert to deny vocational training in Britain's black work force. Rather, the point has been to suggest a broader and less conspiratorial thesis. The MSC has grown faster than any other department of state (of course, it is *not* a department of state in the literal sense but a departmental adjunct with some Quango-like properties). As it has grown it has sought a role, other than administering Job Centres. Its 'training' function has been extended along two paths. First, to intervene to stem the receding tide of skill training supported by industry itself, which it has chosen to do by concentrating on broad, generic and transferable skills with particular reference to the so-called 'quarternary sector'. In fact, as I have shown, this development is still in its earliest phase and *vocational* training is declining as a proportion of the overall budget. This is because the Commission has tried, secondly, to respond to the overwhelming problem of unemployment. It has attempted to promote better chances of employment, not by arguing the case for job creation (although STEP and community industry do go some small way in this regard) but by seeking to rectify perceived deficiences in employability. More particularly, the Commission has promoted the value of 'work experience' in order to encourage familiarity with the disciplines and constraints of work, particularly for the young.

The academic literature on migration and specific knowledge of Caribbean and Asian cultures, would lead one to predict that young people from such backgrounds, like their parents before them, would be the last to benefit from this second form of intervention, possessing as they do the aspirations of the recent migrant and the disciplines of firm family traditions. However, racism has emerged as a powerful factor and dominant assumptions have been shown to be more in line with popular stereotypes than with the academic literature. In defining ethnic minorities' 'needs' in these terms, the MSC has let pass unchallenged the apparent replication of labour-market inequalities through YTS. But if greater intervention is implicitly *dualistic*, and ethnic minorities are channelled into the secondary sector, then the danger must be that current training policy will help cement and confirm second-class citizenship, despite an apparent commitment to 'equal opportunity'.

6

The space between words: local authorities and the concept of equal opportunities

KEN YOUNG

The Race Relations Act 1976 placed new responsibilities upon local authorities. Section 71 of the Act requires them to ensure that the legislative goals of eradicating direct and indirect discrimination, tackling racial disadvantage and promoting good race relations are met in their own operations. In 1977 a joint departmental circular offered anodyne advice about the interpretation of these new duties. That the Act and the circular did little in themselves to promote the questioning and review of local authority policies and practices has been well documented (Young and Connelly 1981). Nevertheless, since that time the services provided and opportunities afforded to black and Asian citizens have become a major preoccupation in a small number of authorities, while rather more of them are making tentative approaches to the adjustment of employment practice and service delivery. The frontiers of practice are becoming increasingly populated and 'racial disadvantage' is now firmly established as an issue within the domain of local government.

This paper deals with a single aspect of the broader trend towards the pursuit of 'equal opportunities': its application to local authority employment practice. The central theme of the paper – that between intention and achievement falls the shadow of misconception – is implicit in my title. My principal argument is that the future success of this new policy commitment is dependent on achieving a greater degree of clarity, explicitness and coherence in policy argument than has so far been seen in local government.

What follows are essentially personal impressions, arising from a study of local authorities as equal opportunity employers funded by the Economic and Social Research Council and conducted at the Policy Studies Institute. That study centres on policy development in ten local authorities, each of

93

which has an avowed commitment to realising equality of opportunity for minority ethnic groups. In some cases that commitment extends to women and to disabled people and (in fewer cases) to gay men and lesbians. But this discussion, like the study on which it is based, is concerned only with race equality, and touches upon other groups only in so far as their inclusion within the scope of equal opportunity policies has implications for the achievement of race equality goals.

Clearly, many factors bear upon the success of any policy for institutional change. Our present research, which will be fully reported in a forthcoming PSI publication, addresses four themes: What is understood by 'equal opportunity'? What is the scope and content of the policy in which that goal is embodied? What arrangements have been devised for handling and progressing it? And what constraints and opportunities attend its implementation? These factors evidently vary over time and between authorities, as do political impetus, financial constraints, trade union and work force attitudes and other considerations relevant to implementation. Other sources of variability include complex and subtle administrative factors: the patterns of political, professional and departmental power, location of change agents, degree of decentralisation in management, distribution of control over the personnel function, and even the size, type and geographical location of the local authority itself. Evidently, the assessment of feasibility is a complex calculation in the case of equal opportunities. Perhaps nothing that local authorities are currently attempting is likely to prove as difficult as this re-patterning of employment. It is therefore all the more important for them to approach the issue in a critical and coherent spirit.

My argument is as follows: Discussion of equal opportunity in employment is bedevilled by ambiguities and confusions which typically characterise areas of public policy where a powerful rhetorical commitment to change exists. In such areas, a shared language may mask multiple and conflicting meanings. These issues are taken up in the first section of the paper. While ambiguities may facilitate agreement at the symbolic level they preclude clear specification of the ends of policy and so inhibit the proper identification of feasible means for its achievement. Ambiguity can assume major importance where – as in this case – it serves to obscure sharply divergent implications for the practicalities of policy. These issues are considered in the second section of the paper.

The disparities between means and ends which arise in the pursuit of equal opportunities matter because local authorities operate in labour markets in which both demand and supply factors shape the ethnic composition of the work force. Accordingly, the third section of the paper discusses the relevance of labour market considerations to one frequently cited policy goal – that of ethnic proportionality. In the concluding section I turn to the broader normative climate in which the fate of equal opportunity policies will be determined. While local authorities are one important forum in which new opportunities for black and Asian people can be created, they are neither of exclusive importance nor themselves insulated from the wider culture and all its value conflicts and ambivalence.

Equality of what? Ambiguity in policy discourse

Where local authorities face social issues in which moral choices are heavily loaded, they commonly approach them with circumspection. Circumspection is encouraged by the administrator's prudent inclination to avoid polarisation and fruitless arguments and it may be a positive feature of policy discourse. But while this approach advances decision-taking it serves, at the same time, to ensure the clouding of the policy arguments and the evasion of basic value choices. In perpetuating ambiguity it enables the adoption of policy positions whose ultimate implications remain unexplored. The decision process in local government, with its high visibility of local issues and fairly direct accountability coupled with the reluctance of administrators to challenge political choices or subject them to critical argument, thus enables an equal opportunities policy to be relatively easily adopted, even where deeply divisive and antagonistic value conflicts lurk beneath the surface.

The specific ambiguity of equal opportunity policies turns on the issue of 'equality of what?' There appear to be two answers to this question in employment issues, while for service delivery, equal opportunities can denote an even wider spectrum of meaning (Connelly 1985). Some argue that equality of opportunity denotes the *equal treatment* of people from different ethnic groups. Others appear to view equal opportunity as the achievement of *equal shares* of that scarce good – employment. The implications for action of these divergent interpretations will be explored further in the following section, but it is worth pausing here to elaborate the point that such profound ambiguity is not unique to equal opportunities, but is characteristic of a type of rhetorical social policy argument where those who profess a commitment to change and those who oppose it can find, in a political slogan, a common vocabulary and an illusion of common cause.

I have illustrated the point elsewhere in respect of two other terms whose political history has been not dissimilar: 'strategy' and 'reconstruction' (Young 1986; Young and Garside 1982). For the purposes of illustration, I will confine myself here to the second. Early in 1916 the thoughts of British politicians and administrators turned to the post-war world. A Committee on Reconstruction was appointed by Asquith, and proceeded in a cautious and incremental fashion to outline plans for meeting the immediate needs of the transition to a peace-time economy. A large-scale housing programme with new legislation and substantial state subsidies was seen as essential. With the coming to power of Lloyd George, reconstruction was tackled in a more intense, even evangelical manner, with the social goals of housing expressed in the famous slogan 'Homes for Heroes'. The Reconstruction Committee was replaced by a Ministry of Reconstruction, set up to frame ambitious plans to create a new post-war Britain 'with fewer grey colours in it'.

Politicians of both major parties united behind the commitment to planning for reconstruction in both the war-time and post-war coalitions. Yet the consensus failed to survive the experience of attempted implementation, in part because there was a considerable gulf between government's reach (its plan-making ability) and government's grasp (its implementation capacity). Disillusionment with grandiose plans soon set in. But failure was also attributable in large measure to the fact that both radicals and conservatives sought sharply divergent goals, a divergence hitherto masked in policy discussion by common adherence to the term 'Reconstruction'. For the former group, the term signified the establishment of a new social order; for the latter, it implied no more than the repair and renewal of a war-damaged fabric.

As with Reconstruction, so too with equal opportunity. First, there is an element of slogan, whose expression invites acceptance across the political spectrum. Second, there is the hidden ambiguity by which a shared and accepted term can encompass a range of divergent and even polarised meanings. Just as Reconstruction could signify 'reformation' or 'repair', so too can equal opportunity signify *equal treatment* or *equal shares*. Here, as with Reconstruction, men and women of conflicting inclination can agree on a common form of words, notwithstanding the absence of a common meaning.

Generally, where a policy is founded upon ambiguity, any apparent consensus is likely to be fragile and incapable of withstanding the stresses and conflicts of implementation. With equal opportunities the normative loading of the values in conflict is such that rancorous and divisive discussions are likely to be deliberately avoided by apprehensive participants, with the result that any feelings of ambivalence cannot be worked through in the course of policy formulation. The normal processes of attitude change through mutual involvement are short-circuited, and deep-rooted feelings surface only in the unfavourable climate of compliance with a previously 'agreed' policy.

Second, different conceptions of the substance of policy embody

lifferent implications for the politics of policy and thus for the feasibility of
ts achievement. Specifically, subscription to 'equal treatment' as a goal
mplies an essentially regulatory policy pursued in the interests of
procedural justice with no logical implications as to who will benefit from its
application. Subscription to the goal of 'equal shares', on the other hand,
mplies an essentially redistributive policy pursued with clear presumptions
as to who will benefit and who will lose from its application. This important
discussion, and its relevance to the implementation process, merits
further elaboration.

Means and ends: the implications of policy choice

Recent writing on the translation of policies into practice stresses the nature
of implementation as a political process, in which disparate resources, conflicting interests and divergent appreciations are mobilised to different
degrees to play significant parts in the shaping of policy outcomes (Barrett
and Fudge 1981; Hogwood and Gunn 1984). The weight of these factors
and thus the prospects of successful policy implementation are affected to
some degree by the nature of the policy itself. A policy or programme may
be regarded as distributive, regulatory, or redistributive in intent, or to have
a blend of these elements (Hargrove 1983). That these three categories constitute a continuum of implementation difficulty will become clear from a
brief elaboration of their characteristics.

Distributive policies
The concern of distributive policies is with public goods for the general
welfare or with those kinds of private goods which are publicly provided to
individuals within the population at large. The traditional concern of local
government, distributive policies are generally universalistic in character
and are seen as non-zero-sum. The notional beneficiaries are diffuse
publics, although the long-term or unintended consequences of distributive
policies may in practice fall unevenly upon different social groups. The
policy choices will usually be framed in quantitative terms: how much or
how many of some defined good should be provided. The diffuse and
indirect nature of the immediate costs and benefits which follow upon such
policies help ensure that they will generally enjoy low levels of conflict, at
least up to the point where the level of public expenditure and its fiscal
burden becomes a politically contentious issue.

Distributive policies in employment are less concerned with who gets
employed, or with the allocation of jobs, than with the overall level or
volume of employment opportunity. The numbers of people employed in
the public sector derive from the level of public service provision, from the

labour-intensity of the specific services provided and from the efficiency with which they are managed. This is not to say that a distributive goal, such as resistance to service contraction, may not be pursued for reasons which are essentially redistributive. For example the Labour Party 'Jobs and Services' campaign appears to reflect a concern both to maintain existing service levels and to secure the position of those lower-paid manual workers to whom local authority employment levels are of particular importance. It is easier, it seems, in practice to pursue distributive policies in phases of expansion (when 'everybody wins') than in times of contraction (when identifiable groups must lose).

Distributive policies for employment represent the soft option in tackling disadvantage for they assume that black people, in common with other groups in a weak labour market position, will benefit from the trickle-down effects of policy. This presumption has been of some historical importance in urban policy but it is increasingly recognised that undifferentiated attempts to enhance aggregate opportunities through the maintenance of high employment levels are likely, in practice, to fall far short of any objective of equality. The perpetuation of existing relativities in employment is no longer seen as a defensible goal and it is more difficult today to ignore the effects of discrimination and disadvantage in restricting even the 'trickled' flow of benefits to ethnic minorities. Thus, while the significance of distributive employment policies for the volume of aggregate opportunity is recognised, attention has shifted to the processes through which employment is allocated. The argument is moved thereby into the realm of regulatory or redistributive policies.

Regulatory policies
The characteristic of regulatory policies is that they specify rules of conduct for individuals and institutions. They are typically concerned with procedures and processes, either because a procedural goal such as 'fairness' is sought for its own sake or because beneficial consequences are assumed to flow (in often unspecified ways) from procedural change. While the enforcement of regulatory policies is in practice unlikely to be without consequences for competing groups, their rationale is procedural, rather than distributive, justice. They seek to ensure conformity with prescribed norms of behaviour. In some circumstances it may seem prudent to adopt such a policy less in order to regulate behaviour than as an affirmation that customary behaviour already conforms to the canons of acceptability. In such instances an equal opportunity policy might be introduced as a declaration or symbolic ratification of 'what we do already'.

The circumstances in which a regulatory policy can bring about significant changes in the distribution of benefits are limited, as a later section of this paper will show. They generally enjoy broad support, or at least tolerance up to the point where regulation itself is seen as irksome. That point is typically reached fairly early by those who stand to lose substantial operating discretion in their professional or administrative spheres of competence from the introduction of a regulatory policy. But serious opposition is rarely more widespread. In employment, a regulatory policy is based on the prohibition of certain specified forms of behaviour. It is essentially a policy of control. However, in order to be fully effective it may be necessary to supplement control measures with those designed to enhance the capacity of individuals to comply with the policy. The prohibition of discriminatory acts, for example, may be accompanied by training for those in positions of responsibility so that areas and instances of potential discrimination may be better understood. In addition, some avenues of challenge to decisions are required, as are a set of remedies and some form of regulatory agency or monitoring system. In these various ways the regulatory approach seeks to provide constraints on employment discrimination and to ensure *equal treatment*.

Redistributive policies
Redistributive policies differ from regulatory policies in their concern with outcomes rather than processes. They are 'targeted' in the sense that they specify the groups between whom the distribution of benefits is expected to change. They are explicitly zero-sum, with winners and losers. As such, they cannot escape the opposition of those who stand to lose from their application. However, opposition can be tempered by incorporating a redistributive policy within a distributive policy, for example by attempting to shift the distribution of jobs within a general expansion of employment.

The goals of redistributing employment may also be sought by regulatory means. For example, the reduction of discriminatory behaviour may be expected to lead to a substitution of black people for white in the overall work force. And, as I shall argue, there are circumstances in which this expectation is reasonable. But, even here, the regulatory means is secondary to the end of achieving *equal shares* in employment. In other instances regulation may be antithetical to the redistributive goal if, for example, it is more easily achieved by administrative action unconstrained by legal challenge or regulatory procedures.

But all policies require some criteria of success against which their implementation may be assessed. Whereas the criteria of regulation are self-evident (if in practice difficult to measure) it is not so for redistributive policies. It is necessary for substantive equality to be defined with sufficient clarity to serve as a policy goal: that is, as an *equality target*. The choice of targets is limited only by the need to maintain the credibility of the policy: they should lie within the tacit limits of feasibility. But the benchmark that comes most readily to hand in practice is that of representativeness, conveniently defined in terms of proportionality to the population in the locality which the organisation serves, or from which it recruits. This is something to which I return below.

Why does ambiguity matter?

The distinctions which I have drawn between distributive, regulatory and redistributive policies reflect alternative routes to the goal of enhanced employment opportunities for black people. They represent a clear continuum of implementation difficulty, for they are arranged in order of ascending unpopularity to those already powerful enough to benefit from the present operations of the labour market. At the same time, the difference between the pursuit of procedural justice (or equal treatment) and the pursuit of distributive justice (or equal shares) is fundamental. They represent two distinct notions of 'equal opportunity' which are commonly blurred in practice. We need to consider first why it should be so and then whether or not it actually 'matters'.

Perhaps the most immediately apparent reason for the persistence of ambiguity with respect to equal opportunity policies is that different conceptions of 'equal opportunity' are subscribed to by different participants in the policy process. For example, personnel professionals are particularly likely to frame their own goals in terms of equal treatment because the procedural implications that follow are consonant with their own professional values; as one personnel director put it to me, the pursuit of equal opportunity through the reform of recruitment was simply 'good personnel practice with the backing of the law'.

In adopting this position, personnel managers stand to reap both the psychological rewards of establishing good practice and the material rewards of increased responsibility and resources within the organisation. An equal opportunity policy implies increased standardisation, consistency, monitoring and training, all of which represent opportunities to enhance the significance of the personnel function. Thus, equal opportunities may constitute a rationale for central personnel staff to expand their 'action space' and capture territory hitherto defined as the province of departmental managements. Such considerations will in many authorities push personnel managers to lead their authority towards equal opportunity initiatives. Their objectives will typically be limited to procedural change and may well be conditioned by personnel's other major responsibility: the maintenance of harmonious industrial relations.

In other authorities elected members will be found to take the lead on equal opportunities. Their goals may be more ambitious. They will often look at the outset for changes in procedure in the interests of securing equal treatment. But they may also define their aims as equal shares. They will often express this goal in terms of ethnic proportionality – the reflection in the local authority work force of the ethnic composition of the locality itself. That is, 'equal shares' are proportionate shares in employment. Proportionality has the attractive quality of immediacy and recognisability. It is made still more acceptable as a concept by the long-standing requirement to achieve a three per cent disablement quota. The availability of numerical data on women in employment from the local authority payroll and the evident disproportionality in the status of and rewards to women similarly serve to encourage the definition of equal opportunities for black and white, as for other groups, as proportionality.

If procedural changes aimed at securing equality of treatment fail to advance the attainment of proportionality, elected members may become critical of the personnel staff and suspect them, and departmental managements, of lack of commitment or even of colluding in covert discriminatory practices. This suspicion can result in a highly confused policy environment or, worse, in an insidious and distrustful atmosphere which can degenerate into rancorous conflict and collapsing morale, with management protesting the lack of suitable candidates and elected members drawing the inference that discrimination is still deeper rooted than had been previously realised.

At this point the dangers of ambiguity become apparent. In the absence of critical discussion, and in advance of disappointing results, it may have been tacitly assumed that there is no goal incongruity and that equal treatment will lead to equal shares. In reality, this outcome could be expected to ensue only where disproportionality in employment can be *wholly accounted for by immediate acts of discrimination*. In so far as it can be only partially accounted for in this way, policy makers must lift their sights from their own recruitment procedures to consider the operations of the wider labour market. As an American economist observes:

> any public policy related to employability, employment and income will be ineffective to the extent that it ignores labour market realities and the demographic, economic and social factors that determine these realities. Not that labour markets are sacred, but they comprise the arena within which the levels and structure of employment emerge: hirings, promotions, layoffs and discharges occur; careers are made, and income and its distribution is, in major part, determined. Policy need not accept the dictates of labour markets, but to be successful policies must be consistent

with, intervene knowledgably in, or supplant deliberately the workings of the labour market. (Mangum 1976: 87)

The force of these observations will become clear from a brief consideration of the processes which determine the ethnic composition of the local authority work force.

Ethnic representation in the work force

The composition of a local authority work force is subject to both labour supply and labour demand factors. Regulatory approaches to equal opportunity seek to ensure equal treatment. As such, they bear only upon the demand side of the process. Assuming that regulation can be successfully enforced, equal treatment will reduce disproportionalities to the extent that they derive from past discrimination. However, equal treatment will be less successful to the extent that disproportionalities derive from inequalities in the labour market itself – that is, from 'racial disadvantage'. Equal treatment of people who do not enjoy competitive equality will be limited in its effect, however desirable it may be in terms of procedural justice for its own sake.

Leaving aside for the moment the question of the appropriate comparator or benchmark of 'proportionality', it is evident that progress towards the achievement of a representative work force can be expected only where four conditions can be met: First, there should be no labour market inequality in the sense of ethnic stratification in the distribution of educational attainment, skill, work record or such other criteria of 'employability' as are operated by the employer. Second, there should be no ethnic differentiation in the overt preferences or covert practices of those who allocate employment. Third, potential black candidates themselves should not regard the employer as discriminatory but see the jobs as being accessible to them. Fourth, a sufficient number of persons in each category should seek employment in the occupation in question. Consideration of these four conditions illustrates the operation of the local authority labour markets.

The manipulation of demand

The effective demand for labour is determined by the size and rate of expansion of the many categories in the labour force and by the rate of turnover within them. It is also affected by the extent to which the employer or his agents discriminate between potential employees on ethnic or racial grounds. Thus, a strict segregationist employer would expect to recruit no staff from particular racial groups and effective demand would be for white labour only. The introduction of non-discrimination practices would go some way towards ensuring that recruitment was 'colour blind', in that formal exclusionary choices by recruiters would not be tolerated. However, demand-modification as a route to equality in employment faces a number of obstacles. First, there are problems of monitoring performance and securing compliance. Many large organisations are not equipped to establish such consistency throughout the organisation. Local authorities in particular are characterised by high degrees of vertical and horizontal differentiation in their structures and by weak integrating mechanisms. This characteristic is particularly true of the larger authority with its territorial and service-based form of organisation. For example, a large county council may effectively recruit at several thousand separate points within the organisation. The personnel function is also less centralised in local government than in much of the public sector and has not achieved the centrality in the organisation necessary to counterbalance the claims to autonomy of departments based on service professions.

Second, and a corollary of decentralised management, is the conflict between consistency in recruitment and the attribution of proper degrees of responsibility to managers. It is often claimed that the pursuit of equal opportunities is 'good management practice', but in reality there are conflicts here *between* equally valued management practices. Personnel departments, even where relatively powerful, may baulk at assuming too controlling a role in appointments on the ground that it is essential for managers to 'own' their decisions and to accept responsibility for their staff. In the more decentralised authority, this attribution of responsibility to line managers may be seen as properly established custom and practice. In such a case, the modification of labour demand cannot be achieved by the exercise of control, but must be won more gradually through changing the perceptions and appreciations of managers at all levels. There are no guarantees that this goal can be achieved.

Third, few organisations can expect to monitor recruitment practice sufficiently closely to eradicate the possibility of unconscious direct discrimination occurring. For some prejudiced selectors, membership of a particular racial group may be seen as an undesirable characteristic and one which can be readily rationalised away in some more apparently acceptable 'employability' criterion. There is no evidence that race-awareness training will be efficacious in tackling this tendency.

Fourth, indirect discrimination is more likely to be perpetuated in local government in the form of unwarranted credentialism. A service built on more than a century of spare-time study and qualification will understandably resist changes in practice that require the justification of taken-for-granted job requirements. In some cases the requirement will not be for the local authority itself to disregard, but will have been laid down by an external professional body.

Finally, and most importantly, certain kinds of informal credentials will continue to be used by selectors who look, at the end of the day, for indicators of employability. Formal qualifications may have been accepted as not strictly related to job performance, but may none the less be read as indicators of stability, self-discipline and commitment. Or they may be accepted as a necessary rationing device to cope with the otherwise unmanageable numbers of applicants for some posts. Even the requirement that candidates should possess 'relevant' work experience will have an exclusionary effect. 'Racial disadvantage' is defined as the disproportionate possession of certain life-chance attributes by minority racial or ethnic groups. But that disproportionality may itself be attributable to past discrimination. No employment policy can remedy this heritage. The discriminatory system perpetuates itself through the disproportionate lack of job experience, track record and other factors that employers will commonly – and legally – regard as the hallmarks of employability.

None of the preceding should be taken to imply that manipulating local authority labour demand by the eradication of direct and the reduction of indirect discrimination will have no effect on the composition of the work force. Some opening up of employment is possible and has been proved possible by those authorities that have regularised their employment practices. For some posts there is scope for regarding a minority background or certain types of community experience as themselves a relevant (or in the words of the Act) a 'genuine' occupational qualification for employment. And to say that acceptable qualifications are under-represented among members of Afro-Caribbean and Asian groups is not to say that there is an insufficiency of black and Asian candidates capable of serving local authority departments as well as the white majority. It is to say only that their proportionate employment will not be achieved by a labour demand policy alone.

Supply factors

That regulatory policies designed to secure equal treatment do not necessarily lead to striking shifts in the composition of the workforce is unsurprising, given that both demand and supply factors are at work. The principal supply-side constraint lies in what is commonly termed racial disadvantage: the less than proportionate possession, by ethnic minority groups, of those attributes which employers will take to constitute 'employability'. As Mangum has pointed out, employability issues (or supply-side constraints) cannot be effectively tackled by employment policies alone. The implication is that education and training policies are at least as important a route to ensuring that black people can attain more equal shares of employment.

At present, ethnic minorities as a group tend to lack the formal skills, educational qualifications and work experience required for many of the administrative, professional and technical grades of local authority employment. The lack of work experience is of particular importance, and among those authorities which maintain records of short-listing decisions for their equal opportunity policies, 'lack of experience' features all too commonly as a reason for excluding black candidates from further consideration. There is an element of circularity here, for unless black people can break through into secure and high-status employment they will continue to be excluded from it on just such grounds. To some extent, then, supply and demand factors are interdependent, for citing 'racial disadvantage' as a supply constraint does little more than describe the second-order consequences of earlier acts of discrimination in labour demand.

There are other, less malign examples of what might be termed 'interaction' between labour demand and supply. Among the circumstantial constraints on supply is the tendency among black people in many areas not to regard local authority employment as open to them. For this reason some equal opportunity employers, however willing to appoint black people, find themselves faced with a shortage of candidates. But employers can intervene effectively on the supply side by signalling their own changes in labour demand. Publicising the adoption of an equal opportunity policy, advertising in the ethnic press, including declarations that applications from black people are welcomed, circulating vacancies to community groups, 'outreach' recruitment in schools and colleges and through the careers service are all examples of beneficent interactions between demand and supply. They are neither to be dismissed as 'mere' public relations, nor evaluated narrowly in immediate cost–benefit terms. Their potential significance lies in the longer term, through the gradual acceptance of and response to the opening up of employment opportunity. Thus there is some scope for positive action to increase the representation of black people in the local authority work force. The problem remains of establishing some yardsticks by which the policy can be assessed. And any attempt to define acceptable and attainable degrees of representativeness leads inexorably back to the convenient yardstick of proportionality.

Ethnic proportionality
The pre-existence of numerical data on gender divisions in the work force and the statutory requirement to employ a defined quota of disabled people incline some policy makers to tackle the problem of attaining more equal shares for black people as proportionality. Often, census figures will be invoked in comparisons between the ethnic composition of the local authority area and that of the existing work force. The temptation to take the

first as an equality target for the second is understandable. To some extent the Race Relations Act appears to encourage it, for Section 38 enables employers to take positive action to provide training for groups which are under-represented in the work force.

But two important points must be made about proportionality: First, it is a meaningful concept only for particular occupational labour markets. Second, the spatial extent of those particular labour markets will vary widely. It is misleading to adopt as a comparator the composition of the local authority area itself; the Act speaks of 'the relevant labour market'. Local authorities employ a wide range of staff from top professionals to unskilled manual workers. The characteristics of the labour market from which senior professional staff are drawn may bear no relation to those of any particular local authority area, for recruitment takes place in a national labour market. On the other hand, the less-skilled grades may be recruited from a limited catchment area, far smaller and perhaps different in composition from that of the local administrative area. Thus the 'relevant proportion' for the first group might be lower than that of the local area. But conversely, it might be far higher for the second. This is not to say that a literal interpretation of labour market proportionality implies the recruitment of professional staff in proportion to some national ethnic pattern. It is open to a local authority to positively seek black professionals on service delivery grounds. But a service-based policy of black recruitment is not an equal opportunity policy: it stems from a different rationale.

The establishment of proportionality targets rarely acknowledges the significance of the age structure of the population. Because the black population is a younger population, any meaningful equality target should be considerably higher than that derived from the characteristics of the population for the area as a whole. Further, even this adjustment to the characteristics of the economically active population will be misleading with recruitment grades. Much more care and analysis is required in the definition of such targets, and crude assumptions about proportionality are a poor foundation on which to rest an equal opportunity policy.

Finally, any discussion of proportionality as a policy goal should pay regard to the distinction between proportionality as an expected outcome of a regulatory policy of equal treatment, and proportionality as a target for a redistributive policy of equal shares. The first is based on a misconception of the nature of regulatory policies, which bear only upon the demand side of the labour market process. While the second is subject to problems of implementation, it has the advantage of directing attention beyond recruitment practices to the larger issue of education and preparation for work.

The cultural setting of equal opportunities

Local authority policies are not constructed in a vacuum and their prospects of implementation are affected to some degree by the wider cultural setting. The policy analyst who attempts to abstract the actors from the broader context in which their actions acquire meaning, ignores the vital interplay of social and organisational factors. The principal issue here is the disjuncture between the group conceptions of equality on which current equal opportunity policies are based and the individualistic terms in which rights are commonly construed.

The shift towards a group conception was implicit (if rarely recognised) in the prohibition, by the 1976 Race Relations Act, of (indirect) discrimination. As Pannick puts it, 'indirect discrimination proceeds on a theory of group entitlements': it provides 'a collective remedy for a collective wrong' (Pannick 1982). I have argued elsewhere that this fundamental change in the legal definition of a social ill has been tempered by a widespread reluctance to be open and explicit about ethnic diversity and by a concomitant unwillingness to grasp the implications of ethnic pluralism: that is, of a society characterised by a plurality of cultures, tongues and faiths (Young 1983). While the last few years have seen some movement towards racial explicitness in political discourse, it has been constrained by the persistence of a deep-rooted and perhaps peculiarly British ambivalence: an ambivalence about ethnic differentiation, about group particularism and indeed about equality itself.

This ambivalence serves to sustain the ambiguities of policy and to constrain the possibilities for its success. Without an acceptance of ethnic pluralism – that is, of a society differentiated by ethnicity – it is scarcely possible to consider the roots of disadvantage or its discriminatory consequences. Still less is it possible to apply appropriate remedies. Some further exposition is required to show why this should be so. First, the concept of indirect discrimination is focused primarily not on individuals as victims in disputes but upon individuals as members of groups which possess – as groups – certain attributes in greater or lesser degrees. For an individual to be a victim of indirect discrimination is to fail to win some benefit (say, a job) solely on the ground of his or her inability to comply with a requirement which a member of another racial group is more likely to be able to meet. Similarly, the individual can be said to be 'disadvantaged' and therefore at risk of indirect discrimination if he or she is a member of a racial group among whom some significant attribute – educational qualification or language skills for example – is absent in *disproportion*. Thus the life-chances of members of such groups (which need not be numerical minorities) are dependent not upon encounters with prejudiced allocators but upon their under-possession of a valued attribute.

Arguments about disadvantage are based on the relative distribution between groups of valued attributes, while arguments about indirect discrimination centre on whether such attributes are used – or should be used – as criteria of allocation to the detriment of the 'under-possessing' groups. In both the concept of proportionality is, as we have seen, to the fore. It follows that neither action nor argument can be advanced far in the face of a resistance to consider the individual's life-chances and deserts in a group context. However, the dominant value orientation in British society is one of individualism. Individualism militates against a group perspective in three important ways.

First, it is maintained that to locate an individual in group terms is to reduce the moral person to an amoral category, a practice which is to be deprecated both as a matter of principle and because a number of uncomfortable moral loopholes appear to follow from it. Second, to ascribe to a 'group' a kind of corporate personality and moral claim is to reify a social construct and thus confuse the discussion of individual rights and obligations. It is on such grounds that Hayekians dismiss the concept of 'social justice', and it is an argument which bears closely upon those doctrines of historical guilt and inter-generational obligation on which some aspects of race equality policy in the United States have been founded. Third, for the law to penalise practices which lead to the 'indirect' exclusion of members of groups in which valued attributes are under-represented appears to abrogate the cardinal principle that moral value attaches to the individual's subjective intention, not to an objective social consequence. Hence the discomfort with the concept of 'institutional racism', a term which appears to be a moral judgement in need of an act to which to attach itself.

Professor Banton's own criticisms of my earlier arguments for ethnic pluralism reflect some of these strands of the individualist position and exemplify the difficulties encountered by the group perspective *on which the law as currently framed is based*. As Banton puts it, British culture 'stresses the rights of *individual* citizens; those citizens resent any sugges- tion that someone is to have greater or lesser rights because he or she belongs in a particular category and has done nothing to deserve different treatment' (Banton 1984: 282). A 'philosophy of individualism', continues Banton, has great strengths as a basis for public policy and the onus is upon the advocates of ethnic pluralism to establish, through some assessment of social costs and benefits, that the group basis of politics is superior. That has not been my task, and, as far as I can tell, only Lustgarten has seriously attempted to confront this issue (Lustgarten 1983).

My own concern here is not with the nature and limits of a culture of individualism but rather with its implications as a social context for a legally sanctioned policy which proceeds on an assumption of group entitlements. The issue is how best to reconcile the moral and political values of individualism with the realities of ethnic differentiation. Neither those who are currently seeking to advance equal opportunity policies in local government and elsewhere nor those who rail against their efforts are convincing in their treatment of this dilemma. Meanwhile, specific proposals for achieving racial equality are often met by a crude and rhetorical version of the individualist case, which none the less strikes a cultural chord, thus sustaining ambivalence and equivocation to the detriment of the conduct of our public affairs. The absence of a practical response to the growing realities of ethnic pluralism highlights an alarming disjuncture between law and politics: that is, between the identification of an ill (inequality) and the remedies which we are prepared to apply to it.

7

Equal opportunity in the private sector: the limits of voluntarism

RICHARD JENKINS

Nearly ten years after the introduction of the legislation concerned, it has, unfortunately, become almost conventional widsom to observe that British anti-discrimination law, if not quite a dead letter, has had very little impact upon ethnic or 'racial' disadvantage in employment. Nor does the contemporary opportunity structure for black people, whether migrants or British-born, give one much cause for optimism. Indeed, as Braham and Rhodes argue in their contribution to this volume, the current economic recession has actually served to intensify the labour-market disadvantage experienced by black workers.

The effects of economic depression aside, there is a growing body of evidence which insists that the influence of the law relating to equality of opportunity has been minimal. Reviewing the impact of the 1975 Sex Discrimination Act,[1] Snell et al. have argued that, 'the legislation as it stands has not been nor is likely to be effective in creating genuine equality of opportunity in employment' (1981: 92). As Angela Coyle has so strikingly put it, the Equal Pay and Sex Discrimination Acts have, 'managed to combine being one of the most significant achievements of the 1970s and one which affects most women's lives hardly at all' (1984: 138). Similarly, Sanders has recently concluded that although 'It is five years since the Race Relations Act 1976 came into force . . . it is clear that much more can be done to eliminate racial discrimination' (1983: 75). Such a conclusion is more than amply confirmed by the present author's research into racism and recruitment in the manufacturing, retailing and public sector industries (Jenkins 1982, 1984a, 1984b, 1986).[2] There is thus a broad body of agreement that the legal measures of the mid-seventies have, in general, failed to achieve their objectives, certainly if those objectives are seen as the achievement of widespread equal opportunity in the labour market.[3]

110

There are, however, no signs of a consensus with respect to how this state of affairs might be remedied. On surveying the literature which relates, more or less broadly, to the topic, four distinct interventionist approaches may be discerned. The first of these argues that the law is inadequate and, consequently, that it is the law which must be altered; this I shall call the *legal* approach. Although it is by no means the only strategy advocated by the Commission for Racial Equality (CRE), the legal approach finds one of its most exhaustive expressions in the Commission's recent consultative paper (1983e), which proposes a series of amendments to the 1976 Race Relations Act. An approach based on the need for legal reforms is also central to McCrudden's discussion of 'anti-discrimination goals and the legal process' (1983a).

Second, there is the *administrative* approach, advocated by Lustgarten in his chapter in this book and elsewhere (1980). His argument is that neither amendments to the existing law nor the introduction of new legislation are necessary. Rather, the state should, through the undoubted power it already possesses as an employer, as a customer for goods and services, as a major influence on the public sector generally and as a general influence on public (and private) opinion, intervene directly to implement equal opportunity. Such an approach presupposes the existence of the necessary political commitment to anti-racism to carry it through.

Both of these strategies are concerned with action at the level of central government. By contrast, however, the third approach de-emphasises the role of law and the state, arguing that equal opportunity in employment can only be achieved on the basis of employing organisations taking steps themselves to reform their own institutional procedures and policies. This I will refer to as the *voluntarist* approach; it has recently been vigorously advocated by Torrington *et al.* with respect to black workers (1982), and, by implication, by Chiplin and Sloane in their study of gender discrimination at the work-place (1982). The major interventionist device advocated by the voluntarist approach is the organisationally specific equal opportunity policy.

Finally, there is that approach to change which, certainly in the first instance, stresses the importance of autonomous political action by black workers and communities. Viewed from this perspective, which I shall characterise as primarily concerned with *struggle*, equality of opportunity is not seen as something to be granted by white society. Rather it is a right which must be wrested from a racist society. In various forms, this approach may, for example, be found in the writings of authors such as Herman Ouseley (1981), on the one hand, and in the pages of publications such as *Race Today*, on the other.

These, then, are four contrasting approaches to the pursuit of equal opportunity. It should not be thought, however, that they are necessarily mutually exclusive. There are, for example, those approaches to the issue which stress the importance of both legal and voluntary measures. The CRE's corporate position, with its dual emphasis upon enforcement and promotion (Ollerearnshaw 1983; Sanders 1983), is a good example of this, as is the attitude taken by the Trades Union Congress, both with respect to gender discrimination (1982) and racism (1981). Similarly, the struggles of black workers are, at the end of the day, concerned of necessity with forcing through action, both from central government, on the one hand, and employing organisations and trade unions on the other. It is also clear that Lustgarten's administrative approach is by no means incompatible with 'voluntary' moves by employing organisations; in fact, it is designed to encourage just such a response from employers.

Thus, it seems that we must think in terms of a mixture of approaches if the issue of equality of opportunity is to be more successfully tackled. In this chapter I am, however, going to concentrate my attention upon voluntary interventions; furthermore, since the public sector is discussed by Ken Young elsewhere in this collection I shall, in the main, confine my discussion to the private employment sector. Although I am centrally concerned, in the context of this volume, with equal opportunity for black ethnic minorities, much of what I will have to say will have some relevance to the case of the other major beneficiaries of equal opportunity initiatives, women workers, and I shall draw upon research into women's employment where relevant.

Equal opportunity policies in organisations[4]

It has been argued above that, in addition to various forms of state intervention, either legal or administrative, there are other approaches which can be taken to the problem of ensuring equal opportunity in employment. With respect to voluntary approaches, the most important development in the attempted amelioration of ethnic disadvantage and the management of 'race relations' at the work-place in the United Kingdom in the late nineteen-seventies has been the introduction of organisationally specific equal opportunity policies (hereafter referred to as EO policies). Across a range of industries and in both the public and private sectors, management has been apparently trying to put its own house in order.

Of course, not all management has attempted to do this. It is doubtful, although it cannot be conclusively demonstrated, whether even a sizeable minority of employing organisations have, in fact, taken such an initiative. The best estimate which can be offered is that of the officers of the Department of Employment who, in 1980, thought that the number of employers in Great Britain 'known to have equal opportunity policies in one form or another' was 'about 250' (Home Affairs Committee, Sub-Committee on Race Relations and Immigration 1981a: 223). However, in as much as EO policies find their way as topics for discussion onto the pages of professional periodicals such as *Personnel Management* and have been publicly adopted by a significant number of 'high visibility' organisations in both the public and private sectors, such an approach must be regarded as a contemporary managerial strategy of some significance.

As a managerial strategy, however, it may be a response to a number of different situations. Indeed, the motives behind this trend appear to be multifarious. To judge from the literature (Ben-Tovim *et al*. 1981; Hitner *et al*. 1982; Torrington *et al*. 1982; Young and Connelly 1981), and from my own research, there are at least seven factors which may lie behind the initial organisational decision to adopt an EO policy. These are, however, rarely effective in isolation; it is typically in their combination that one witnesses the genesis of an EO policy in a particular employing organisation.

In the first place, an EO policy may represent a straightforward response to a 'race' problem, such as, for example, pressure from the Commission for Racial Equality, an unfavourable Industrial or Employment Appeal Tribunal decision, or a 'race'-related industrial relations problem. Second, the formulation and implementation of an EO policy may, however, be an attempt at a pre-emptive strike, to prevent difficulties of the sort mentioned above happening in the future. It should, of course, be recognised here that the distinction between admitting to the existence of an actual 'race' problem, and recognising the potential for future difficulties may be a fine one in concrete situations. Third, such an initiative may be nothing more than a public relations strategy, aimed at improving the organisation's standing in the eyes of a particular constituency, be that its employees, its customers or its paymasters. Looked at together, these three factors may be categorised as *defensive* or *reactive*. Impressionistic evidence leads one to believe that, certainly in the private sector, they are among the most characteristic reasons for EO policy formulation and implementation.

Coming now to the public sector in particular, a fourth factor which may underlie EO initiatives – one which is not unrelated to the public relations strategy discussed above – is the *political* appeal of such a problem. This is particularly the case in local government and especially in those cities with a concentration of the black vote in a number of inner-city wards, and where the electoral results from these wards may be decisive for political control of the council.

A fifth reason relates to the fact that the equal opportunity issue has become part of the professionalising rhetoric of personnel management specialists, an integral component of the profession's claim to the custodianship of employment policy and legal issues (see, for example, IPM Joint Standing Committee on Discrimination 1978: 43–5). An important part of the personnel profession's enthusiasm (such as it is) for EO policies lies in the general insistence upon 'best practice' in employment procedures generally; an EO policy is seen as an extension of this principle.[5] There are two dimensions of the professional personnel model of 'best practice' which require emphasis here: one, it offers a *technical* rationale for formal, 'rational' employment procedures, that is that in this manner the best possible recruits are selected and the optimum utility derived from manpower resources; and two, it is also a *moral* rationale, that is that such an approach serves to ensure the fairness of the process. The two are, in fact, opposite sides of the same coin: the technical justification is an aspect of the personnel function's defensive ideological repertoire, to be drawn upon and mobilised in the internal struggles for power and influence within the organisation; the moral component is an essential part of the personnel specialist's public relations role. As such, EO policy formulation and implementation is a good illustration of the convergence between technicism and welfarism in the work of the personnel profession (Watson 1977: 52–63).

Related to this is a sixth factor: the use to which individuals and, particularly it seems, personnel specialists, can put an EO policy in their personal mobility strategies within or between organisations. This however, is not restricted to those in managerial positions; an EO policy can serve the same useful end for trade unionists (for example, Torrington *et al.* 1982: 25–30). These last two factors may be categorised as more concerned with *career* than *organisational* issues.

Finally, one other influential factor which deserves mention is the impact of *external* organisational policy. This can take three forms. The first of these is found in multi-national organisations; here one may find policy imperatives and even, in some cases, the *minutiae* of policy and procedural detail (Torrington *et al.* 1982: 18–24), being imported by an American or European controlling organisation and imposed on its United Kingdom subsidiaries or operating divisions. Second, policy may be formulated by management in the United Kingdom, although more with an eye to satisfying the requirements of top management elsewhere than anything else. Third, even in wholly United Kingdom-owned organisations, policy may be developed centrally at a senior corporate level and passed down to, or imposed upon, subsidiary organisations.

There are thus four different factors which may result in pressure for an EO policy impinging upon, or developing within, an employing organisation: the *defensive*, the *political*, the *career* and the *external*. The important point to be borne in mind, however, is that these are not exclusive influences; it is to be expected that pressures from two or more of these areas will combine to plant and germinate the seeds of an EO policy. Equally noteworthy, perhaps, it should be emphasised that good intentions seem to play only a small part, if indeed any at all, in paving this particular road to hell!

Reflecting on this diversity of motivations and influences it is clear, perhaps not surprisingly, that there is also a wide variety in the details of the organisational postures and procedural arrangements which pass as EO policies. At one extreme, there are those organisations who express a public commitment to 'equal opportunity', in their job advertisements for example, but make no further moves towards the operationalisation of such a commitment. Similarly, there are those employers who appear to think that it is an adequate concession simply to adopt the Trades Union Congress 'model clause' in their agreements with trades unions.[6]

At the other end of the spectrum, however, there are highly elaborate policies which include a wide variety of topics from training, promotion and recruitment, to the provision of special facilities for particular ethnic minority groups, to systems for the detailed ethnic and gender monitoring of the work force. Good examples of this kind of comprehensive approach to EO policy formulation and implementation are the packages adopted by the Ford Motor Company[7] and Thames Television,[8] although other organisations could also have been cited. In between, there is a wide variety of 'half-way house' approaches to the issue.

Such diversity in practice characterises the United Kingdom's tradition of voluntarism in *all* areas of industrial relations and employment policy generally; there are no reasons for expecting that the issue of equal opportunity should be handled differently. However, in order to set the comprehensive approach to equal opportunity apart from other, less thorough-going, approaches, I shall, in the rest of this chapter, distinguish between two different approaches to policy: EO *statements*, basically superficial expressions of intent, and EO *programmes*, detailed packages covering such things as routine employment procedures, the role of trades unions and employees, training and ethnic monitoring.

Formulation and implementation: some problems

So far in this chapter I have distinguished voluntarism as one possible approach to the production of equal opportunity in employment, and discussed the reasons which appear to underlie this voluntary approach in the context of the United Kingdom. Further, a distinction has been drawn between superficial EO statements and comprehensive EO programmes. In the above discussion, I have deliberately talked about policy implementation and formulation in the same breath, as aspects of the same process. This I believe to be the correct approach if one is to avoid the fallacy of saying, for example, that an organisation's problem is simply that it has a good policy which it is failing to put into practice. That kind of interpretation misses four important points. First, policy-making is a practice in its own right and may, in some organisations, actually be an active substitute for 'doing something' about discrimination (Hitner *et al.* 1982: 25). Second, part of any employment policy is, or ought to be, the means by which it is to be implemented. In other words, the distinction between the formulation of policy content and the design of the means of its implementation may be difficult to maintain in specific instances. This is particularly the case in those situations in which training is an integral part of an EO policy. Third, the content of an EO policy, the nature of the organisational changes proposed therein, may constrain the degree to which such changes can be effected. Finally, once a policy is in effective operation, there will be some feed-back to policy-makers and, as a consequence of inadequacies or difficulties which then become apparent, changes in the content of the policy may be made. These are all compelling reasons for considering policy formulation and implementation (or, indeed, the lack of it) as aspects of one unified process. In the rest of this section, I shall draw upon the published research of other authors and my own research in the West Midlands to discuss some of the problems which may be encountered during this process.

Perhaps the best place to start such a discussion is the research carried out into the problems of 'managing the multi-racial work force' by a group from the University of Manchester Institute of Science and Technology (Hitner *et al.* 1982; Torrington *et al.* 1982). Based largely on case-studies of twelve organisations, which ranged from a textile mill to a hotel, a supermarket to a foundry, this research, although regrettably uncritical of the taken-for-granted managerial ideologies which it documents, does usefully examine some of the central issues involved in organisational EO policies. On the basis of their comparison of the EO initiatives in the case-study organisations, the authors come up with eight issues which critically affect the degree to which an EO initiative succeeds or fails.

In the first place, they argue that it is important to avoid generalised, packaged solutions to the problem of equal opportunity. Organisations differ one from another in a host of ways; what is appropriate and workable in one organisational setting is possibly not going to be a successful innovation in another. Therefore, EO policies should be individually designed for specific organisations. Next, following from this, EO policy must be contextually defined and relevant; it is, according to Hitner, Torrington and their colleagues, neither sufficient nor sensible to simply 'read off' a set of proscriptions or prescriptions from the appropriate legislation and impose it on the work-place. It follows from these conclusions that the development or introduction of EO policies as a result of *external* organisational factors is unlikely to make much impact on the day-to-day affairs of the organisation.

Third, it also seems to be clear from this research that, in order for an EO policy to be effective in any sense, some system of ethnic (and, by implication, gender) monitoring is necessary. Furthermore, it is equally clear that precision with respect to procedure and objectives is considerably easier to monitor than vague good intentions. This, of course, highlights the need to have an EO *programme*, in the sense in which I am using the term here. However, fourth, this does not obviate the necessity for an organisational EO *statement*; the authors argue that a generalised – and public – organisational commitment to the principles of equal opportunity is important. However, they also argue that such a commitment is most likely to emerge as part of the working-out of solutions to perceived organisational problems.

The fifth point in their argument concerns the need to have procedural controls built in to an EO policy. In essence, this amounts to a defence of the importance of general 'good employment practice', in the professional, personnel management sense. Their next two points are an extension of this: the need to avoid the use of arbitrary selection criteria; and the important role of training, in particular in the area of language and communication, in the operationalisation of a successful equal opportunity initiative. Once again, these conclusions point to the desirability of a detailed, co-ordinated programme. Finally, the research emphasises the importance of employee involvement, both formally, at the trade union level, and informally. Unless the co-operation and participation of the work force has been secured, an EO initiative is likely to encounter difficulties, if not overt obstruction.

There are, therefore, a number of obstacles to the successful formulation and implementation of organisational EO policies which are identified, either implicitly or explicitly, by the Manchester research team. Research by Chiplin and Sloane, into 'tackling (sex) discrimination at the workplace' 1982), has produced a broadly similar set of conclusions. The starting-place for intervention against discrimination, according to these authors, must be an awareness of the relevant legislation and case-law and an appreciation of the obligations thus placed upon the employer. In order to satisfy these legal requirements it is necessary for an organisation to have a monitored EO policy. There are two main aspects to the notion of 'monitoring' put forward by Chiplin and Sloane: one, it is important to maintain a constant awareness of the distribution of differing gender (and ethnic) categories of employee in the work force; and two, it is equally necessary to continually monitor the 'reasonableness' of the criteria for selection decision-making.

However, Chiplin and Sloane are adamant that, with respect to monitoring ethnic and gender distributions, the simple collection of statistics is *not* enough to decide whether or not discrimination exists in a particular setting. It is necessary to collect precise and detailed information; with respect to gender, this entails the use of variables such as marital status, presence and number of children in the home etc. On the basis of this monitoring exercise it is vital that the organisation consciously pursue remedies to the distributional disparities thus identified. These conclusions are further arguments for the necessity of an organised programme of intervention if the issue of equal opportunity is to be effectively tackled.

These are both useful pieces of research, particularly in as much as they complement and endorse each other with respect to their findings and recommendations. However, they also share two significant and related shortcomings. In the first place, they exemplify what is probably a dominant trend in managerial thinking, namely the view that the provision of equal opportunity can largely be guaranteed simply by the introduction of certain employment procedures. In other words, equal opportunity is defined as a *technical* problem, for which technical solutions are appropriate: monitoring systems, more 'rational' selection criteria, 'best practice' in general.

At one level, this is undoubtedly true; indeed, it is the view of the present author that such organisational innovations are vital and necessary conditions for any successful anti-discrimination intervention. However, a purely technical approach to equal opportunity misses an important – indeed crucial – aspect of the issue: attacking discrimination and promoting equal opportunity, both for women and black workers, are political measures whose legitimacy, either in the 'nation at large' or in the public domain of politics, cannot by any stretch of the imagination be regarded as either secure or consensual. Indeed, it is true to say that such consensus as there is, is largely negative; furthermore, there is good reason to suspect that in the present economic and political climate the notion of equal opportunity is becoming less rather than more publicly acceptable. Within organisations, this trend is manifest in overt racism or harassment, at worst, and stealthy opposition to EO initiatives, at best. With respect to ethnic monitoring, it is perhaps worth recording here that recent research by Jewson and Mason (1984–5, and this volume) argues that such an innovation may be used as a smoke-screen behind which discrimination continues to flourish.

Second, both of these analyses appear to rely, either explicitly (Hitner *et al.* 1982) or implicitly (Chiplin and Sloane 1982), on innovations and interventions stemming from, or administered by, professional personnel specialists within organisations. As the people who profess to skills in the field of employment procedures, employee relations and the law, the personnel profession is the obvious, or indeed perhaps the only, custodian of an EO policy within most organisations. Having recognised this, however, one must then also acknowledge the inescapable fact that within the political networks of the majority of organisations the personnel function has limited influence, authority or resources. Furthermore, the commitment of many personnel managers and officers to the professional personnel model of equity and equal opportunity is, to say the least, lukewarm.[9] These factors conspire together to ensure that, if equal opportunity is left in the care of the personnel profession, the prospects for women and black workers are likely to remain gloomy.

Some of the issues discussed here were also prominent in my own case-study of the formulation and implementation of an EO policy at KingCo, a large manufacturing company in the West Midlands. Since I have written the research up in detail elsewhere (Jenkins 1986:200–18), I shall do no more here than briefly adumbrate the case-study's broad outlines and conclusions.

King Components Ltd (KingCo) is a division of MMI, a larger manufacturing group. In response to the legislation of the mid-1970s, MMI introduced an EO policy. Following several unfavourable Industrial Tribunal decisions and some pressure from the CRE, an updated, more comprehensive, EO programme was developed and issued to companies within the group in 1981. The 'new' policy is a much more wide-ranging attempt to deal with the issue, both in terms of its scope and its rigour; it was produced as a direct result of difficulties experienced by MMI, particularly legal problems. As such, the new programme, the changes in procedure which it introduced and its accompanying training package, are largely intended to prevent further legal difficulties arising. In two senses, therefore, MMI's 1981 EO programme is *defensively* oriented. However, as experienced by the management and work force of KingCo, it is an *external* imposition.

As communicated to KingCo's employees through training sessions (for managers and supervisors) and documentation, the EO programme can be summarised as follows. First, the documentation and the training sessions are mainly concerned with the requirements established by the 1975 and 1976 Acts and the subsequent case-law. Second, the programme emphasises the need to avoid both direct and indirect discrimination with regard to 'race', ethnicity or gender.[10] Finally, the programme is impressively detailed at the procedural level; many routine aspects of employment practice, that is interviewing, application forms, promotion procedures, and so on, are affected by the policy's requirements. This procedural detail is given further force by the fact that infringements of the EO policy's requirement may lead to disciplinary action.

Here it is necessary to introduce a distinction between the *central* policy and the *local* policy. A clear illustration of this difference of emphasis concerns the degree to which individual employees may be held legally responsible for their actions. In reflection of Section 32(3) of the 1976 Race Relations Act, the MMI documentation points out that if the organisation take steps recommended in the Codes of Practice of the CRE or the Equal Opportunities Commission (EOC) to prevent its employees practising discrimination, then this might enable the company to avoid legal liability for that discrimination. However, this is a very small facet of a complex body of policy documentation; on balance, there is no reason to suspect that MMI, in formulating and implementing the policy, was actually trying to slough off its legal responsibilities.[11]

On examining the local version of the policy, as presented to managers and supervisors during the KingCo training sessions, a rather different picture emerges, however. Considerable emphasis was placed upon this aspect of the EO policy; they were told that having been acquainted with the company's requirements and the details of the policy they were personally legally responsible for their actions. Thus, although the issue of individual responsibility is not a major feature of the central policy, it is very important in the local version. The most plausible reason for the disjuncture is that KingCo's training department produced this particular reading of the central policy in order to give the issue of equal opportunity more weight, in an attempt to make the policy 'stick' in the minds of their managers.

With respect to the differences between the central and local policies, three things must be emphasised. First, there is little doubt that the manner in which the EO policy was presented in training sessions at KingCo, far from encouraging managers to take it more seriously, actually induced hostility to the policy and to the idea of equality of opportunity in general. Second, it is not simply the case that a policy requirement or a legal possibility was being misinterpreted, distorted or ignored by the training specialists at KingCo. If the architects of the 1976 Act had not created the possibility that an organisation might shed its legal responsibility in this fashion and if that possibility had not subsequently been written into MMI's EO policy, albeit unobtrusively, then it could not have figured in the training sessions at KingCo. It is not simply, as MMI senior personnel people insist, 'a dysfunctional aspect of implementation'; the problem was created in the initial formulation of the policy.

In this sense, therefore, both the central and local versions of the policy are, despite considerable differences of emphasis, recognisably part of the same body of policy. However, what MMI presents publicly as its Equal Opportunity Policy is not necessarily the same thing as the EO policy which its employees at KingCo understand to be in operation. In terms of a useful distinction recently put forward by Brewster *et al.* (1983), the central ersion is the *espoused policy* and the local version the *operational policy*.

Finally, the formulation and implementation of MMI's EO policy should be understood in the context of the organisation's broader industrial relations policies. In particular, it should be understood in the context of a strategy which has as its objective the enhancement of managerial control of the work-place, through strengthening the role and responsibilities of foremen and superintendents and undermining the power of the trade unions. The EO policy, in as much as it is partly concerned with increasing managerial control over decision-making, and given that the unions have been a source of 'race'-related problems for MMI in the past, is congruent with this broad strategy. This is not to say, however, that MMI's EO policy is a deliberate anti-union policy, simply to suggest that it 'fits in' with the tenor of the company's industrial relations strategy. In a different industrial relations climate one might imagine the development of a very different EO initiative.

Looking at the views held by the managers and supervisors who I interviewed concerning the equal opportunity issue, the situation may be summarised as follows. First, there is *at least* a large minority of both personnel specialists *and* managers at KingCo who disagree with all or part of MMI's EO policy. In particular, strong opposition was expressed to any accommodation being made over spoken and written competence in the English language. Second, the policy was seen as an external imposition, irrelevant to the situation at KingCo (although possibly relevant to other parts of MMI). Finally, there was a degree of confusion in the minds of some of the interviewees, including members of the personnel function, as to what MMI's policy (and, by implication, the legislation) actually says. Despite the documentation and the training sessions, some of them, for example, understood the policy to introduce reverse discrimination or 'quotas', as discriminating against native whites, or as open to abuse by black people. It is perhaps worth emphasising the similarity between the views of the line managers and those of the personnel specialists in KingCo. The most important reasons for this similarity appear to be the relatively low level of professional training of the personnel specialists and their career backgrounds, most having been either supervisory or administrative staff, or union officials promoted as 'poachers turned game-keepers'.

There is thus a considerable disjuncture between the organisational EO policy and the views of managers of KingCo. This disjuncture is partly a reflection of the difference which exists in all organisations between the formal bureaucratic rules and procedures and the contingency-constrained practices of individual actors as organisational members and as members of informal work-place cultures. However, the gulf between policy and the views of local management is also a reflection of the fact that the majority of the United Kingdom population have yet to accord legitimacy to the active pursuit of equal opportunity by and on behalf of their black fellow-citizens. In addition, there is also the problem, discussed earlier, of the imposition of an EO policy by management outside the organisation under immediate consideration. Lastly, it should be recognised that the contradictions within MMI's EO policy communicate themselves to managers and personnel specialists at KingCo, who react accordingly. On the one hand, the policy insists that MMI's goal is to ensure that all employees, regardless of race or gender are allowed to develop their talents and abilities to the full. On the other, however, an equally plausible interpretation – and this is the view of some of those who I interviewed – would focus upon the policy's defensive preoccupation with avoiding legal trouble and the perceived emphasis upon the responsibilities of individual employees and agents. The contradiction between the espoused intentions of the EO policy and its local presentation generates cynicism and disenchantment among KingCo's managers.[12]

Finally, to look at the views of the local trades unions, it is apparent that there is a complete lack of consensus on this issue. Split between those stewards who reflect the predominantly racist and anti-equal opportunity stance of the (almost totally white) shop-floor and those who are closer to the more liberal position of the unions nationally, the unions locally are largely inactive on this question. Even had they been able to form a consensual platform for action, however, the company has taken no steps at all to consult with the local unions. This has only served to deepen the hostility to the EO policy which was present in the first place.

This then is something of the situation within KingCo at the time of the research. It should come as no surprise that MMI's EO policy had, as yet, to make any impact on the day-to-day practices of local management. In addition to the factors discussed above, however, three other aspects of the organisational situation contributed to this state of affairs. In the first place, the absence of monitored ethnic record-keeping served to make the policy largely unenforceable with respect to promotion or recruitment. MMI had, however, recognised this problem before I started to do the research and taken steps to remedy the situation. Second, some aspects of routine formal and informal employment practices at KingCo had hindered the operation of the EO policy. Specifically these were single-person interviewing (which undermines the accountability of selection decisions) and 'word-of-mouth' recruitment, which is potentially indirectly discriminatory and may create the conditions wherein direct racist discrimination may flourish. Third, the current economic recession also limited the practical impact of the EO policy. Due to low levels of recruitment and promotion, managers at KingCo were effectively putting the EO policy to the back of their minds.

ince, given the ethnic composition of the factory, it rarely comes up as an ssue in other contexts. This low level of visibility of the equal opportunity ssue in the eyes of managers combines with a strongly felt sense of the policy's external imposition to make it appear irrelevant to most managers and supervisors. Short of regular refresher training sessions, there is probably little that the company can do to improve matters. A solution of his nature might, in any case, prove to be counter-productive, simply increasing managerial resistance to the notion of equality of opportunity.

The politics of equal opportunity

n this paper I have discussed some of the variety in the voluntary responses o the issue of equal opportunity which currently exists in the private employment sector in the United Kingdom. In the main, I have concentrated my attention upon organisationally specific equal opportunity policies and programmes. I have also outlined the many organisational obstacles which such voluntary EO initiatives encounter during the formulation and implementation process. As a consequence of these obstacles and impediments it is probably true to say that voluntarism has, at best, severe limitations as a strategy for combating ethnic or gender discrimination and disadvantage in the labour market.

To concentrate upon the technical aspects of EO policy formulation and implementation, although vitally necessary, is not sufficient if we are to understand the limits to voluntarism. Nor is it enough to embrace the organisational politics of the relationship between the personnel function and line management, important though that relationship is. If the limitations of a voluntarist response to racist discrimination are to be fully appreciated, it is necessary to look outside the boundaries of individual organisations, to national politics and popular racism.

It might, of course, be argued that national politics are irrelevant to the important issues within organisations. This is manifestly not the case, however; it is clear from the speeches, writings and parliamentary answers of major politicians, particularly within the Conservative Party,[13] that they deeply distrust the principle of equality of opportunity, seeing it as a brake upon free enterprise and the market and as something which will disadvantage white Britons or disrupt the sanctity of 'traditional' family life. At the national institutional level, this distrust has resulted in the under-resourcing and political undermining of the Commission for Racial Equality, in particular, although the Equal Opportunities Commission has had its fair share of vicissitudes.

These oppositional views are shared by many – perhaps the majority – of the nation's managers and workers.[14] The public pronouncements of politicians and newspaper leader-writers do not create popular racism; they do, however, serve to grant legitimacy to those in all walks of life who continue to regard their black fellow-citizens as alien and undeserving outsiders. Within organisations such a political stance provides support for those who would oppose the promotion of equal opportunity for black workers. To a lesser degree much the same can be said with respect to the linked issues of equal pay for women and the employment of women outside the 'traditional' areas of 'women's work'. Until it is recognised that equal opportunity is a political issue of the first magnitude and not simply a problem of employment practice, which can be met and solved solely by the use of certain management techniques or the introduction of new employment procedures, it is unlikely that the labour-market position of either women or black workers is going to improve.

To say this is to recognise that the legal, administrative and voluntarist approaches are entirely constrained by the limitations imposed by a white populace and political establishment which has little enthusiasm for greater equality of opportunity. High unemployment can only serve to exacerbate this situation. Although something can probably be achieved within these political constraints, it seems, therefore, that the only effective source of pressure for equal opportunity is likely to be the black community. Such a conclusion, however, overlooks the possibility that in the present political climate the most likely state response to black resistance is increased repression, rather than the extension of greater equality of opportunity. To reiterate: the evidence of this chapter suggests that significant advances could be made by changing the organisational processes and procedures of employment. Whether or not these changes will materialise is, however, largely dependent upon the political climate, both within organisations and at the national level.

8

Monitoring equal opportunities policies: principles and practice*

NICK JEWSON AND DAVID MASON

Introduction

The object of this paper is to explore and clarify a number of conceptual issues concerned with equal opportunities policies and their monitoring. It is not intended either to offer a set of concrete proposals about the minutiae of policy implementation or to present a detailed research report. Nevertheless, our experience of attempting to advise a manufacturing company on the monitoring of an equal opportunities policy, and of subsequent research we have conducted in a local authority, strongly suggests that numerous 'down-to-earth' practical problems and difficulties arise from misunderstandings and confusions about the philosophy underlying equal opportunities policies. Thus, different sections of the work force may have varying expectations of such policies and of the social practices which they entail. It is under the pressure of practical problems that participants in the policy-making process frequently fail to identify and to recognise either the various conceptions of equal opportunities invoked by different sections of the labour force or the different conceptions which the same individual may employ in varying contexts and circumstances. We have observed situations in which these different definitions have been in contradiction with one another, or have had implications which those who held them had not thought through at the outset. Puzzlement, suspicion and anger have, on occasion, been generated by the simultaneous operation of these different taken-for-granted assumptions. It is with these social processes that we are concerned in this paper. (See the more extended discussion of these issues in Jewson and Mason 1986b).

The need for effective monitoring as an integral part of equal opportunities policies is widely agreed (EOC 1978; CRE 1978a, 1978b). Monitoring is, however, almost always conceived as a statistical exercise;

125

that is the keeping of records concerned with applications for jobs, short-listing, appointments, promotions and progress and the like. It is generally suggested that such record keeping has two functions. First, as a diagnostic tool which may reveal *primae facie* evidence of discrimination. Secondly, as a means of charting the subsequent progress of black[1] or women workers within an organisation which has adopted an equal opportunities policy. There is a potential confusion here. Progress towards greater represen-tativeness has clearly on occasion been taken as an indicator of the pro-vision of equality of opportunity. This is a view which is clearly taken by many of the *participants* in policy making. In other words it is very easy for equality of outcomes to be regarded as one – or indeed the only – criterion of equality of opportunity.[2] The presence or absence of equality of outcomes becomes the yardstick by which the provision of equality of opportunity is measured. In so far as this confusion is widely shared it has the consequence of giving ammunition to those conservative thinkers who, like Anthony Flew (1984), would wish to attack the very existence of bodies like the CRE. It also gives rise to a potential for considerable disappointment and disillusionment among those involved in policy making. The intended beneficiaries of the policy may feel cheated but unable to identify the means by which the deception has been perpetrated. Sections of management may feel aggrieved at being the object of continuing and intensified accusations of discrimination, despite having developed employment procedures which appear, at least, to be scrupulously fair. It may even be that following the implementation of an equal opportunities policy, frustrated and contradic-tory expectations have the consequence of increasing bitterness and tensions. Thus, in our research company an elaborate policy had been developed in relation both to racial and sexual discrimination which was widely regarded, inside and outside the company, as embodying fair procedures. Nevertheless a significant body of black and women workers on-site claimed that it could not possibly be fair because black people and women were still under-represented in skilled and supervisory positions.

Lest we be misunderstood, we should make it clear that we are not arguing that statistical monitoring is an inappropriate procedure. Nor would we deny that it may be essential to reveal some forms of disadvantage and/or discrimination. However, we believe that taken on its own it may both create the potential for misunderstanding and fail effectively to ensure policy implementation. Moreover, both the wider literature and our research indicate that statistical monitoring is neither widespread nor easy to carry out. A central feature of our argument is that this should not be allowed to become an excuse for lack of political will in the pursuit of equality of opportunity. Accordingly, part of what we do in this paper is to propose a wider conceptualisation of monitoring than is usual. Our conceptualisation includes a range of issues which are central to the success of equal opportunities policies but which are frequently not seen as requiring the systematic and continuing surveillance that we are suggesting. Whilst we would not suggest that our broad conception of monitoring is easy to put into practice, it does offer wide scope for up-dating policy and for exposing and confronting differences of view. In addition, we feel that some aspects of the monitoring process more broadly conceived may facilitate the important book-keeping exercises included under narrower definitions by gaining the confidence of the work force and creating a climate of co-operation. Effective monitoring is crucial to the existence of a dynamic policy. An equal opportunities policy thus becomes a practical forum in which employers and employees together resolve a range of managerial and workplace problems and so make good the widespread claim that effective equal opportunity programmes contribute to the general profitability and efficiency of an establishment. Certainly it is clear to us that, in the company we have researched, the equal opportunities programme arose out of a specific set of problems and indeed remains a serious practical concern for workers and management. In other words, it is bound up with such vital matters as the general climate of industrial relations, the profitability and efficiency of the organisation, its capacity to attract investment of funding, and its ability to respond effectively to changing conditions in the market-place or political system. As a practical problem it is not most readily dealt with by the imposition of theoretical blueprints drawn up apart from the day-to-day context in which they must operate (though this is not to say that externally developed guidelines may not be helpful as a starting point for policy formation). What is required are policies tailored to the particular needs of the organisation and its employees. However, this makes it all the more important to be clear about such elements as are integral to all equal opportunities policies.

Elements of equal opportunities policies

In the course of our research we found it necessary to distinguish the following dimensions of equal opportunities policies:

(a)   The existence of a formal programme embodying procedures which can be demonstrated to be fair. This covers such matters as procedures for filling vacancies, promotion and recruitment, grievance and discipline.

(b)   The implementation of this programme; that is the translation of the formal policy into day-to-day practice.

(c)   The effectiveness of the programme; that is the consequences of implementation for patterns of recruitment, promotion, etc.

(d)   The perceptions of the programme by the work force; that is the extent to which the work force believes the formal policy to be fair, to have been implemented and to be effective.

Each of these four elements of equal opportunities policies entails a different procedure for investigation.

The key issue with regard to the existence of a formal programme is whether work-place procedures are in accord with principles of equity and fairness. The relationship between the formal programme and principles of justice may, as we shall see, be difficult to determine in the abstract and in advance. For example, principles which seem unequivocal in themselves may be ambiguous in relation to specific situations and circumstances. It is necessary, therefore, constantly to review and reconsider such principles in light of experience.

The key issue with regard to implementation is whether all parties concerned are adhering to the established procedures of the equal opportunities programme. In this context it is often suggested that training has an important part to play in achieving conformity to procedures.

The key issue with regard to effectiveness is whether agreed procedures produce an equitable distribution of black people and women among the work force. Two indices of equity are often conflated. One is proportional distribution within the work force measured against some chosen standard. The other refers to the use of non-discriminatory procedures. These, we shall argue below, represent two quite different conceptions of fairness.

The key issue with regard to perceptions of equal opportunities policies is whether justice is seen to be done; that is the ways in which various parties evaluate the fairness, implementation and effectiveness of the policy. There is a potential here for disagreement and misunderstanding *both* about the objectives of a policy and the extent to which they are achieved.

Monitoring in our conception, then, draws attention to the links between the various elements of equal opportunities policies. The paper will now examine each of these elements in turn.

The formal programme

The existence of the policy itself is not usually regarded as a matter for monitoring. Nevertheless, there are at least two senses in which such a view is inadequate. First, there may well be outside bodies interested in whether a particular institution has a formal policy. These might include the CRE, the EOC, local community groups and, perhaps, trade unions. (We may note in this context that a survey of 500 leading employers by the EOC revealed that only 25% of respondents had written policy statements (EOC 1978).)[3] Second, the process of monitoring necessarily implies a willingness to change and modify policy. If it is not to be merely a pious statement of intent or a piece of tokenism there must be a commitment to continuous review.

At the heart of an equal opportunities policy is the question of what are to be the principles of equity and fairness which are enshrined in the formal programme. There appear to us to be two quite different and opposed interpretations which are, none the less, often confused with one another. On the one hand fairness may be said to refer to an absence of racist or sexist criteria of decision-making. This interpretation is a *procedural* one. It suggests that providing unfair discrimination is removed from the procedures of selection at work, over the generations the members of disadvantaged and minority groups will acquire the qualifications and resources necessary to carry them into the highest reaches of society. Many of those who subscribe to this view would regard themselves as of 'liberal' outlook, yet it should be clear that the roots of this position are to be found in a form of nineteenth-century economic liberalism well-expressed in the following remark by Enoch Powell: 'Perhaps the Free World has too long denied itself the right to proclaim that the market economy it opposes to communism is the most effective enemy of discrimination between individuals, classes and races' (quoted in Foot 1969: 129). In essence this view asserts that equity is guaranteed by the unfettered operation of the capitalist free market in labour. It follows that the objective of equal opportunities policy should be the elimination of obstacles to 'free competition' at work which, it is assumed, prevent individual talent and skill from expressing themselves and from determining the rewards of labour.[4] (If underrepresentation persists over a period of time this may be explained in terms of either a lack of effort or the inhibiting effects of cultural values and family structures (see Flew 1984; Honeyford 1984).)

On the other hand, a more radical conception understands fairness to exist when members of different groups are distributed in proportion to their presence in the wider population.[5] The achievement of such a state of affairs may involve a willingness to intervene in the operation of the labour market. Such intervention would require the more or less explicit setting of quotas and a reassessment of the significance of qualifications. The latter may take the form of questioning the necessity or relevance of some qualifications for a job. It could even entail a willingness to set aside some relevant qualifications in order to achieve what is regarded as the more urgent or important goal of racial and sexual fairness. In other words, some disadvantaged people would be given an opportunity, which they would not have obtained by virtue of the free operation of the labour market, on the grounds that in the past other members of the groups to which they belong have been severely discriminated against.

The different conceptions of fairness entailed in the liberal and radical views lead to two very different practical indices of the successful operation of equal opportunities policies. The first interpretation emphasises that a formal programme must ensure that non-discriminatory criteria of selection and decision-making are institutionalised at work. This is the yardstick by which the fairness of formal policy is judged. The second view, in contrast, concentrates on the distribution of the relevant population throughout the work force. In this case the formal fairness of an equal opportunities programme is judged by reference to the ensuing distribution of black people and women within an establishment.

As already noted, these two principles and indices of fairness are often confused with one another. To assume that the first leads automatically to the second is mistaken (cf. Chiplin and Sloane 1982:42). The dilemma for equal opportunities policies at the work-place is that the elimination of both direct and indirect discrimination cannot necessarily be expected to lead to equality of distribution. This is because of more deep-rooted structural disadvantage, of which the discontinuity of work experience typical of the life-cycle of female workers or the 'underachievement' of black people within the British education system are particularly relevant examples. In other words, this conception of the relationship between 'fair procedure' and 'equality of distribution' makes a series of unjustified assumptions about the existence of and access to meritocratic competition for rewards and status in society as a whole.

Given these limitations, the only way to achieve equality of distribution would be by reverse discrimination, that is forms of intervention which go far beyond those currently envisaged by the CRE and EOC and which are contrary to British law. In these circumstances it is effectively the case that both employers and review bodies can only adopt a procedural approach to the design of equal opportunities policies: that is, fair criteria of selection and decision-making. Even those who pursue radical policy objectives, therefore, are forced to operate within the framework of liberal rhetoric and legal constraints. This has implications for the other issues which we shall discuss below under the monitoring of effectiveness and perceptions.

Before we proceed to these matters, however, it is necessary to draw attention to the significance of the organisational context in which policy emerges and is developed. The formulation of an equal opportunities policy may well entail a formalisation of employment practice within an establishment, which may have implications for the success and failure of the policy. It is frequently noted that the existence of informality and the 'old-boy-network', the absence of explicit criteria for decision-making and the failure to keep records all contribute to a situation in which it is both easy to discriminate and to conceal such discrimination. Secrecy and informality are frequently cited as the enemies of equality of opportunity (see, for example, EOC 1981b: para. 329; Jenkins 1982). However, it should not be assumed that there is a straightforward connection between greater formality and greater equality of opportunity.[6] (These and other issues are discussed at length in Jewson and Mason 1986a.) There are two aspects to this question. First, consideration should be given to whether the formal procedures are implemented, a matter which is discussed in the next section. Second, it is rarely noted that there may be positive advantages to the maintenance of some aspects of informality. To cite an example from our own research company, the development of a formal equal opportunities policy, following a change of ownership, was part of a wider process of formalisation and bureaucratisation within the plant. These developments were associated with the creation of a detailed formal programme intended to deal with a proliferation of allegations of racial discrimination. One of the consequences was that a leader of the Asian work force on the site had his hitherto close informal liaison with the personnel manager effectively terminated, with the result that he suffered a loss of prestige and influence in the eyes of both management and Asian workers. With the breakdown of these informal relations, complaints of discrimination took an increasingly formal and legalistic form. In other words, not only was a valued channel of communication lost but also the change was seen as indicative of an intention to discriminate. Interestingly, it now appears to be the case that the personnel department is seeking to re-establish informal contacts in order to reinforce and facilitate the operation of the equal opportunities programme.

The question of informality must also be considered in another context. There are crucial aspects of relationships at work which cannot be subject to bureaucratic forms of control. Equality of opportunity may well include equality of access to these informal channels of communication and activity which are intrinsic to the operation of all organisations. For example, ethnic minorities may seek equality of access to 'word-of-mouth' systems of recruitment (cf. Dex 1978/9); or female managers may require access to the leisure and informal business relationships in which important work-related contacts and deals are made (cf. Cooper and Davidson 1982). In short, informal channels of communication among ethnic minority or female workers may have advantageous consequences for the population concerned. We should also note, however, that their very existence is frequently indicative of the exclusion of these groups from involvement in other channels, both formal and informal, which are of far greater significance.

Implementation

The existence of a formal equal opportunities policy does not guarantee that any steps will be taken to promote equality of opportunity. There are many examples in the literature of equal opportunities policies which have not been implemented. This may be because policy is imposed from the outside and is not seen as relevant (Torrington *et al.* 1982: 23), because it is not communicated to the work force by senior personnel (Torrington *et al.* 1982: 28), or because trade unions specifically oppose and frustrate the policy (EOC n.d.: 113; Snell *et al.* 1981: 66).

All of these are examples of situations in which equal opportunities policies are not implemented. However, even in cases where a formal policy has been developed and communicated to their work force, as recommended by the CRE and EOC, there remains the possibility that individuals and groups who have responsibility for selection, grievance and disciplinary decisions may be able to circumvent formal procedures. Such circumvention may simply take the form of neglecting to operate prescribed practices. More subtly, however, in addition to 'circumvention by neglect' there may also be 'circumvention by manipulation'; that is, the letter of formal procedures may be followed in order to frustrate the spirit behind them. Discrimination occurs through the misapplication of anti-discriminatory measures and practices. Some examples will illustrate the point. Our own and other studies have come across the practice of 'fixing' job descriptions and advertisements so that they may freely circulate among the work force without danger that black people or women will apply. At one of our research sites we have been told that an internal job advertisement called for 'O' level English and Maths *and* experience as a fork-lift driver: only one person in the plant fulfilled the criteria (cf. the discussion of 'genuine occupational qualifications' in EOC 1982: paras 12–15). Another example of circumvention by manipulation is that of employers who exclude women from certain categories of employment, or select them for redundancy, on the grounds that they are prevented by protective legislation from undertaking certain kinds of night-work and shift-work (EOC 1981b: para. 3.28, see also para. 3.26; EOC 1980: para. 3.11). Employers can apply for exemption orders but it may suit their interests not to do so. Attempts at circumvention by manipulation may also make use of spurious appeals to exemption clauses within the legislation: for example there appears to be a widespread but quite erroneous belief amongst employers that the absence of lavatory facilities justifies the recruitment of one sex only. Sometimes such appeals are patently absurd, as in the case of a firm which employed only men on full-time work and only women on part-time work, but claimed this was not discriminatory because they had six of each! (EOC 1980: para 3.10).

Training is frequently seen as a central feature of the process of implementation. A number of authors have shown, however, that there is some doubt about the effectiveness of such training, that its character and consequences are subject to variation, and that the efficacy of training depends to a large extent on its perceived relevance as well as on the vigour with which it is pursued by those in managerial authority (Peppard 1980, 1983; Shaw 1981/2). In the course of our research we have come across evidence which is in line with these observations. We have encountered three broad types of training activities: those concerned with the explication of the law and of organisational procedures; those concerned with extending awareness of differing cultural backgrounds and requirements (particularly where these are seen as relevant to the recruitment process); and racism-awareness courses which appear to have as their aim the unmasking of explicit or implicit racism.

The question of training in procedural matters need not detain us here, although it is necessary to note that if it is to be effective such training must reach a broad spectrum of the work force. We have found evidence that cultural background training was well received in our research company and was felt to be helpful and relevant for those involved in selection procedures. We should note here, however, the extent to which commitment to equal opportunities policies is related to the existence of perceived managerial problems. In our research company the equal opportunities policy was supposedly concerned with both racial and sexual disadvantage but had clearly been developed in response to the organisational consequences of complaints about racial discrimination. Thus attempts to parallel cultural awareness training in the field of race with lectures about the position and special difficulties of women were clearly seen by all concerned as largely irrelevant. Hence, although a session on the cultural backgrounds of different ethnic groups was allowed to run on for some fifteen hours, a ninety-minute talk on women was clearly regarded as more than enough.

In the local authority, racism-awareness courses have been less well received. A highly didactic approach was clearly resented by senior managers to whom we have spoken. In addition attempts to draw attention to implicit racism and to the pervasiveness of racism in British society were clearly seen by the audience as a personal attack in which, both as individuals and as representatives of white society, they were 'in the dock'. The relevant issue here is not whether the observations made in the course were justified. Rather the point is that they appear to have had a counter-productive effect upon the attitudes of managers towards the equal opportunities policy as a whole. There was clearly a feeling that both training in cultural backgrounds and procedural instruction would have been more job-relevant and more acceptable. A final and crucial point to note is that the consequence of all forms of training are unpredictable and therefore themselves require to be constantly monitored. For example, training might contribute to 'circumvention by manipulation'. Thus, as we were forcefully reminded by a trade union official at one site, training which is not ultimately backed up by sanctions is unlikely to be effective.

This takes us into the question of intra-organisational power struggles. Relations between different levels of management and of the work force, and the power struggles resulting from these, will have a direct effect on the capacity to implement policy. The relationship between line management and the personnel department is of particular importance. The issue of the involvement of the personnel department in equal opportunities policies is not simply one of the degree to which personnel is *willing* to extend its responsibilities, as Torrington *et al.* imply (1982: 114–15). Rather it is a question of the extent to which the structure of the organisation, and the pattern of power struggles within the establishment, allows, or indeed impels, the personnel department to become involved. As Jenkins (1982) in particular has noted, in the case of manual and routine non-manual occupations in manufacturing industry and the public sector, line managers almost always have the final say in recruitment decisions. Resistance to equal opportunities policy may be indicative, for example, of hostility to increasing formalisation which, it is feared, will reduce the general autonomy of lower line management. By the same token equal opportunities may be employed by some groups, such as the personnel department, as part of a general strategy for increasing their influence within the organisation. Both of these features were evident in the company which we have studied where, as we have seen, the development of the policy coincided with generally increased levels of formalisation. (We are not, of course, seeking to argue that equal opportunities policies are never resisted in their own right. Some individuals and groups do wish to discriminate. Routine racism and sexism certainly flourished at our research site and that of Jenkins (1982).)

In conclusion, then, we may note that the heavy emphasis of many authors on the need for collecting data and records only makes sense in the context of rigorous and continuous review procedures operated by senior managers who have the authority to insist upon implementation (Department of Employment 1972). Otherwise, it is a purely cosmetic exercise. The implementation of equal opportunities policies, then, requires the analysis of and sensitivity to the complex pattern of formal and informal relationships which constitute the organisation. It implies that the policy must be tailored to the organisation and that different types of organisation may require different types of policy.

Effectiveness

We do not wish to reiterate here points commonly made in the literature (see, in particular, Chiplin and Sloane 1982: chs. 4 and 5). Moreover, a number of the relevant issues have already been raised in the section on formal programmes. There are, however, some further matters which warrant comment. Just as there is a potential for confusion between the liberal and radical principles of fairness described above, so the judgement of effectiveness is itself open to misunderstandings deriving from the same source. Firstly the presence of black people or women in supervisory or management positions cannot be taken as a sufficient indication of procedural fairness. For example particular individuals might be selected for such positions precisely because they are atypical members of the groups to which they belong. They might, for example, be particularly acquiescent or deferential. Their presence in the middle or higher echelons of the establishment may be a product of discrimination rather than its absence. It is always necessary, then, to check the fairness and implementation of formal policy, whatever the distribution of the relevant population may be. A second point is that equality of distribution of black people and women within the work force can occur as a result of specific employment practices which may be regarded as ill-advised. Hitner provides an example in his case study of Threads Ltd., where promotion was made available to a number of Asians who happened to speak the language relevant for communicating with some members of the work force. This ultimately led to a variety of organisational and managerial problems (1982: 9).

Where equal opportunities policies fail to achieve a proportional distribution of black and women workers in the work force, attempts may be made at direct intervention (cf. Bindman 1980). Two different principles may be invoked in achieving this objective. We may call these 'positive action' and 'positive discrimination'.[7] Positive action aims to increase the numbers of people in the disadvantaged population able to benefit from formal procedures; that is to say, in the classic liberal tradition it seeks to remove educational and other forms of disadvantage which prevent individual members of particular groups competing in the market-place on an equal basis with individual members of other groups. It would, therefore, include such measures as the provision of crèche facilities for women workers or language training for members of ethnic minorities. (For other suggestions see EOC 1982: 11, 12). Behind this strategy lies the assumption that its successful implementation will have the consequence of eradicating differential patterns of distribution but it does not invoke such principles as the imposition of quotas. It thus remains committed to individual achievement whilst directing policy action towards the removal of collective barriers to such achievement.

By contrast, positive discrimination involves the more radical policy of deliberately manipulating selection procedures and standards so as to ensure that a proportional number of the members of specific deprived groups receive relevant occupational placings and rewards. A commitment to minimum standards may be retained but individuals are selected because of their group membership rather than because they are the best qualified candidates. What is not often recognised, however, is that a very large number and wide range of occupations require few or no functionally specific qualifications. This is the case in the bulk of manual and routine non-manual occupations. As Jenkins (1982, 1986) has pointed out, in such occupations acceptability criteria (whether or not a person will 'fit in') are of much more salience than suitability criteria (technical or functionally specific qualifications or experience). It is often argued that such a situation facilitates racial and sexual discrimination. We would only note here that it, *ipso facto*, makes possible the strategy of positive discrimination.

Positive discrimination, then, is collectivist in conception but individualist in action, since it involves positive *discrimination* between individuals at the point of selection. This form is, of course, prohibited under the Race Relations Act (1976) and the Sex Discrimination Act (1975). The fact that the principles of individualism and collectivism are simultaneously involved in both positive discrimination and positive action to some extent explains the frequent confusion between the two and the mistaken assumptions that the policy measures derived from one type can achieve the policy objectives of the other. It also explains the extreme hostility which proposals for positive discrimination often evoke, since they simultaneously involve the imposition of a collectivist conception on a sphere of social life usually associated, in capitalist societies, with extreme forms of individualism and, at the same time, they reverse the principles of legitimation normally applied at the point of individual selection.

An important point to note is that positive action, as we have defined it, does not necessarily lead to a situation in which members of different groups are equally distributed throughout the occupational structure. This is because the social sources of variation in individual ability and aspiration are many and varied and it is difficult to conceive of a positive-action policy which will deal with all of them. Those who see the goal of equal opportunities policy as completely equal distribution should recognise that the logical implication is positive discrimination in our sense. This indeed may account for the fact that people in our research examples frequently perceived the introduction of an equal opportunities policy as the prelude to positive discrimination. For example, we have come across a situation in which white employees refused to fill in ethnic self-classification forms because they believed this to be a prelude to the dismissal of some workers in order to increase the number of black employees. We have also come across the case of a senior local government officer who believed that the confusion between equality of opportunity and equality of outcome was leading to pressure on him to engage in positive discrimination. This was because only an increased proportion of black and female workers was regarded by his political superiors as satisfactory evidence of his operation of the equal opportunities policy. He claimed to be under intense informal pressure to engage in positive discrimination.

What we find in this example, then, is not simply the bureaucratisation of decision-making but also its politicisation. Political decision-makers had radical policy objectives but were forced to operate within the constraints of liberal procedures. They may well have resorted to 'behind-the-scenes' pressure in order to achieve the desired result. Thus we would argue that the confusion of the two conceptions of equal opportunities discussed in this paper may not always be entirely accidental.

Perceptions

In the literature the monitoring of perceptions is occasionally dealt with, typically under such headings as 'felt discrimination' (Hitner 1982) or the 'monitoring of reactions' (Tavistock Institute 1978). The consequence is that perceptions of equal opportunities policies are relatively narrowly defined and considered. For instance, under the heading of the 'monitoring of reactions', the Tavistock writers are principally concerned with letters of complaint. However, such analysis begs the question of who complains and under what circumstances. This points us towards a monitoring programme which actively seeks out perceptions and enables participants to define what they regard as relevant parameters. In this context we may note that the frequent claim that black people and women are over-sensitive to discrimination may result from a failure to understand the situations in which certain acts are perceived as discriminatory, whatever the real motives may have been.

Some aspects of equal opportunities policy intrinsically entail a subjective element in their definition. Sexual harassment is a case in point. Whilst at the extremes few observers would have any doubts, in many cases whether and when remarks or actions constitute sexual harassment is not self-evident and cannot be bureaucratically defined. Does the use of obscene language and the telling of 'dirty' jokes constitute sexual harassment? Or, indeed, might exclusion from such activities itself be held to be a form of unfair sexual discrimination? Here monitoring of equal opportunities can only be conducted by means of active search for and collective discussion of the perceptions of participants.[8]

Certainly, whatever formal procedures are devised, people should have the right not to be subject to insulting racist and sexist ideologies. This issue is complicated, however, by the relationship between the formal and informal aspects of equal opportunities policies noted above. Sexist and racist ideologies may offer managers and supervisors a means of controlling sections of the work force. These are forms of control which may mask or legitimise inequalities of power and authority within the plant. However, if we consider the example of sexist ideologies, these may offer those workers who are subject to them a type and degree of countervailing power. Just as male supervisors may seek to control female workers in the context of sexist joking relationships, so members of the female labour force may under certain circumstances turn these personal contacts to their advantage (Pollert 1981: 139–45). In her study Dhooge (1981) has also noted how Asian women workers took advantage of the racist and sexist assumptions of their employers to exert a limited degree of control over their working conditions.

Monitoring of perceptions is also of significance in evaluating the effectiveness and implementation of equal opportunities policies. For example, the absence of applications for promotion from certain sections of the work force may not be due to the failure of the programme to eliminate formal or informal unfair practices. Rather it may be a function of the meanings and perceptions of work that are current in the labour force. Thus, low occupational aspirations may be unaffected by the removal of obstacles to occupational advancement. It is for this reason that radicals would see a major function of policy as the raising of consciousness. Here equal opportunities policy is conceived as part of a longer term political struggle.

Perceptions of work are not simply derived from within the plant. Nevertheless such perceptions may be influenced by the way in which management treats the work force. Thus for example, as the EOC has noted, the different titles for jobs performed by men and women may reflect not merely the nature of the work performed but also the management's attitude to male and female employees. Thus men may be employed as salesmen, chefs and personal assistants; women as shop assistants, cooks and secretaries (see EOC 1981a: 40).

As we have seen, one of the complexities of operating an equal opportunities policy is that participants may use a variety of different criteria by which to judge the effectiveness and implementation of a programme. In this context, where equality of opportunity and equality of outcome are confused, equal opportunities policy may even be regarded by some as a cover-up for racist and sexist practices, a view which may be reinforced by activities such as circumvention by manipulation. In addition, the fact that equal opportunities policies arise in an organisational context, where groups are competing for power, gives rise to further sources of confusion. Thus, in our research company, we have come across some evidence which suggests that lower line management and supervisors are concerned to devise ways of maintaining their autonomy in the face of increasing pressure towards formality and bureaucratisation. One of the ways in which they may seek to do this is by clinging onto their 'traditional' right to make recruitment and promotion decisions. In exercising this right they appear to be seeking to develop networks of personal allegiance and dependency in order to bolster their positions, whilst deliberately resisting the demands of formality, including those associated with equal opportunities policy. The question arises of how such behaviour is to be interpreted. It may not have had discrimination as its principal motive although it was discriminatory in form and in consequence. This may help to explain why, in some cases, both victims and 'beneficiaries' of selection decisions were black. These decisions were certainly perceived as deliberate racial discrimination by those in the work force who suffered as a result. In so far as senior management is unwilling or unable to control such behaviour they may be seen as accomplices in racial and sexual discrimination. This may in turn result, as in our research company, in the whole of the formal programme being seen as a 'white-wash' or no more than tokenism.

Power struggles between groups are not simply matters of the manipulation of bureaucratic procedures. They may, as in the case of our local authority, involve overtly political confrontation. Here again the radical approach both utilises and celebrates politicisation as a means of furthering policy objectives. In the local authority the growth in commitment to equal opportunities policy, which was associated with a change in political control, was paralleled by a shift in the relationship of officers and councillors. The new controlling group challenged the independence of officers as providers of impartial technical advice and redefined their role as the implementation of political decisions made by councillors.

Conclusion

This paper has sought to clarify and extend the concept of monitoring. In the course of our discussion we have pointed to ambiguities in the character and objectives of equal opportunities policies and to the kinds of policy action which are advocated in their promotion. Not only do liberal and radical conceptions differ in their underlying principles and philosophies, they also imply different policy objectives and actions. In everyday situations, however, both principles and policy practices are routinely confused. This may not always be a matter of accident. In particular, we have suggested that liberals frequently promote their programmes by promising radical outcomes whilst radicals often legitimise their policies by reference to the rhetoric of liberal procedures. In this process, we believe much confusion, hostility and disappointment is created. In the long run, the cause of equality would be better served if the proponents of policies were to 'come clean'. This would, of course, bring into the open latent conflict and disagreement but it may be that genuine confrontation and honest debate generate deeper and more fruitful understanding of social processes. Certainly there is no reason to believe that the present confusion gives rise to harmony and consensus.

9

Training and organisational change: the target racism

GLORIA LEE

When considering the contribution of training towards the implementation of equal opportunity for ethnic minorities, there is a basic distinction to be made between the experiences of first-generation immigrants from what has become known as the New Commonwealth and Pakistan, and that of their children. For the first generation, learning opportunities have come largely through training provisions. In the case of the second generation, where training has a role to play, it follows on from previous exposure to the British education system.

The 1976 Race Relations Act identifies training as a mechanism for promoting equal opportunity in employment. The Act *enables but does not require* certain specified bodies – employers, trade unions, training bodies, employers' organisations etc. – to provide special training to members of racial groups, who are either absent from or under-represented in certain areas of work. The rationale for such provision is to enable ethnic minorities to catch up with the experiences of white applicants and employees. It is recognised that even if discrimination in selection and promotion were to be eradicated, ethnic minorities would still be disadvantaged due to past discrimination. Thus, as a stop-gap measure, 'positive action' can be taken to provide special training programmes for ethnic minorities in order to widen their job horizons.

Training in Britain has traditionally been seen as a separate activity from education. Basically, education is to develop character and intellectual abilities, whereas training is concerned with standards of efficiency in particular areas of employment skills. Although the state has taken responsibility for the provision of education for well over a century, government intervention in the field of training has only developed rapidly during the last two decades. Dating back to the medieval guild system, employers

141

have been the traditional providers of training. Notwithstanding the rise and fall of the training boards and the growth in influence and resources of the Manpower Services Commission, employers continue to be accorded a central role in the provision of work-related training. In the 1984 government White Paper 'Training for Jobs', the roles of employers and government in training are reaffirmed. Treating training as an investment for the future, the White Paper calls for further development of cost-effective methods of giving and assessing competence:

> These improvements are all attainable provided industry and commerce play their part. Most depend on the decisions of employers. It is for them to make the investment in training people to do the work that they require . . .

> It is for central and local government at the expense of taxpayers and ratepayers, to ensure that general and vocational education are provided in such a way as to improve the transition to work and respond to the changing needs of employment. (Cmnd 9135:5)

Thus government still looks to employers to make the decisions to train, in ways that are effective for their organisations. This is an important parameter when considering the role of training in implementing equal opportunity.

Since the mid-1970s and the rise in youth unemployment, government attention to training needs has focused heavily upon the youth scene. The Youth Opportunities Programme was followed by the more ambitious Youth Training Scheme, announced in the 1981 Training White Paper (Cmnd 8455) fully launched in September 1983 and extended to a two-year scheme in the spring of 1986. Studies of YOP (Cross, Edmonds and Sargeant 1983), apprenticeship provision (Lee and Wrench 1983) and more recently YTS (Fenton *et al.* 1984; NATFE 1983; Pollert 1985) all catalogue over the years the disadvantage of black youth seeking training.

Far fewer resources have been devoted by government to adult training generally, and less attention has been given by pressure groups and researchers to the implications of adult training provisions for ethnic minorities outside the field of language skills. The MSC's provision for adult training under the Training Opportunities Programme was designed to assist the re-training and re-deployment of adult workers necessitated by structural changes in the economy and consequent unemployment. Although adult ethnic minority workers have been particularly severely hit by the recession, Smith (1981) demonstrated that they were less likely to benefit from government re-training schemes than indigenous workers. Poor command of English was identified as compounding their problems

The deepening recession saw cuts in TOPS but recently the MSC and government have directed more attention to the need for adult training. Following the MSC's consultative document in April 1983 on adult training, in November of that year recommendations were made for a major initiative to improve adult training and these were largely taken on board in the 1984 White Paper. The particular needs of specific disadvantaged groups are not singled out however for attention of specific provisions. In the MSC consultative paper, only passing reference was made to ethnic minorities in a sentence on disadvantaged groups generally and the need for openings for the unemployed: 'But we believe that basic (non-occupational) education and training opportunities must be preserved and improved for those who have been out of employment for some time or who, like the disabled, ethnic minorities and women returning to work, may suffer disadvantage, which can be remedied by training, in getting a job' (MSC 1983a: 11).

The 1984 White Paper distinguishes between the training needs of the employed and the unemployed but training to combat disadvantage within any specific group like ethnic minorities or indeed women is not part of any explicit or coherent government policy. The whole focus of the MSC's Adult Training Campaign, launched in June 1985, is upon skill shortages and the need to heighten awareness of the potential and value of adult training. The Campaign publishes a regular newsletter 'Focus on Adult Training', which highlights successful training initiatives with the emphasis upon new skills, efficiency and effectiveness. It seems that equal opportunity is not part of the message of this government-backed campaign and there is no central thrust to promote equal opportunity through training.

In the specific field of race, the Commission for Racial Equality was created to work towards eliminating discrimination and providing equal opportunity for ethnic minorities but it is in no way a training body. Realistically, the CRE puts its limited resources into pressing employers to adopt equal opportunity policies and ethnic monitoring and into the investigation of alleged discrimination. As equal opportunity policies are adopted, training needs can be more readily identified. American experience suggests that progress is possible along this route, although there are many differences between the British and American situation (Wainwright 1980; Lee 1983).

In the absence of coherent government policies, the adoption of training to combat racial disadvantage rests upon the unco-ordinated initiatives of various bodies. Fairley and Jeffrey (1982), in their study of the training needs of disadvantaged groups, aptly describe the situation:

> One characteristic of the British training system is that it is highly fragmented, involving a plethora of agencies, statutory and volun-

tary, government and non-government. This fragmentation means that national objectives only exist for certain individual parts of the training system. At regional and local level the fragmentation of the training system is acute. Typically the only co-ordination which can be found at local level is within the programme of provision under particular labour market policies e.g. YOP. (Fairley and Jeffrey 1982: 49)

This paper reviews some of the initiatives which have been taken recently to address the implementation of equal opportunity for racial groups through adult training, with special reference to provision within the West Midlands area. This review provides the opportunity to evaluate the potential effectiveness and implications of attempting to redress racial disadvantage through training. The situation for ethnic minority youth has been considered in a separate paper by Malcolm Cross.

When considering the role of training in the promotion of equal opportunity for ethnic minorities, two distinct approaches need to be identified, in terms of the recipients and purposes of training. There is 'positive action' for ethnic minority employees and various forms of race-relations training for white employees. Under 'positive action' organisations adopting an equal opportunity policy can provide training specifically for a disadvantaged group. Thus ethnic minorities excluded from a particular area of work or promotion may, through special training provisions, improve their job prospects.

The disadvantage in employment faced by ethnic minorities is, however, more specifically a consequence of direct and indirect discrimination. Institutional racism still holds back ethnic minorities, even if they are suitably qualified, as demonstrated by Lee and Wrench (1983) in the case of apprenticeships. One approach to combating institutional racism has been to direct training towards white employees, to heighten awareness of the ways in which discrimination operates. Race training for white employees is also concerned with improving inter-personal relationships between white and ethnic minority employees or clients.

This paper will outline approaches to the training of blacks and the training of whites in order to evaluate the role of training in promoting equal opportunity. The themes of language needs, economic recession, technological change and social unrest will inform the discussion.

The inability to speak English was identified back in the 1960s as a major barrier to assimilation and integration by New Commonwealth immigrants. Whilst language and communication needs still underpin a great deal of the adult training provision for ethnic minorities, during the last decade certain other factors have had an impact upon the scope and extent of race-relations training, as well as the methods used. Economic recession and techno-logical change have influenced training provisions for ethnic minorities in particular, whereas what have become known as the 'riots' of 1981 can be seen as having an impact upon both training for blacks and training for whites.

Training for blacks
Language and the recognition of 'special needs'
The first official recognition that the presence of immigrants necessitated special provisions came about within the educational system. Facilities were provided to teach the children of immigrants English as a second language, in order for them to be able to benefit from the British education system. At this period, attitudes towards race still reflected the belief in integration and assimilation, consequently an ability to communicate was crucial. However, it was not until the 1970s that there was any official recognition of the need for immigrants themselves to be able to speak English as well as their children. The Slatter Report, as it became known, pointed to the pioneering work of the Pathway Industrial Unit in Ealing, which provided in-company language training courses. The report called for major resources to be made available to further language training facilities for industry. In the introduction to the report, it was estimated that some 100,000 Asian workers had little or no English. A case was made for the need for language training, as a contribution towards improved indus-trial relations and safety in the work-place, as well as in terms of the benefits to the individual (Slatter 1974). The report provided fuel for a campaign and the need for language training was accepted by a number of local authorities, who took the initiative in setting-up local Industrial Language Training Units (ILTs), based initially on Section 11 funding.

Since 1978, the MSC has taken over responsibility for the units. This has provided continuity for their activities through national funding on a ten-year basis. There are now about thirty such units and in response to chang-ing economic conditions their work has expanded beyond the work-place setting. Their activities are nationally co-ordinated, through the National Centre for Industrial Language Training, which also provides support services, including a range of training materials.

In the employment field, the ILTs remain the largest providers of race-related training and communication continues to be treated as a key parameter in good race relations. Whilst not denying the handicap faced by anyone in Britain unable to speak English, this is essentially a first-generation Asian problem. Also the focus on language in adult training provision tends to divert attention away from the training needs of Afro-Caribbeans.

The 'Asian orientation' in the work of ILTs is inevitable, as companies typically seek help when they are having difficulty in communicating with their Asian work force. Murray and Chandola (1981) in their review of the work of ILTs acknowledge that the provision for Afro-Caribbeans is much more limited. Trainees from this background are normally only found on advanced courses involving a strong emphasis on literacy. Changes in the economic climate have had a major impact upon the provision of training generally but the ILTs have broadened and adapted their work in a number of ways to meet new demands.

Economic recession and technological change
Economic recession has a number of implications for training and equal opportunity. Training budgets are often an early victim when business becomes more difficult, so there is less employer-funded training generally. In the case of Asian and Afro-Caribbean workers the paper by Rhodes and Braham (below) details the differential impact of unemployment in comparison with white workers.

Whilst lack of English can be a handicap in employment, the problem becomes far more acute for the unemployed seeking work. With the recession ILTs lost much of their company-based work but have moved into providing training for the unemployed, having effectively argued the case for language barriers to re-employment. (For a detailed study of these difficulties see the report by the Lancashire Industrial Language Training Unit, CRE 1983.) The ILTs have attracted MSC funding for various courses which incorporate language and vocational skills training. Some of these courses are designed to lead on to TOPS courses at a Skillcentre or into further education.

Many Asian workers had previously been employed in older contracting industries like the foundries, forges and textiles. The ILT's Computer Opportunity Language/Keyboard Skills (COLAK) Course is an example of an initiative to re-train workers in response to the demands of new technology. Here trainees divide their time between learning to program and operate office-type computers and learning the specific language/ numeracy skills related to the computer skills training. This attempt to enable workers to move into an area of new technology has, not surprisingly, attracted mainly women.

Whilst unemployment has provided a major new focus to the need for language training for Asians, technological change has also heightened awareness in some cases concerning those in employment. For instance, a new production process may call for the re-training of employees. Whereas employees' lack of English may not hitherto have presented particular difficulties in the work situation, this is not the case when re-training is required. Again this has on occasion provided a role for ILTs.

Although technological change can provide an impetus for training, more usually in the case of ethnic minorities, non-work-based training provision has developed in response to the plight of the unemployed. An example in the London area is the Tower Hamlets Training Forum, set up following the impact of the recession in the garment industry upon the local Bengali community. The Forum offers courses on clothing skills and language training, coupled with other provisions like an out-reach service and a crèche, which serve the community as a whole.

The Greater London Manpower Board was set up by the GLC in recognition of the anarchy in the field of training. The Board provides advice and information and assists a variety of initiatives to help various groups, including ethnic minorities. One example is the Open Access Project which provides an ethnic minority service, covering counselling, placement and the negotiation of access to apprenticeships and professional bodies. A particularly useful function of the Board is the provision of information on available funding. The GLC and the County Councils have been important sources of funding and with their demise, unless new sponsors come forward to take their place, important initiatives could be lost.

One of the most striking features of the 1980s training scene has been the growth in size, resources and influence of the MSC. Although the MSC does not have any particular brief regarding ethnic minorities and it is not proactive in promoting equal opportunities, it does undertake to fund training solely targeted at a particular racial group, as in the case of some ILT courses. In the Midlands there have been MSC-supported courses for black managers and those wishing to enter this field. The MSC are no longer prepared to continue TOPS occupational training courses where there is little likelihood of trainees entering that area of employment. They do, however, encourage provisions to help people to become self-employed and to set up small businesses. There has been a substantial growth in Asian businesses in the Midlands during the last few years and the MSC are now funding courses to encourage and assist the setting up of black businesses. The GLC's Greater London Enterprise Board also provides advice as well as financial support to foster ethnic minority businesses.

Training and social unrest
Another factor having an impact upon the provision of training for ethnic minorities is the often unofficial or unacknowledged response to the social disturbances of the summer of 1981. Whilst there has been a gathering momentum towards improving and extending race-related training during this decade, the 'riots' have heightened awareness of the issue of race, with

an increase in general support and, most importantly, funding for training programmes. Some of the initiatives have been directed towards ethnic minorities but the real growth-area has been in terms of training white people to work more effectively in a multi-racial society.

In the case of ethnic minorities themselves, in addition to the types of provision already outlined, there has been a growing recognition of the under-representation of ethnic minorities in areas of professional work, in organisations like the police, the prison service and in central and local government. Alternatively where blacks are represented in an area of work, they are often unsuccessful when seeking promotion.

Cheetham (1982b), discussing the under-representation of ethnic minorities as social workers in America and Britain, points to the greater efforts made in America to redress this situation, where there is a 'scorn for people who proclaim their burning commitment to minority interests but, wringing their hands, say there are no suitable applicants' (1982b: 208). She outlines ways in which greater use of access courses could be made to enable people to enter a variety of occupations which require higher education qualifications, providing, of course, the funding is forthcoming to support these extra years of study. The paucity of support for such initiatives suggests a reluctance in many areas to do more than pay lip-service to the value of such schemes.

In Birmingham, for instance, a 'New Way' Course provides an alternative to the normal 'A' level route into higher education. It can give ethnic minorities a path into professional social work or teacher training. Although the course is staffed on Section 11 funding, its potential is limited, as there are no grants made available by the local authority to study on a full-time basis.

Many social services departments serving inner-city areas have unqualified ethnic minority staff working in residential and day-care centres. Along with other unqualified staff, they can apply for day-release to take the Certificate in Social Services (CSS). Although this provides some basic training, it is not a professional qualification in social work and rarely provides a route on to the professional Certificate of Qualification in Social Work.

More posts are being established by local authorities for ethnic advisers or trainers to promote equal opportunities in social services and other departments. However, when selection and recruitment takes place for these posts, ethnic minority candidates are often unsuccessful and white candidates with higher formal qualifications are appointed.

There has been growing criticism within the trade union movement that unions do little for their black membership. Also black trade unionists rarely hold official positions above that of shop steward. The Trades Union

Congress has been active in stressing the role of education for encouraging more black members to participate in the affairs of their union. Once again, language is identified as a major barrier and the TUC and a number of unions have provided funds for translating their written materials into Asian languages. In the West Midlands shop stewards courses have been organised by the TUC Regional Education Service for Asian members in the mother tongue, using trained Asian tutors. Such initiatives are important as an indication of union concern but they only reach a small proportion even of the Asian membership and, of course, ignore the needs of Afro-Caribbean members. For trade unionists, participation in educational provisions has been a traditional means of progressing within the movement but the very small number of black members generally on trade union courses indicates that language is not the only barrier to participation.

In 1981 the TUC published what has become known as the Black Workers Charter, which set out a variety of ways in which unions should further equal opportunities for their black membership. Many unions have, however, been reluctant to respond to this challenge. Afro-Caribbeans and young Asian members in particular are critical of the lack of union response to their needs. Since 1981 there has been a growing call for black caucuses within unions and for the kinds of proportional representation that has already been acknowledged for women in parts of the movement. Greater educational provision for black members will not divert this challenge, which can only be met by structural changes within unions (Lee 1984).

Within the public sector in particular, some progress has been made in the direction of equal opportunities in that more local authorities and parts of the Health Service have begun to examine their recruitment and training practices. However, it is difficult to foresee many immediate gains for black people. Ethnic record-keeping and ethnic monitoring provide, amongst other things, a means of identifying training needs but even where organisations do move in this direction, the policy is often to limit ethnic record-keeping to new appointments. If no attempt is made to record ethnicity for existing employees then progress along this path will be very limited and the case for more funds for targeted training more difficult to make.

Whilst certain pressure groups like the ILTs and other committed trainers continue to seek funding to improve training provisions for ethnic minorities, progress is both limited and very piecemeal. There is neither a basis for a co-ordinated assessment of adult ethnic minority needs, nor a clear focus to existing training schemes, other than the underlying theme of language and communications which only applies to a specific category of recipient. The situation generally is one of little interest and attention given to the development of positive action as a means of promoting equal opportunity.

Race training for white workers

Although positive-action training remains limited in scope and application, following the social unrest of 1981 there has been a marked growth in race-relations training provision for white people. In various ways this is directed towards enhancing their ability to work effectively in a multi-racial context.

In recent years, a number of organisations have declared themselves equal opportunity employers. Some have moved on to examine their recruitment and selection procedures and have provided training programmes for those in personnel departments which demonstrate ways of avoiding direct and indirect discrimination. The CRE's Code of Practice published in 1983 sets out guidelines for employers and trade unions for promoting equal opportunity.

Various approaches are taken by organisations to race-relations training. Many favour working to enhance professional competence amongst their staff, as in the case of training personnel managers to avoid discriminatory practices. Other organisations seek to alter the attitudes of their employees towards ethnic minorities. The techniques adopted by trainers vary too, ranging from a non-confrontational approach of supplying information about other cultures in order to promote understanding, through to a highly confrontational stance which challenges trainees to examine their own attitudes and beliefs in order to face up to unconscious racism.

In the area of education, local authorities with ethnic minority populations have a long tradition of providing English as a Second Language (ESL) teachers. In more recent years the focus has been upon the development of a multi-racial curriculum and many such authorities have established in-service training units to foster this work. This is not the occasion to enter into the debates about the validity of multi-culturalism, but given the support for the approach in a number of local authorities, the work of the Schools in Service Unit in Birmingham provides an interesting example of one of the newer approaches.

The Schools in Service Unit was set up in 1979 to develop school-based in-service training for teachers, unlike the more usual pattern of centre-based courses. The team go into a school for a term and spend the bulk of their time working with teachers in the classroom. They assist them in their approach to ESL pupils and to deal with the curriculum implications of multi-cultural education. This is an example of trainers not addressing racism awareness directly but in the course of their work tackling issues of racism as they arise, as part of the on-going programme, to enhance professional competence.

In their early work with white employees, ILTs stressed cultural understanding as an aid to communication but in recent years some ILTs have developed racism-awareness training. Even when trainers are committed to this approach, however, resistance can come from the organisation whose wishes, as clients paying for the service, cannot be ignored. Whether for practical or professional reasons, others like Murray and Chandola (1981) favour a less confrontational approach, aiming 'to encourage positive attitudes, and to disturb existing negative attitudes to the multi-racial society and to the ethnic minority groups' (1981: 10). Realistically they acknowledge that in the industrial context a six-week course cannot in itself change attitudes built up over fifteen or twenty years working in a multi-racial factory. They see long-term attitude changes coming through post-course involvement in the work of trainees.

In contrast to the indirect approaches, the Racism Awareness Programme Unit make a frontal attack upon racism in daily life. The unit was established by people involved in education, community and human-relations work, who were concerned to change attitudes to race. RAPU acknowledge that their original approach relied heavily upon developmental work by Judy Katz in the United States but they have since developed techniques and materials appropriate to the British context. Their work is based upon three premises: that Britain is a multi-racial society; that Britain is a racist society; and that racism is a white problem. They use a variety of techniques, including role-play and role-reversal exercises to assist trainees towards an understanding of racism at the personal, institutional and cultural levels. They provide courses and workshops for statutory and voluntary services, church groups, the Home Office, university departments, trade unions, community groups, and so on. They will also train trainers, which could be an important resource in an area where the formal provisions to help trainers develop their approaches to race issues are extremely limited.

RAPU is London-based although they also do work in the provinces. Similar approaches are developing in other parts of the country, including the work of David Ruddle in Birmingham, who is a founder of the West Midlands Racism Awareness Unit. A number of professional groups have been attracted to this approach, but one of its limitations is that it tends to attract the 'converted' on to its courses. Evaluation studies are required to establish the effectiveness of this approach in achieving attitude change which carries over into the work situation.

Binstead *et al.* (1980) and Burgoyne *et al.* (1978) working in the field of management education, indicate some of the complexities in this type of learning situation. Trainees can have problems of translating from their own experiences, what has to be learned and/or transferring what has been learned into the work situation. Unless both processes take place, affective learning will not result. There is also the danger with experiential training in particular, that if it is inadequately presented, the training may be counter-productive to the original aim. In the case of race training, this could mean the reinforcement of racist attitudes and beliefs.

A previous paper by the present author on equal opportunity and training commented upon the limited recognition of the need to improve services to ethnic minority clients in the Health Service (Lee 1983). At that time the introduction of training packs on Asian diets and Asian naming systems was noted as the beginning of an initiative. The availability of this material and the work of pressure groups has encouraged the development of in-service training on race issues for a variety of health workers. Following the pioneering work of Alix Henley and others, a national body, Training in Health and Race, has been established by the National Extension College and supported by the Health Education Council to provide training and resources for health workers in a multi-racial society. In addition to their Project Co-ordinator, they have Research and Development Officers centred in Birmingham, Leeds, Leicester and London. They are examining the existing provisions to assist health workers in various areas of activity, in order to identify race training needs. They are also examining the policy implications of developing race training on professional training courses. They work closely with NHS trainers and run local training courses, which provide information in various forms.

Despite the clear implications for patient care, the nursing profession has been slow to incorporate a race dimension into their training courses. For a long time the philosophy was that nurses care for all their patients regardless of colour, creed etc. Training in Health and Race have been working with the English National Board on the inclusion of race topics in the curriculum of SRN basic training, midwifery and health visitor training. The Royal College of Nursing is also offering courses for senior nursing staff on the care of ethnic minority patients. In 1984 Training in Health and Race published an extensive checklist on Providing Effective Health Care in a Multi-racial Society. This covers the different aspects of health service provision, like health education, family planning, the elderly, psychiatric services and so on, and gives examples throughout of good practice.

This work should help to improve the service provided to ethnic minority patients. However, the NHS also has ethnic minority workers who could benefit from specialist training, to improve their professional competence. For instance, interpreters have traditionally been recruited on the basis of their knowledge of minority languages and their need for training has been neglected. The importance of their work is now receiving some attention (West Midlands Regional Health Authority 1985; Schackman 1985). Also in East Birmingham Health Authority, for instance, there is a growing recognition that resources should be put into interpreter training.

Both the Home Affairs Committee Report on Racial Disadvantage

(1981a) and the government's reply comment favourably upon the work of the Race Relations Employment Advisers. The Committee recommended that their work should expand to cover local authorities and this was accepted. In practice, however, this is a very limited operation with only twenty-six Race Relations Employment Advisers to cover the entire country. Their remit is to promote harmonious relations in a multi-racial work-place and they do this by providing an advisory service to employers. In particular they advise on the requirements of the 1976 Race Relations Act. However, they have also developed a training role and provide typically fairly short inputs into training courses for the private and public sector. Unlike the ILTs, the Race Relations Advisory Service does not charge employers for the training they provide.

The work of the ILTs has also reflected the growing demand for race inputs into training programmes and specialist short courses. They have broadened out from their original industrial employer focus and now work with staff in the public and service sectors. Local authorities, banks, building societies, hospitals, trade unions and Citizens Advice Bureaux etc., are increasingly recognising the need to train their staff for work with ethnic minority clients. The ILTs now provide courses on 'Working with the Multi-racial Public' for many public service organisations. Occasionally courses are also offered to give training in minority languages, for example, basic spoken Hindi or Urdu for police officers. There is, however, a limited potential for such courses, as a very high level of motivation is needed to sustain progress in such languages and the ILTs can only provide an introduction, which would have to be pursued over a much longer period of time, probably through Further Education Courses, to achieve fluency.

The Prison Service has also extended its race-relations training. Race Relations Liaison Officers have been appointed and some of these are Training Officers. Both initial training and development training for governor and officer grades now has a race-relations input. There are also specialist sessions which are attended by governors and inputs on courses for others like chaplains, education officers, civilian instructors and so on, who work for the Prison Service.

The Police, particularly as a response to the Scarman Report, have also become more prepared to introduce race relations into police training for different grades, covering induction courses and subsequent 'in-service' training for the different ranks of officer. However, doubts have been expressed as to the effectiveness of some of the training offered. For example a report by the Home Office Research and Planning Unit on probationer training in West Yorkshire is very critical of the content and time made available for the topic of race relations. This report also points to the importance of the attitudes and behaviour of senior officers in the daily

work situation and the 'informal' police culture for conveying the importance of race issues to young officers.

Training in race relations can only enhance professional or occupationa
competence, if the approach can be sustained in the work situation. That i
why it is essential that senior personnel receive training and recognise thei
role in fostering effective race relations.

The Probation Service in the West Midlands is providing anti-racisn
training for all its officers in an attempt to promote a new approach toward
black clients. The scheme has not just received support in principle but alsc
active participation by senior officers, which serves to underline the
perceived importance of the issue to the Service. An innovative aspect o
this training is to use black officers as a resource in ways that acknowledge
the validity of their experiences as black people and as probatio
officers.

Green (1986) has argued that when probation officers found that the
had no role in the court proceedings immediately following the stree
disturbances of 1981 this served to begin to alert the Probation Service tc
the ineffectiveness of its relationship with black clients. He contrasts the
response of the Service at that time with its much more proactive stance
following the disturbances in Handsworth in September 1985. A
professional service or organisation where there is a lead from the top is in a
stronger position to take a radical approach to the use of training to figh
racism than an organisation like the TUC or individual unions where
participation in training relies more heavily upon individual interest anc
motivation. The study of trade unionism and race cited earlier points tc
factors like the need to make courses 'popular' with members, which blunt
the effectiveness of training as a source of change in the field of race (Lee
1984: 4).

Does training matter? – some concluding thoughts

This paper examines the role of training as a strategy for promoting equa
opportunity and combating racial discrimination for ethnic minorities
Essentially training is a tool operating within an existing system. It cannot
in itself, achieve the kind of fundamental structural change required tc
achieve equality of opportunity for a minority group. Nevertheless, trainin
does clearly have a contribution to make towards these aims by enablin
people to operate more effectively in terms of a particular system. Trainin
will not change the existence, size or positioning of the hurdles erected b
society. It can, however, assist certain groups or individuals to negotiat

them and in some circumstances find an occasional path around them, as in the case, say, of access courses which provide an alternative to the 'A' level route into higher education.

Another role for training is to attempt to change attitudes, with the long-term aim of challenging existing value systems and creating a new ideology. Racism awareness training is one attempt to use training in a more radical way but, as an approach to improving race relations, it is clearly very limited in scope where it relies upon voluntarism. In any case, the scale of the problem is too great to be solved at the level of the individual. Training becomes a more effective means of tackling racism where an organisation has adopted an equal opportunity policy. The existence of a policy can open up the role of training in the organisation and strengthens the authority of trainers, as experts in the field. An equal opportunity policy charges the organisation with certain responsibilities to promote equal opportunity and training provides the vehicle for both heightening the awareness of managers and employees of these responsibilities and for providing understanding of appropriate courses of action. Equal opportunity then ceases to be a matter of goodwill and enlightenment but a requirement of the job, for which people can be held accountable. Once trained, employees cannot plead ignorance of the requirements of the policy. To be effective in practice, there has to be a demand for accountability and here those in senior posts (together with members, in the case of local authorities) have particular responsibilities to ensure that practice equates with policy. In these circumstances training can be an effective means of implementing equal opportunity policies by enhancing 'professional' competence to avoid discriminatory practices or to provide a better service to ethnic minority clients.

It is perhaps useful at this point to take an approach used by many trainers and to consider training in terms of the aims of the activity and the needs which it attempts to serve. These can be distinguished at the levels of society, groups and individuals.

At the societal level, Britain has never had a co-ordinated training policy. Training is still traditionally seen as the responsibility of the employer. The growth of the MSC has come about largely through the government's inability to ignore the rise in youth unemployment. Something had to be seen to be done and training was put forward as the ostensible solution. Employers could not be expected to meet the bill for this training, so funds were provided nationally. Training in the field of race, or indeed in terms of gender issues, has never been part of any national programme.

The Commission for Racial Equality was created to work towards eliminating discrimination and providing equal opportunity for ethnic minorities but it is in no way a training body. Another national initiative in the field of race relations, the Race Relations Employment Advisory Service is very small indeed. Although individual officers respond to requests for training, it is not in their brief to co-ordinate race training or to ensure that such training takes place. The ILTs are nationally funded, but they have to go out and 'sell' their training to employers, which circumscribes many of their initiatives. The MSC does fund training, which, as positive action, benefits ethnic minorities, but it does not so much seek out these schemes, as respond to proposals put up by other agencies and groups.

Various government departments and local authorities have race-relations advisors but, as their title indicates, they can advise on and participate in race training yet they do not have the authority to require such training to be undertaken. Section 11 funds are the only source of national finance specifically ear-marked to meet the needs of ethnic minorities. These funds can now be applied in the field of social welfare, and some social services departments have taken this opportunity to provide trainers with a special ethnic minority brief.

Training related to issues of race, then, relies very much on the interest and commitment of different organisations. Legislation allows some of them to take certain initiatives, there are no specific requirements. As Young and Connelly have pointed out, local authorities interpret Section 71 of the Race Relations Act in 'widely varying ways' (1981: 146). Section 71 declares the duty of every local authority to eliminate unlawful racial discrimination and promote equality of opportunity and good relations between persons of different racial groups. Local authorities are generally important providers of training but in the case of race issues, initiative usually depends upon the enthusiasm of particular trainers and/or the interest in this area by certain councillors who are prepared to push for resources. The recent growth in the provision of training for white staff on race issues has already been noted in the case of the public sector. These organisations have, however, been much less ready to examine the training needs of ethnic minorities within their organisation.

As in the case of youth unemployment, there is the real danger of race training being used as a panacea. It may be seen as a means of placating the conscience of those who express concern over social injustice to ethnic minorities, without seriously challenging the *status quo*. It can also be used to allay the fears of those who are alarmed by media coverage of events depicting social unrest. Training can be substituted for other measures, which would provide a more direct challenge to existing status preserves. Thus, positive action is seen by many as an acceptable alternative to reverse discrimination for a variety of reasons, not the least of which is its limited impact.

Turning to training in terms of the aims and needs of groups, it is useful to distinguish between ethnic groups and other types of group, in particular, occupational groupings. The need for language training has enabled some Asian groups to receive work-related training opportunities at the same time. This has occurred in the work situation and in the case of unemployment. These provisions are far from extensive but nevertheless, it is still an opportunity that does not reach Afro-Caribbean groups in the same way. In the case of the unemployed, the proportion of Afro-Caribbean and Asian men in the 25–64 age-group is very similar, but their exposure to ILT training opportunities is not comparable. The language base of ILT work has inevitably led them to focus on the needs of Asian workers. However, as major providers of training in the race field, this also has implications for their work with white trainees. The 'Asian orientation' comes over in the work of ILTs with white groups, as the professional staff have some Asian members and others have extensive knowledge of Asian cultures. The practice has been to draw upon 'resource people' from the Afro-Caribbean community to contribute to their programmes but the alternative is also to recruit from this community.

In the case of in-service training, organisations generally have been far more ready to put resources into training their white staff to work in a multi-racial context, than to train their ethnic minority employees to improve their job and promotion opportunities. These training opportunities for white staff are intended to promote equal opportunities by, for instance, improving recruitment and selection procedures to avoid direct and/or indirect discrimination, by extending the service to ethnic minority clients and by fostering more effective management of a multi-racial work force. In as much as such training does lead to changes in practice and behaviour, benefit should accrue to the minorities – although there are also certain problems and limitations to its effectiveness. In the case of specialist courses, for instance, participation is often voluntary, so to some extent they attract those who have a particular interest in or sensitivity to the issues anyway. Others, who may be in greater need of this sort of training, will not apply. In these circumstances, their managers should encourage or require their attendance, but this, of course, will only occur if the managers themselves are alive to issues of race.

Where a race element is included in an induction course or subsequent regular re-training courses, the extent to which these training sessions do influence behaviour in the direction of improved race relations will vary considerably with the quality of the training and the motivation of the individual trainees. There is always the danger, as suggested earlier, of racist attitudes being reinforced.

This points to another dilemma – that training in this area is not always undertaken by professional trainers. Trainers do not always have any expertise in the field of race and so they have to bring in others. These people may have no particular skills as trainers; also their contribution may be from one particular perspective, due to their own background and experiences. This presents considerable problems of balance in devising training programmes. There are no systematic courses or programmes available to train trainers on matters of race, or indeed to train those who have competence and expertise in the field or race, to become skilled in the task of training. It is usually a matter of attending any limited formal programmes mounted from time to time by various institutions like universities, colleges and interest groups etc. There are also now a few private consultants who provide advice on training in race relations. Beyond this, a great deal rests with the enthusiasm of trainers to develop their skills by self-instruction, through reading and, in some cases, setting up interest groups amongst colleagues.

At the level of individual aims and needs motivations will vary, clearly amongst trainees as well as trainers. Some may see training as a path to career development but find their opportunities very limited, as it is often difficult to get access to training from low positions within an organisational hierarchy. Also the price of training can be high, for instance, if it has to be undertaken at the expense of doing overtime. The attitude of managers as facilitators is important too. The approach of senior personnel is also very critical in the case of white people who have been exposed to race-relations training. Behaviour is unlikely to be modified, unless the actual working environment is anti-racist. This puts considerable responsibility upon senior personnel to provide an appropriate work culture. They may be prepared, for instance to send their staff on race training courses but fail to recognise their own need for such training.

In conclusion then, training will not eliminate racism and it is important that it should not be 'passed off' as the solution. Training can, however, make some contribution to wider efforts towards this end, although it is circumscribed by various difficulties and limitations. The training scene in Britain is fragmented and initiatives rest with interested parties, also funding relies heavily upon voluntarism. To date, ethnic minorities themselves have received only very limited benefit from training provisions and there are differences between ethnic groups in the opportunities available to them. Training does not provide jobs for trainees, but it can improve their market position, ready for a situation where there is some increase in the demand for labour. Training is very much an investment in the future for society, groups and individuals.

Training in race relations for white people has provided an additional focus for a number of training bodies. It has generated work for more trainers but ethnic minorities, especially Afro-Caribbeans, have not themselves been well-represented in this growth of activity. If such training does lead to improvements in practice and behavioural changes which endure in the work and other situations, then benefit will in time be felt by ethnic minorities. Training can also contribute to improving the quality of life for individuals, through the opportunity to develop personal potential. A more active approach to positive action is required on the part of employers to provide these opportunities.

Training alone will not alter the structures of inequality, which require changes in policies and *in practices* in organisations. If there are such changes, training can hasten their implementation and effectiveness. Also, those engaged in training, when they have expertise in equal opportunity issues, can provide an important source of pressure to challenge the *status quo*.

10

Unequal comrades: trade unions, equal opportunity and racism*

JOHN WRENCH

We are convinced that trade unions are more decisive than any other organisations in the struggle to uproot racist prejudice, check racist discrimination and help our country to achieve true equal opportunity in jobs, promotion, education, housing and the whole of the social services.[1]

In much of the literature and the debate on equal opportunity within organisations it is true to say that trade unions themselves do not figure prominently as examples. Yet it could be argued that, more than any other public or private employers, local authority or government agency, trade unions are a key sector where equal opportunity and anti-racism should be addressed with the utmost priority. There are two broad divisions to this activity: first, trade unions have an essential role to play in the promotion of racial equality in work-place negotiations with employers; second, within their own organisations themselves, trade unions must be seen to be embracing equal opportunity and anti-racism, both in the treatment of a union's own employees, and in the organisation and servicing of its own membership (activity which must include tackling racism amongst union members). And if, as the opening quotation suggests, trade unions can be more effective than other organisations in furthering the struggle for racial equality, then it also follows that a shirking from equal opportunity issues and a connivance in racism by trade unions must have particularly severe implications for black people.

This chapter looks at the record of trade unions in the area of equal opportunity and anti-racism. It describes the progress that has been made, as well as showing that there is nothing to be complacent about. The paper looks first at the unfortunate history of trade unions in relation to black labour

within this country. It describes the early open racism of white trade
unionists, the poor example set by trade union and Labour leaders, the early
resistance by black workers to their treatment and their organisation among
themselves to fight the racism of both employers and unions. It describes
the development of TUC initiatives on race and the continuing reality of
racism in more subtle and varied forms. It considers the factors influencing
the participation of black members within unions, the growth of separate
black support organisations, and the ways in which some unions have
responded positively to pressure for change by black and white activists.
The fight for equal opportunity within unions is put in the context of
unemployment, recession and structural change in the economy. Finally it
considers some of the most recent investigations, criticisms and proposals
for change and union responses to these, and concludes that further
progress in the area of equal opportunity will be achieved only through the
continuing momentum of organisation and pressure by black members
themselves.

The fallacy of 'cheap labour'

Trade union membership amongst migrant workers is one indicator of
whether or not they are being employed to undercut indigenous working-
class standards. In Britain in the late 1940s and 1950s, the common reaction of white trade unionists to black migrant workers was to see them as a
'cheap labour' threat and as potential strike breakers.

The 'cheap labour' argument is explored by Fevre (1984) in the case of
Asian textile workers in Bradford. He found, in fact, no evidence of Asian
workers directly undercutting prevailing wage rates by taking jobs in
Bradford's mills at lower rates of pay than those who preceded them. It
could be argued that Asian workers provided 'cheap labour' only if the term
is used to describe a situation where workers are employed at a rate of pay
which the employer would normally expect to result in an eventual labour
shortage: 'More often ... the employer of cheap labour does not reduce
wages, but rather refuses to increase them' (Fevre 1984: 4).

Such circumstances do not readily enable the label of 'scab labour' to be
attached to black migrant workers, particularly as white workers were not
noticeably in competition for these jobs at a time of labour shortage. If there
was any truth in the assertion that black workers were commonly undercutting white rates and strike breaking, this would have been reflected in
lower rates of union membership. In fact, there is much evidence to suggest
that Afro-Caribbean and Asian workers have had an *above* average propen-
sity to join trade unions. The observation of Radin in 1966 that 'coloured
workers were as receptive to overtures to join the union as were English

workers if not more so' (Radin 1966: 166) was confirmed by the surveys of Smith in 1977 and 1981, and Rex and Tomlinson in 1979. More recently, the PSI survey found in 1982 that 56% of Asian and West Indian employees were union members, compared with 47% of white employees (Brown 1984: 169). Although much of this difference today is explainable by the different types of job done by black and white workers, historically the greater inclination for black workers to join unions held true regardless of occupational differences (Brown 1984: 182).

Not only were black men and women good 'joiners' of unions – they also demonstrated, from the early days, that they were not afraid to protect their interests in collective action. Radin described this as the 'impatience of the newcomer' (Radin 1966: 172). However, many of the black migrant workers were not new to organisation and struggle – they brought with them a tradition and experience of militant collective action gained in their countries of origin, both within trade unions and, when such unions were perceived to be reactionary, outside them. Added to this, some black communities (like some mining communities in Britain) have had the benefit of strong support in their struggles from their own local communities. For black workers this has proved invaluable in those many cases over the last 30 years when their struggles were ignored or abandoned by the local union branch.

Collective action is, perhaps, more significant than union membership, which, as Phizacklea and Miles argue (1980: 35) could only be an expedient form of action. In fact, black workers have demonstrated a much greater willingness to support their white workmates in collective action than white workers have shown in return. As one black trade unionist told Lee (1984: 2): 'They know that when they call us out we will be solid, but the rest of the time they don't want to know.'

Unions and race: an unfortunate history

This leads us to the poor record of the trade union movement in this sphere: to put it bluntly, black workers in this country have served the unions far better than the unions have served black workers. According to the features that are normally associated with trade unions: comradeship, solidarity and a desire to bring about improvements in the conditions of working people, this should not have been so.

In reality, history shows the record of the trade union movement to be characterised, at worst, by appalling racism and often by an indefensible neglect of the issues of race and equal opportunity. Between the two World Wars, there was an effective colour-bar in British industry, supported openly by individual unions. Apparently the greater 'tolerance' which operated towards black workers during both wars was clearly understood by white workers and their unions to be temporary. For example, in the spring of 1919 about 120 black workers who had been employed for years in Liverpool sugar refineries and oil cake mills were sacked because white workers refused to work with them, and from 1918 onwards the seamen's unions formally and openly opposed the employment of black seamen when white crews were available (Fryer 1984: 299, 298).

Although such incidents are written off by trade unionists today as 'history', the uncomfortable fact remains that some of the most notorious cases of union hypocrisy and racism have occurred since the Second World War. Some of the most dramatic instances – those which have entered the Labour movement's chamber of horrors (such as Coneygre Foundry, Mansfield Hosiery, Imperial Typewriters) – are discussed below. In as much as such disputes surface only intermittently, they too are dismissed within a couple of years as the 'bad old days', an attitude which ignores the enduring injustices experienced by black union members.

Some of the main failings of the trade union movement with regard to its black membership may be summarised as follows:

(1)   The failure of the trade union leadership to entertain the idea that black members were faced with any different problems from those of the ordinary white membership, or that this necessitated any special policies.

(2)   Cases of direct and active collusion of local shop stewards and officials in arrangements of discrimination. (In addition to this, in some notorious cases, the union withheld support from striking black workers who were protesting about this adverse treatment in relation to white workers.)

(3)   Cases of more passive collusion of union officers and shop stewards in practices which were demonstrated to have been discriminatory in outcome, along with a resistance to change these practices.

(4)   Individual cases of racism by unsympathetic, unenlightened or even racially bigoted shop stewards and local officials, and a reluctance on the part of unions to take disciplinary action against racist offenders.

(5)   A general lack of awareness of the issues of race and equal opportunity and the particular circumstances of ethnic minority members, which may not manifest itself as racism but in effect lessens the participation of black members in the union.

These failings are set in a background history of years of prejudice and ignorance by white trade unionists and officials who have been ever ready to categorise black members in terms of simplistic stereotypes, whether as scabs and strike breakers, or as unreasonably militant hot-heads.

Setting a bad example from the top

The sluggish and blinkered reaction of the trade union leadership to its discovery that the movement possessed black members was quite consistent with the earlier response to black immigration by the leadership of the Labour Party. It was during the time of the post-war Labour government that attitudes towards black people in Britain underwent something of a change. During the war traditional antipathy towards black workers had been tempered by an appreciation of their effort in industry and the services in a 'common cause'. After the war, even though this was a time of labour shortage, it was trade unionists and Labour Party members who were the first to voice objections to 'coloured immigration'. Meanwhile the Labour government was washing its hands of any responsibility or guidance on the reception of immigrants. The Labour government was 'blind' to racism – it was seen to be the concern of those involved with colonial affairs, 'something external, not germane, to the main-stream of the labour movement' (Joshi and Carter 1984: 55).

The government's *laissez-faire* attitude was to set the pattern for later Trades Union Congress (TUC) inaction.

The Labour government's view was that to make any special welfare or housing provision would be to discriminate against the indigenous population; this view was echoed by the TUC in the 1950s and 1960s. As one TUC official told Radin, 'There are no differences between an immigrant worker and an English worker. We believe that all workers should have the same rights and don't require any different or special considerations' (1966: 159).

The trade union leadership saw no differences between the problems faced by black migrant workers and those by the white working class generally, and their inability to perceive any particular implications for unions of increasing numbers of black members led to a failure to develop any special policies. Rather than concerning themselves with the problems of racial discrimination, the TUC seemed to be more preoccupied with the necessity for the black immigrants to integrate with the host society (Radin 1966: 161). The first statement of a different tone to come out of the TUC General Council was in 1965 when 'immigrants lacking an adequate knowledge of English and British customs' were seen as a growing problem. At the time that she was writing, Radin noted that the TUC was continuing to hold on to its 'rather muddled' position, alleging that immigrants caused problems but refusing to do anything because 'all men are brothers' (Radin 1966: 161).

As late as 1970, Vic Feather, the then General Secretary of the TUC, could insist that 'The trade union movement is concerned with a man or woman as a worker. The colour of a man's skin has no relevance whatever to his work' (quoted in *The Sunday Times*, 3 December 1972).

In 1955 the annual Trades Union Congress had passed a resolution condemning all manifestations of racial discrimination or colour prejudice and urging the General Council to give special attention to the problems of racial friction. Similar resolutions were affirmed at the Congresses of 1959, 1966 and 1968. However, there was a noticeable gap between formal policy and practical action. As McIlroy writes (1982: 4) the obvious racism practised by rank and file and union officials and the TUC's policy of opposition to race-relations legislation made the TUC's exhortations seem rather hollow.

White exclusion attempts and black resistance

Post-war attempts at racial exclusion by white trade unionists took forms which were sometimes surprisingly blunt. In many industries white trade unionists insisted on a quota system restricting black workers to a maximum of (generally) 5%, and there were understandings with management that the principle of 'last in first out' at a time of redundancy would not apply if this was to mean that white workers would lose their jobs before blacks (Fryer 1984: 376). In 1955 Wolverhampton bus workers banned overtime and West Bromwich bus workers staged one-day strikes in protest against the employment of black labour on the buses. That year there were motions from transport workers to the TGWU annual conference asking the union to ban black workers from the buses. Similarly, hospital branches of the Confederation of Health Service Employees passed resolutions objecting to the recruitment of coloured nurses (Bentley 1976: 135). There was a 'determined effort' by the National Union of Seamen to keep black seamen off British ships after the war. The Assistant General Secretary told the 1948 conference that Liverpool and other British ports were to be 'no go' areas for black seafarers (Fryer 1984: 367).

In reality it did not need overt, public motions and statements of racism for black workers to become consolidated into limited areas of work and for lines to be drawn around those jobs where they were not expected to go. Their jobs were often low paid, menial and dirty (and disproportionately dangerous – as shown by Lee and Wrench 1980). The assumption by white workers that black workers should be the first to be made redundant was aided by this job segregation, as it could always be argued that particular classes of *jobs* were being shed, rather than particular groups of workers.

Sivanandan has catalogued early black resistance of this treatment. To start with, he argues, resistance was 'more spontaneous than organised' (1982: 5). Early attempts to form work-based groups were frustrated within the factory walls and so black workers had to establish themselves outside – this was one reason why black organisations developed as more 'community-based' rather than simply work-based groups. In the context of trade union racism this was to be a strategic strength, as later disputes would show. Throughout the 1960s a series of industrial disputes demonstrated that rank and file black men and women were not going to passively accept racism at work. What Sivanandan calls the 'first important "immigrant" strike' took place at Courtaulds' Red Scar Mill, Preston, where white workers and the union had collaborated with management in the attempt to force Asian workers to work more machines for proportionately less pay (Sivanandan 1982: 15). Later that year a strike by Asian workers at the Woolf Rubber Company was lost through lack of official union backing. In the late 1960s there were a number of strikes characterised by a strong support of Asian workers by local community associations and an equally noticeable lack of support by the local trade union.

There then occurred a number of disputes which generated adverse publicity and shook the complacency of the trade union movement. Perhaps the best-known of these are the disputes at the Coneygre Foundry in Tipton in 1967–8, Mansfield Hosiery in Loughborough in 1972 and Imperial Typewriters in Leicester in 1974. At Coneygre Foundry management precipitated a strike by Asian workers (members of the TGWU) through racial discrimination in its redundancy procedures: management refused to operate the generally accepted trade union principle of 'last in first out' and instead selected 21 Indians – and no whites – to go. The TGWU refused to make the strike official and rejected the idea that racial discrimination was involved; the white workers in the Amalgamated Union of Foundry Workers crossed the picket line and were supported in this by a local AUFW official, who explained that his members were not involved in the redundancies and therefore not in the strike. However, the strikers received support from other Asian workers and the Indian Workers Association, and eventually management was forced to take back all those of the 21 made redundant who wished to return (Duffield, forthcoming).

At Mansfield Hosiery, the 500-strong Asian work force had been effectively denied access to the best-paid jobs on knitting machines and the union had failed to support the Asians in their attempts over many years to gain promotion. When, in 1972, a strike was called over this and other anomalies in the payment system, the management, supported by the white workers and the local union, recruited 36 outside trainees, all white, for the knitting jobs. Eventually – and belatedly – the National Union of Hosiery

and Knitwear Workers made the strike official, but without calling out its
white membership. The eventual success of the strikers was made possible
not because of the help of the union but because of the support of local community organisations and political groups and Asian workers from other
factories.

The success of the strike at the Mansfield Hosiery Mills was one factor
among several which encouraged black workers in further collective action.
One outcome of the dispute was a conference of Trade Unions against
Racialism, held in Birmingham in June 1973, one aim of which was to
pressure the trade union movement to match its words with action
(Sivanandan 1982: 35–6). One year later what Sivanandan called 'the
apotheosis of racism . . . and therefore the resistance to it' was reached with
the Imperial Typewriters dispute. This Leicester company employed about
1,100 Asians in its 1,650-strong manual work force, a large proportion of
these being women from Uganda. From a background of long-standing
grievances over low pay, bad conditions and racial discrimination, a strike
began over the bonus system involving 40 workers. After an ultimatum by
management and a public denial of support by the union, about 400 workers
came out on strike. The dispute lasted three months, with no support from
the strikers' union, the TGWU, even though the strikers had discovered
that the company had been cheating on its bonus payments for over a year
(TUC 1983b: 37). Instead the strikers found an alternative source of
support from within their own community (see Parmar 1982: 264).

1974 – signs of change

The disjunction between TUC policy and trade union action at this time
was still marked. Smith, in his Political and Economic Planning Report, set
out a list of eight points of action which should have been implied by the
TUC's formal position: for example, one of these was 'energetic representation of any workers from minority groups who are being discriminated
against by management' (Smith 1974: 66–7). By comparing these points
with actual practice, as revealed in his survey, he concluded that little or
nothing was being done in this respect. For Smith there were both positive
and negative sides to his findings: 'On the one hand the unions have seldom
made formal representations against ethnic minorities. On the other hand
they have seldom made positive representations either' (Smith 1974:
68–9).

However, in the light of evidence, the 'absence of formal representations
against ethnic minorities' was less reassuring than it might initially have
seemed. With the discrimination that was clearly happening in the 1970s
there was no need for the sort of *formal* representations that took place in

the 1950s. A study of the processes which excluded black school leavers from apprenticeships found the discriminatory processes operating quietly and systematically in the routine practices of institutions, often disguised as custom and practice agreed with unions – for example, an agreement not to advertise widely and to give preference to the family of employees when recruiting (Lee and Wrench 1983). In fact, Smith's own evidence illustrates a number of the quiet agreements between union and management so effective in excluding black workers (Smith 1974: 69).

Around 1974 changes could be detected at the official trade union level with the official stance of many unions increasingly acknowledging the need to move away from a *laissez-faire* position towards a more active role. A number of factors might have contributed to this change. First, there were the increasingly public criticisms voiced by black trade unionists frustrated by the union neglect of their interests. Second, there were the recent embarrassingly well-publicised disputes in the Midlands which had produced damning evidence of union racism. Third, the TUC was still, as McIlroy put it (1982: 5), 'smarting under the verdict' of a House of Commons select committee which stated in 1974 that: 'the record of the TUC is similar to that of the CBI in that both organisations have declared their opposition to racial discrimination, but have taken wholly inadequate steps to ensure that their members work effectively to eradicate it'.

Fourth, there had been a growing lobby of grassroots' activists in the trade unions, local trades councils and the Labour Party who regularly voiced their criticisms through delegates at annual conferences. Finally there was the worrying growth of the National Front in the early 1970s. Thus the TUC, having dropped its opposition to race-relations legislation, now started active campaigns against racism in the movement.

The continuation of racism in practice

Of the five 'failings' of the trade union movement mentioned earlier, the first – the failure of the leadership to produce any special policy – had begun to change by 1974. With respect to the others, change is less easy to produce centrally and there is much evidence that the institution of active campaigns at the top does not necessarily produce much change lower down.

The second of the five 'failings' was that local union officials and shop stewards actively participated in racist practices. Examples in the 1970s and 80s are easy to find. For example, in July 1977 a black Birmingham-born man applied for a job at British Leyland's Castle Bromwich plant as a machine tool fitter, a job for which he was well-qualified. Some of the tool-room maintenance fitters asked the AUEW shop steward to arrange a meeting and a motion was passed that they would not accept a coloured fitter. Consequently, Mr Jones, the black applicant, was rejected for the job. The case came to light after a white employee informed the CRE some nine months after the event and a formal investigation by the CRE found that BL Cars Ltd and the two AUEW shop stewards had contravened the Race Relations Act (CRE 1981). (It is important to note that at that time BL was supposedly an 'Equal Opportunity' employer and was colluding in discriminatory practices with a union which had passed a number of conference resolutions on the importance of equal opportunity.)

In 1981 two black electricians employed by the GLC complained that they were getting lower wages and bonuses and less overtime than equally qualified white workers, as a result of being consistently allocated the least remunerative work. At the enquiry the black workers refused to be defended by the EETPU (indeed, the EETPU senior steward had allegedly threatened to expel the black workers from the union), and they turned for help to the Black Trade Unionists Solidarity Movement. The enquiry lasted five days and found in the black electricians' favour on almost every point.

These cases illustrate a more general point: that members of craft unions in particular have long been willing to practice racial discrimination. Lee and Wrench (1983) found resistance to black co-workers particularly strong in skilled areas, for example in tool-room, maintenance and sheet-metal working areas.

Another 'failing' was the more passive collusion of union officers in practices which were discriminatory in their outcomes and a reluctance to change these practices. Inertia and indirect discrimination can be just as effective in excluding black workers as can direct and open racism and with the higher profile of the TUC on racism, along with the passing of the Race Relations Act in 1976, it could be argued that this more covert racism has increased in significance. Such practices were shown to be a large part of the reason for the finding that within a cohort of fifth-form school leavers who (realistically) aspired to a craft apprenticeship, only 13% of Asian and 15% of West Indians were successful, compared to 44% for white boys (Lee and Wrench 1983: 61).

One of the practices that worked against black applicants was the reliance of companies on word-of-mouth recruitment, as opposed to advertising or using the careers service. (Word-of-mouth recruitment is apparently a remarkably widespread management practice – see Jenkins 1984a, 1986.) Sometimes recruitment took place only from white catchment areas, and preference was frequently given to the sons of existing employees. Although many managers were quite happy to go along with this practice of recruiting from the family of employees, in many cases the main instigators of it were the workers themselves and their shop stewards, with the approval of the unions (Lee and Wrench 1983: 33–5).

The effectiveness of such practices in creating systematic racial exclusion could be seen in the case of Massey Ferguson, investigated by the Commission for Racial Equality (CRE 1982). At the Banner Lane plant in Coventry in 1975, out of 6,800 employees only 10 were black, and out of 200 employees recruited in 1977 none were black. The main reason for this was the company's policy of not advertising hourly paid jobs, but relying on letters of application from people who had heard of jobs by word-of-mouth. In quite a large part of the engineering industry (as well as in printing) recruitment is carried out through the trade union itself, which helps to perpetuate white work forces.

This discriminatory custom and practice is not just characteristic of manual unions. An attempt at the Greater London Council to widen the recruitment base for GLC staff in line with its Equal Opportunities Policy was opposed by the main white-collar staff union. Previously, movement up the staff hierarchy was usually restricted to internal appointees. When recruitment was opened up to outside, the staff unions took industrial action – under the old system their members had benefited from the exclusion procedure.

Bill Morris, Deputy General Secretary of the TGWU and CRE commissioner, writes: 'Many of the conventions practised in industry, to which trade unionists are themselves party, were not designed for a multi-racial workforce and could well be resulting in indirect discrimination' (CRE Employment Report, July 1984). He argues that practices such as family recruitment would come under this heading 'although they were not designed with this intent'. However, the extent to which such practices are unintentionally discriminatory is debatable. Certainly it would be a mistake to see a racist motivation in these practices when they first developed: they often represent hard-won elements of creditable work-place control conceded by management over years of negotiation and struggle. However, in the present circumstances it would be equally erroneous to see all such practices as 'neutral' and entirely accidental in their discriminatory effects. Mere 'inertia' can be a highly conscious and effective device for racial exclusion: such practices, although established before the work force was 'multi-racial' could well take on a new life precisely because of the arrival of black workers in the labour market.

This brings us to a consideration of the individual racism of union officials and members. With a combined membership of millions, trade unions will inevitably reflect within their membership the prejudice and racist attitudes endemic in the overall population. It would be strange if among shop stewards and full-time officials there were no active racists as well as anti-racists. However, even if the proportion of bigoted individuals was regarded as 'normal', this does not make their existence any more tolerable. This is because such individuals are in positions of *power*. A racially bigoted man or woman in the street could be regarded as unfortunate; a bigoted shop steward or union official is an issue of serious social concern.

Manifestations of prejudice on an individual person-to-person level are the most directly felt by individual black workers, but the most difficult for an outsider to see (though occasionally hints may emerge at an industrial tribunal). Less dramatic than open bigotry, but equally problematic, is the ignorance displayed by shop stewards and officials subscribing to what Barker (1981) has called the 'new racism', the 'reasonable', and 'acceptable' racism of the 'I'm not racist but . . . oil and water don't mix' kind. Sometimes in the course of a dispute an incautious official will let slip a remark which reveals the problems that black workers may have to suffer with their white representation. For example, after a dispute in a Smethwick factory in 1978, during which Asian workers had received less than adequate support from the National Society of Metal Mechanics, a union official remarked: 'Don't get me wrong, I'm not racist but I think everyone who enters this country should be given a test to make sure they can read and write English properly. I don't blame employers being selective about whom they employ' (Bishton 1984: 50).

As Bishton remarks, a union official who sympathises with management even when he is aware how badly exploited the Asian workers are (often coming to this country to do dirty jobs where the ability to speak English was not needed), is hardly the man to help them achieve much (Bishton 1984: 50).

The role of trade union education

Cases such as those discussed above demonstrate the need for, at the very least, programmes of education for shop stewards and officials. The TUC has now recognised the need for resources to be allocated to anti-racist education courses. In 1977 it produced a 19-page booklet for use on a 10-day-release shop stewards course, and in 1983 it produced 'Race Relations at Work' and the 'TUC Workbook on Racism'. (However, critics argue that this particular arm of the anti-racist struggle is still under-resourced: see McIlroy 1982: 5.)

At the best of times tutors involved in race relations courses for trade unions have found it difficult to do justice in the subject. Trade unionists on the courses often begin with a less than receptive attitude to the material. One tutor involved in running courses in the West Midlands on Race Relations and Communication for shop stewards from different unions writes that three issues were usually upper-most in shop stewards' minds when they began the course:

> The issue of immigration was always raised, often emotively, and without any knowledge of the economic causes (especially in Britain) of immigration. Secondly, cultural differences were emphasised, sometimes with racist jokes or derogatory anecdotes. Thirdly, the issue of unity, participation and communication in the union came up, sometimes with reference to some of the bitter disputes (especially in the Smethwick area) on either side of 1970 when both English and Asian strikers claimed that they were not getting support from the other group. (Murray 1981: 38)

Educators in a situation of this kind find themselves faced with a dilemma: because of the 'normal' racism within many shop stewards there is a danger felt by tutors that an over-emphasis on race within courses could jeopardise the other areas too. This in turn, of course, makes it less likely that racist assumptions will be challenged.

There are differing views on the best approach to race-relations training: some feel that, in order to give it the weight it deserves, race relations require separate courses; others argue that this will attract only the 'already committed' and that a race relations component ought to be one part of a wider course covering a range of issues that are important for shop stewards.

Another side of education is the provision of special courses directed towards black workers themselves. The most common in the past have been courses of language training when needed by Asian workers, often through Industrial Language Training Units. Some courses are designed to increase the awareness of Asian workers to union activities, with information printed in ethnic minority languages. Some have the aim of encouraging the participation of black workers to become lay officials and be active within the union structure. The need for such courses is recognised more readily now than it was ten years ago, when a more likely reaction from many unions would have been that to make special provision for any one group of members was to be sectionalist and divisive. Arguments that certain groups of workers suffer particular problems and need special resources were won first by women and later by black members.

There are a number of reservations that must be borne in mind on the role of education in the pursuit of equal opportunities. First an *over*-emphasis on 'special needs' education carries the implication that if only the black workers had better language ability and more knowledge of the movement they would be able to participate fully in the union. The experiences of English-speaking and second-generation blacks have shown that there are undamental barriers to participation in the unions, other than those of anguage. Secondly, race-relations education for shop stewards is beset with problems. Through the resistance of shop stewards themselves it may become a neglected part of the course. Furthermore, those particularly bigoted shop stewards and officers who would benefit most from attending such courses tend to stay away as they feel that such provisions are a waste of time and money (GLC Anti-Racist Trade Union Working Group 1984: 5).

In the current economic crisis shop stewards are being granted less time away from work to spend on courses, and with new employment legislation and other threats to the work of trade unions from central government and employers it becomes easy for 'race' to slip down the list of priorities in trade union education. Also, it must be remembered that, in itself, education is unlikely to produce fundamental changes in attitudes and behaviour. It needs to proceed hand-in-hand with other measures such as positive equal opportunity measures and active strategies in opposition to racism.

Further TUC initiatives

In 1977, Congress called upon the General Council of the TUC to conduct a campaign against racialists in the unions. In 1979 the TUC sent out a circular to all its affiliated unions recommending that they should adopt a policy on racialists. In 1981 the TUC published 'Black Workers: A TUC Charter for Equal Opportunity'. This encourages unions to be active in equal opportunities instead of just talking about it, and stresses that they should review their own structures and procedures. The Charter's main points include: the removal of barriers which prevent black workers from reaching union office and decision making bodies; the need for vigorous action on employment grievances concerning racial discrimination; a commitment to countering racialist propaganda; an emphasis on personnel procedures for recruitment and promotion being clearly laid down; the production of material in relevant ethnic languages when necessary; and the inclusion of equal opportunity clauses in collective agreements.

The TUC has also co-operated with the CRE in the production of a Code of Practice' (1984) and is encouraging unions to make use of the code.

Some unions are setting up Race Relations Committees and national officers responsible for encouraging the participation of black members and furthering equal opportunities. (For a list of those who have set up bodies to monitor race issues and have issued positive statements against racism, see GLC Anti-Racist Trade Union Working Group 1984: 13 and Labour

Research July 1983.) Increasingly, collective agreements are being made which include the model equal opportunities clause of the TUC.

The participation of black members in unions

It remains to be seen, however, whether any of these measures will help to increase the participation of black members in unions. Recent evidence suggests that they remain under-represented in union posts: the Policy Studies Institute survey found that black members are much less likely to hold an elected post than white members, even though they are more likely to join unions than white people and attend meetings with about the same frequency (Brown 1984: 170). To explain the low participation of black workers in unions the Runnymede Trust in 1974 wrote that 'there are forces at work which make it more difficult for coloured and immigrant workers to play their full part in the movement. These include factors such as language differences, shift working, ethnic work groups and lack of trade union experience' (Runnymede Trust 1974–5: 24).

This explanation puts much of the emphasis on the characteristics and special needs of the black workers themselves. There is no mention in this explanation, for example, of the experience of racism. In 1980 Miles and Phizacklea did take account of this, arguing that an awareness of racial discrimination and racism at the place of work and within the union was a factor in explaining the lower level of black participation in work-place union activity (Phizacklea and Miles 1980: 125; see also Phizacklea 1982). The reason there were so few black shop stewards was not because they were 'new' – they weren't – but rather because they weren't 'invited' through the usual informal processes. Alternatively, a black worker who felt that racism was a feature of the work environment would be less likely to take on a position which entailed making 'personal sacrifices for the collective good' (Phizacklea and Miles 1980: 125).

It was the perception that, despite the range of initiatives over the last few years, black members still have relatively low rates of participation in unions, that prompted an initiative by the West Midlands Regional TUC. As one full-time officer put it: 'Despite the thousands of black members they don't seem to participate in trade union activism outside work. We want to be active in wider social concerns for ethnic minorities as well as for whites. At the moment there is a void.'[2]

Thus the West Midlands Regional TUC sponsored a research project (with financial support from the Economic and Social Research Council) on 'Trade Unionism and Race' (Lee 1984). In this, black union members reported a lack of confidence in trade unions to look after their interests, a view born out of their own day-to-day experiences as well as a recognition of the recent past history of trade union failings. One complaint was that trade union officers were reluctant to take action over racial discrimination and did not perceive race issues as something to fight about with management. Racially aware white officials admitted that there was a reluctance in the movement to act on race issues, one reason being the fear of losing white support.

Lee concluded that, at present, trade unions are only really tackling the problems of black workers if they are those also faced by white workers. They are not acting on issues such as under-representation in certain areas of work, promotion, the differential impact of redundancies, or racial abuse. She argues that union officers only feel comfortable with the idea of treating everyone alike, regardless of colour, and feel that giving any special attention to the grievances of black workers is to give them 'two bites at the cherry' (Lee 1984: 12).

White trade unionists tended to explain the lack of participation and involvement by black workers as primarily due to their inertia and lack of interest. Black members themselves argued that, after years of racism within the unions, and with day-to-day evidence of its persistence, it is not surprising that they were reluctant to put themselves forward. They dismissed union efforts on equal opportunities as 'a front', 'tokenism' or 'lip-service'. One talked of 'subtle ways of discouraging black people' from becoming involved in the union – for example, black members might not have the requisite insight into union history and internal politics if they did not already have certain informal links with long-standing trade unionists. Or the barriers might be more practical, such as holding meetings in public houses, which deterred many Asian women from participating.

When black workers did get themselves involved in meetings they would often feel that 'their' issues were being excluded. 'Unpopular' race items would be left late on the agenda, or would be omitted altogether because of the apathy of the white majority. The fact that black workers are usually in a minority at meetings means that it is difficult to sway opinions to get race on the agenda. This was found to be one of the fundamental problems: that of being a minority in an institution run by majority interest: 'How are you going to work within a democratic system where by the sheer virtue of a majority they can prevent progress by the minority?' (black trade unionist, quoted in Lee 1984: 9).

It was, as one respondent put it, 'the kind of democracy which is holding back progress' (Lee 1984: 19). This kind of experience had converted many black trade unionists to support the establishment of a black caucus within individual unions, and the relative success of women trade unionists in getting the caucus principle accepted reinforced their views. Others pressed for proportional representation or reserved seats, pointing to women's success in gaining these too, and arguing that this in itself would encourage black participation (Lee 1984: 21).

White officials, however, were more resistant to this idea, claiming that it would be sectarian, divisive, or even patronising to black members. Lee concludes:

> It is with great reluctance that (black) members have come to believe that such a move is necessary. Black people want to be elected to positions on their merit, in line with custom and practice within trade unions. It is only through sheer frustration that more are now coming to the conclusion that, as a minority, they cannot beat the exclusionary tactics which a majority can operate within a democratic system. (Lee 1984: 24–5)

Towards separate black organisations?

At the TUC 1983 conference, Ken Gill, speaking on behalf of the General Council, warned that unless there was an urgent response from unions over equal opportunity and racial inequality, there was a danger that black workers would lose whatever confidence they had in the willingness of trade unions adequately to represent their interests (CRE Employment Report, October 1984: 11). The TUC is understandably worried that black members may drift away from the main body of the unions. The formation of a separate black trade union is something which black trade unionists have so far resisted, though many acknowledge that this may be a future option if nothing changes.

The move for a separate black trade union poses a real dilemma for black activists. At the present time they see their particular interests being ignored by unions; however, there would be dangers in creating a separate union specifically to cover these interests. A separate black union might become isolated and relatively easily ignored by other unions and management; internal pressure on other unions to act on race issues would be weakened, and the end result could be a *reduction* in the collective power of organised black labour. The fact that black trade unionists have not yet set up their own separate trade union does not mean that they have been satisfied with the record of trade unions – rather that they are aware of the problems of separatism. None of the black trade unionists interviewed by Lee were in favour of a separate union.

One of the founder members of the Black Trade Unionists Solidarity Movement was insistent that there was no question of forming a separate black union because 'we don't want to let the unions off the hook' (*Morning Star* 25 January 1983). The more effective option is seen to be the formation of pressure groups and organisations to influence the existing trade unions, something that organisations such as the Indian Workers Association have been doing for years. The IWA acts not as a black trade union but through existing unions; it expects its members to belong to unions and be active within them, and makes representations at branch, district or TUC level. The IWA believes that over the years it has had an effect on the unions and has contributed to changes in attitudes to race issues within the movement.

More recently, new work-based black groups have been started, with the aim of putting pressure on unions – for example, black workers in the National Health Service have formed an association to influence the range of unions to which they belong. Sometimes black organisations have sprung up in response to specific events, such as the one formed after the incident at BL's Cowley plant when, after a black contract worker was arrested on suspicion of theft, the Chief Security Officer sent a memo instructing his staff to 'check the identity of every black trying to enter'. The black workers, with the support of the shop stewards committee, succeeded in getting the memo withdrawn and the incident led to the formation of a Black Workers Rights Committee (McIlroy 1982: 4). After the 1981 summer riots, the Black Trade Unionists Solidarity Movement was formed by black trade unionists 'who were concerned at the racist reaction in the Labour Movement to the disturbances in Brixton, Southall and other parts of Britain'. The aims were, amongst other things, to work for changes in trade union structure to enhance the participation of black workers, to act as an advice and support resource for black members, and to work for equal opportunity by positive action in the work-place.[3]

The movement held its first conference in London in June 1983. The organisation was to be a 'pressure group within the trade union movement' to 'expose racism in the unions through the media and by picketing union conferences'. The BTUSM stressed the value of racial awareness courses, 'employing specialists to overhaul union rule books and expunge discriminatory practices', and checking whether the procedures for the recruitment of union officers were indirectly discriminatory.

Other groups are more locally focused: for example, the Camden Black Workers Group formed in 1983 to put active pressure on Camden Council as employer and on the relevant unions, to put teeth into their equal opportunity policies. As a group they insist that their full members belong to a trade union, covering with their membership both manual and white-collar unions. The group has lobbied the National Association of Local Government Officers over adequate black participation at annual conferences and over seats on the NALGO Executive, and has gained the right to represent black workers at grievance and disciplinary hearings (GLC Economic Policy Group 1984).

NALGO itself had a National Working Party on Race Equality which produced a report for its June 1984 Annual Conference, recommending, amongst other things, changes in the union structure to strengthen ethnic minority representation, race-training priority for stewards including advice on how to take up discrimination cases, recommendations for negotiators to include a policy whereby posts are simultaneously advertised internally and externally, and a recommendation that the rule book is changed in order to make it clear that deliberate acts of unlawful discrimination are 'incompatible with NALGO membership and racist activities in the workplace should be subject to disciplinary action' (CRE Employment Report July 1984).

NALGO has responded better than many unions to race issues: nevertheless it, too, has come under criticism from black members over lack of consultation. A meeting of 250 black NALGO members in Birmingham in May 1984 refused to recognise the race-relations working party because of inadequate black representation on it. One complained: 'We are angry and disappointed at the lack of representation in our own union. The white members are the riders and we are remaining the horses. Now we want a go at the reins as well' (*Birmingham Evening Mail* 10 May 1984). As the Camden Black Workers Action Group put it: 'Freedom and equality cannot be given from the top. They can only be secured by people who suffer subordination' (GLC Economic Policy Group 1984).

The recession, the unions and equal opportunity

It is striking that the period when black workers have finally made some progress in the battle for influence within the union movement is the same period when the unions themselves have seen their own influence in society seriously decline. Government and many employers are taking full advantage of the recession and unemployment to reduce shop-floor strength and weaken trade union organisation; public sector employers are responding to government cuts by making an assault on public sector unions. Some employers are employing 'union-busting' consultants; others are tearing up long-standing union agreements, and new employment legislation has on occasion made it difficult for unions to carry out their traditional role effectively whilst remaining within the law. The introduction of the Youth Training Scheme has further eroded hard-won union control in the area of recruitment and training, and the very structure of YTS has made it difficult for unions to make their influence felt.[4] Legislation to protect the low-paid is being eroded and, all in all, there has been something of a shift in power away from the shop-floor and the unions to management.

In 1984, for the first time since 1975, less than half of Britain's workers were organised in unions affiliated to the TUC (*Labour Research* 1984:

192). The *level* of trade union organisation has also fallen: the decline is not only due to the overall fall in employment, but also because the recession has hit hardest many of those industries such as manufacturing, and in particular engineering, where unions have been most effectively organised. These are also sectors where black workers have been concentrated.

As might be expected in a time of recession, traditional manufacturers have in part been replaced by 'sweatshop' manufacturers. Since the late 1970s these establishments have mushroomed in inner-city areas of Birmingham and the Black Country, taking advantage of cheap premises, central locations and access to a reservoir of local labour with few alternative employment prospects. In clothing sweatshops it is often Asian women who are exploited (often by Asian employers) in these illegal working conditions, in small, dirty and unsafe premises where fire regulations are ignored and sanitary and safety provision negligible, working long erratic hours for low pay without union protection (see Hoel 1982).

> These women are quite literally sweating. They are under constant pressure. It is hard to believe that we are living in the 1980s. Industrial conditions are more like the 1880s. (Raghib Ahsan, West Midlands Low Pay Unit, *Birmingham Evening Mail* 20 October 1984)

The growth of sweatshops poses a whole new challenge to trade unions in their relationship with black workers. Previously these workers had been relatively neglected by unions as a fringe sector, perceived as difficult to organise, not only because of the many dispersed and transient locations of production but also because Asian women in particular have been seen by white male trade union officers as lacking a knowledge and tradition of trade unionism and as possibly being resistant to organisation. Union officers are just as prone as anyone else in white society to stereotyped views of ethnic minorities, in this case the view that Asian women are passive, inhibited and exclusively family-centred. Such a view is implied, for example, in a feature article on sweatshops in the *Birmingham Evening Mail* (20 October 1984) where Asian women were described as 'ideal sweatshop fodder' because of, amongst other things, their 'non-union traditions' and 'limited understanding of employees' rights'. To apply this view to Asian women in general is an oversimplification which displays an ignorance of the many Asian women who have been at the forefront of collective workplace struggles for many years. Two of the 'classic' disputes – Imperial Typewriters and Grunwick – concerned *mainly* Asian women; more recently there have been a number of important disputes in the sweatshops of the West Midlands which have demonstrated the readiness of Asian women to resist what the general secretary of the Indian Workers Association called 'feudal draconian working conditions' (*Birmingham Evening Mail* 20 October 1984).

Without full union support and the access to the media that often comes from it, such struggles are often unnoticed by the wider trade union movement. More recently some union officials in the West Midlands have belatedly recognised the importance of this particular category of potential members. For one thing, this sector is seen as one source of replacement members for those lost in the collapse of metal-based manufacturing in the area. For another, the very existence of a significant and increasing number of low-paid, non-unionised workers in the heart of the region constitutes a long-term potential threat to the conditions of trade unionists outside the sweatshop sector. However, as in so many other instances, the record of trade unions in supporting black workers in the sweatshop sector is mixed – and often lamentable – and knowledge of this has been one barrier to overcome when convincing vulnerable workers of the wisdom of joining a trade union.

In recent years in the West Midlands there has been a number of disputes in this sector: for example, Reeve Polishing and Plating, Smethwick in 1978; R. J. Vickers in 1980; Raindi Textiles in 1982; Sadhar and Kang in 1982; Kewal Brothers in 1984; G & M Plastics, Redditch, also in 1984. (Some of these disputes are described in detail in Bishton's report on sweatshops, 1984.) All of these disputes involved Asian workers, often women, and most had as one precipitating factor management strategies to thwart union organisation.

In some of the earlier of these disputes union support was at best half-hearted (Bishton 1984: 58). In more recent cases, union support has been more forthcoming (although sometimes appearing a little late). For example, at Sadhar and Kang the TGWU aided the picketing by getting its member drivers to black deliveries from the large companies who supplied Sadhar and Kang (Bishton 1984: 55), and the strike did have a degree of success.

Union responses to criticism

Unions have moved from a position of not supporting black workers in their employment struggles because they were black, to a position of being more likely to support black workers because they are trade unionists. This is progress. But this is often still in a context of being 'colour blind'; of seeing black workers as faced with exactly the same problems as white workers. This position displays an ignorance of all the kinds of circumstances which have been described in this paper so far, and renders meaningless any idea of equal opportunity.

In a survey by the GLC's Anti-Racist Trade Union Working Group this colour blind' attitude was found to be one of the main problems that black workers had to face in unions: 'The fact is that black workers suffer from all the problems experienced by white workers but also from problems associated with racism which are manifested in prejudice, discrimination and harassment' (GLC ARTUWG 1984: 6).

The Working Group sent questionnaires to 50 different unions requesting information on their stated position and activities in the area of race and equal opportunity. About a half failed to respond, leaving the researchers to infer a low priority in this area. The evidence from those who replied was that although there were from a number of unions some encouraging 'signs and symbols of commitment to combating racism', as yet rather little had been achieved.

Nine unions had adopted formal anti-racist policies, but many others still felt it unnecessary formally to declare their opposition to racism as they felt that equal opportunity had always existed in their organisation. For example, the respondent from the NUR wrote: 'Most of the questions in the questionnaire appear to me to be irrelevant to the situation in this union as all our members have equal opportunity and there is no discrimination against any member for any reason whatsoever' (GLC ARTUWG 1984: 14). Yet the Working Group was aware of incidents and case histories in this and other unions which had responded similarly, demonstrating that discrimination was 'frequently conspicuous'.

Several unions had made internal provisions for combating racism, such as working parties, day schools and advice sheets. Six unions, however, stated that they had implemented no provisions to combat racism because it was unnecessary.

The report criticised the record of unions as employers themselves. Many of the unions did not see the need for an equal opportunity programme for its own employees, even though the same unions could well find themselves pushing for such a policy for other employers. Most unions were not in favour of monitoring the ethnicity of their own work force, which demonstrated a lack of awareness of the potential contradiction in their own failure to keep ethnic records whilst demanding that employers with whom they bargain should carry out such measures (GLC ARTUWG 1984: 17).

The Working Group argue that there is a 'vital need' for records, not as ends in themselves, but rather as means to highlight the procedures of unions as employers and any possible detrimental effects these may have on black applicants: 'Without the information to demonstrate that equality is a fact, it remains a fallacy' (GLC ARTUWG 1984: 19).

The findings of the GLC survey confirm the suspicions of many activists:

that despite the history of disputes and struggles, the research, the educational material and the prosecutions, there remains a body of trade union officers who simply do not understand – or are unwilling to acknowledge – what racism and racial inequality are, what their effects are, how they operate, and what sorts of measures are needed to oppose them. A critical response to the GLC survey by John Torode (*Guardian* 17 December 1984) demonstrates a number of the 'classic' defensive positions argued by union officers when confronted with criticisms of union failings on race. For example, he writes, 'the embittered and all embracing distaste for trade union orthodoxy which the working group displays is an insult to those trade unions who have made honourable colour-blind efforts to absorb minorities'.

This argument displays an ignorance of the way that an 'honourable colour blindness' has long been one of the rationalisations for a refusal to support black workers in struggle, a refusal to acknowledge or oppose racism, and a neglect of many of the real needs of one whole section of trade union membership. Torode also puts forward the 'standard' opposition to ethnic monitoring: 'How many of us want our ethnic origins ("Jewish", "Black", "half-caste" even) stamped on our union files? We sense it as degrading and potentially dangerous. It smacks too much of National Socialism or the anti-semitic internal passports issued by the Soviet Union.'

Again, this argument shows an ignorance of the equal opportunity litera- ture and of the aspirations of the black membership. As the GLC Working Group argues, there is an important distinction to be made between ethnic monitoring carried out by trade unions for the purpose of improving its anti- racist practices, and that carried out by official agencies such as the DHSS where there is no such aim, no control over the data, and real fears about its misuse (GLC ARTUWG 1984: 18).

Like others have done, Torode defends the unions' record on race by pointing to their 'brave and successful stands' against National Front activity. However, to criticise a union's record on race is not to ignore or denigrate this important part of anti-racist activity. But, as Phizacklea and Miles argue, while such campaigns are important, they bring little if any material improvement in the position of black workers (Phizacklea and Miles 1980: 35).

A proper test of a union's commitment to equal opportunity is its willing- ness to take on-board policies which involve ultimately the re-allocation of *resources* to its black members (and where these resources are fixed this will inevitably mean a reduction in their availability to white members). Examples of such resources could be *time* – making space for black issues at union meetings; *money* – making funds available for ethnic monitoring, for black conferences and literature; *jobs* – assisting black workers to over-come barriers around positions occupied by whites, and so on.

The final set of arguments of the 'old guard' are those in reaction to the development of black pressure groups and caucuses within unions, argu-ments which are also going on within the Labour Party. Opponents of these developments often talk of 'discrimination in reverse' or 'racism by blacks'.

For example, in September 1984 a meeting of 70 black delegates at a conference at Birmingham's Afro-Caribbean Resource Centre agreed to set up a Black Trade Unionists Solidarity Group, to represent the rights of black trade union members and appoint liaison officers to deal with race matters in unions. This was condemned by Labour Councillor O'Keefe who was quoted in the *Birmingham Evening Mail* (21 September 1984) as saying: 'I have never seen so much racialism – I will oppose it entirely. It is apartheid in reverse.'

Again, such arguments would only make sense in a world where black trade unionists had not had a history of the kinds of experience described in this paper. For years black workers have seen the failure of unions to take up their issues. Time and time again black trade unionists have attempted to use normal union procedures to get action on the sorts of injustices which have been described above, but without success. Often, the very fact that unions are relatively democratic organisations has meant that the majority voice has predominated and minority groups get over-ruled. Consequently, black workers have learned that the way to make their voices heard is through *self*-organisation within unions. Their success in this has produced change in some unions in the discrepancy between yearly conference motions on equal opportunity and complete inactivity on a practical level. The removal of this major inconsistency between policy and practice, and the shake-up of union procedures and rhetoric resulting from pressure by organised black members, has been in the interests of *all* members and should not be dismissed as a victory for sectionalism or 'apartheid' within unions. (In many cases, where majority-votes in union branches have been necessary for changes in branch rules to enable the setting up of black sections, this has only been made possible through the active support of white members too.)

The ultimate excuse for inaction by a union official is the statement that 'whilst I agree with you, I can't take on this because the white membership won't wear it'. From a historical perspective there is some irony in the defence that it is the membership, not the leadership, who are racist. It could be plausibly argued that one reason for the widespread racist attitudes amongst trade union members today is the absence of a good example from the leaders in the past. It was the leaders of the Labour movement who originally helped to structure the view of 'race as a problem' in previous decades.

When black workers began to arrive here in some numbers in the 1950s there was no progressive, anti-racist political/ideological framework which would have enabled the working class to 'make sense' of a black presence in Britain. Before the working class could fashion a response from within its collective traditions and experiences of poverty and hardship, its reformist leadership had structured such a response around 'colour as a problem'. (Joshi and Carter 1984: 5)

Thus, this defensive position by union officers sounds rather hollow: at the risk of sounding trite, one might re-interpret their stance as 'because over the years we have failed to take a lead in anti-racism, our membership has been encouraged in its own racism, which means that we cannot take a lead in anti-racism'.

Obviously there *are* occasions when a progressive white official has been hamstrung by a reactionary white membership. But it is equally obvious that this excuse is used far too easily by officials, even when there is little basis for this opinion. Part of the role of officials or shop stewards is to inform and educate the membership when necessary – has every shop steward who has raised this defence attempted to do this? (Such an excuse may well reflect badly on his or her previous record on race issues.) What is more, there have been many cases in union history where trade unions have led campaigns in *advance* of the views of their membership – in some areas of health and safety, for example, a work force has appeared to be reasonably content with arrangements which a union has found intolerable: in such circumstances the union has led the way in change and the attitudes of the work force have followed.

The conservatism of unions on race is all the more galling given the knowledge that in many other areas of employment reform – such as health and safety – it is the unions which have taken the initiative against management. Yet in some local authorities we see the phenomenon of management pushing progressive race-employment policies onto reluctant unions. After a decision in 1984 by the education authority in Birmingham to monitor the ethnic background of teachers as part of its equal opportunity in employment policy the deputy general secretary of the Birmingham group of the National Association of Schoolmasters/Union of Women Teachers complained 'We do not see why the authority needs to know the composition of the existing workforce for its equal opportunities policy' (*Birmingham Evening Mail* 24 September 1984). The question to ask the union in return is, 'How can the effectiveness of an equal opportunity policy be measured *without* knowing the ethnic composition of the workforce?' For example, how could the success of the recent initiative in the London Fire Brigade be known without the statistics to show that in 1984, 70 out of 6,000 uniformed staff were of ethnic minority origin compared with only seven in 1981? (GLC 1984: 12). As the GLC Working Group argue, monitoring is not an end in itself but a means to an end; one more tool in the struggle for greater equality, and indispensable for any consideration of whether an organisation is functioning fairly (GLC ARTUWG 1984: 19). In some local authority unions, local branch practice lags behind formal union policy at a national level. It is very important that local unions take on a racial equality commitment: not only are existing equal opportunity strategies by a local authority likely to fail if they do not have union backing, but there is also the possibility that an authority currently committed to such strategies may undergo a change in political control at a future election with a corresponding decline in the impetus on equal opportunity policies from the top. The union may then become the major custodian and guardian of good racial equality policy.

Conclusion

It might be argued that this discussion has been too negative in its concentration on the many illustrations of union failings on race, to the neglect of those occasions when unions have taken positive action in support of black members. To this the reply would be that, despite the progress of recent years, it is still not the time for complacency and self-congratulation, particularly in the light of the dangerous view still widespread amongst many trade unionists that there is 'no problem here'.

This article began with a brief reminder of the unfortunate recent history of trade union treatment of black workers. Again some progressive trade unionists might argue that to dwell on these events has been a rather negative exercise. If they subscribe to the dictum that one should 'Look not mournfully into the Past' but 'Wisely improve the present',[5] then a critical scrutiny of history may in turn be defended by the warning that 'Those who do not remember the past are condemned to relive it'.[6] The overall conclusion is mixed: there are both positive and negative aspects of the current picture. The trade union leadership has made progressive shifts from an archaic position; progressive activists have made their voices heard; some unions have devoted some resources to equal opportunities and anti-racism. On the other hand, it is clear that a real barrier to future progress is still the ignorance, the defensiveness, the misguided colour blindness and indefensible racism of some men and women in positions of power and influence in the trade union hierarchy, as well as within the rank and file.

There are a range of arguments which could be drawn on by 'pessimists': these include whole new areas of sociological debate which the current paper has no room to address. Arguments from this point of view refer to the 'natural' sectionalism of unions, their reformist character in relationship to capital, the ossifying bureaucratic procedures and remote leadership of unions (as described by Michels), the endemic racism of the British working class, as well as the views that the recent interest of union leaders in black members is based on expedience rather than ideological commitment, and that this interest will serve to absorb and deflect the radical energy of black groups. To do justice to these debates would require a whole new paper. Nevertheless, a totally pessimistic view is often founded on somewhat simplistic reasoning. For example, there is a common assumption that in a recession 'scapegoating' racism will automatically increase. The view of prejudice based on economic and political competition is summed up by Aronson: 'Prejudiced attitudes tend to increase when times are tense and there is conflict over mutually exclusive goals' (1972: 208). However, it is not at all clear that racism, at least in the work arena, has increased in the recent years of recession. As many white workers have been thrust into positions of under-privilege and hardship along with black workers, there has been an awareness of common cause and common interest. A simple 'recession increases racism' assumption neglects the role of political education and the experience of struggle. The 1984/5 miners' strike saw instances of striking miners standing on black workers' picket lines outside Birmingham sweatshops, of black groups sending speakers to miners' meetings, of Asian women workers organising collections for the miners, and so on. This is part of one positive development of recent years – the increasing organisation of black workers and their success in making their influence felt within the Labour movement.

Along with the miners it is the black working class who have often had a strong ideological basis to their struggles and a powerfully supportive community base from which to fight. Like the miners, they have the potential for making a greater than average contribution to the struggles of organised labour. But in complete contrast to the miners, they have not had the advantage of a committed union organisation behind them. Black workers are organising themselves in order to change this neglect by unions, and it might well be argued that until greater racial equality is achieved within working men's and women's own organisations there will be little chance of success in other spheres.

PART THREE

The prospects for equal opportunity

11

Equal opportunity in the context of high levels of unemployment

ED RHODES AND PETER BRAHAM

The concept of equal opportunity in employment

In this paper we are concerned with the implications for equal opportunity in employment of persisting high levels of *un*employment. We seek to identify how far rising unemployment has increased the extent of black inequality in the labour market and to what extent it may provide the underlying context for any attempt to develop and extend equal opportunity policy and practice.

However, as a starting point, it is important to consider the assumptions which are implicit in the concept of equal opportunity, particularly those which relate to employment.

The emergence of equal opportunity as an issue and the thinking which surrounded the development of equal opportunity policies in the political, legal and employment contexts, owes much to experience and political action in the USA. The precise nature of the American influence is an issue which need not detain us here; what we wish to examine are the political and economic conditions which prevailed in the USA and the UK and in other industrialised countries as legislative and other action took shape.

The period from the mid-1940s onwards is often characterised as one which was dominated in the political arena and elsewhere by a consensus, variously described as a 'conservative consensus' or a 'liberal–pluralist consensus'. Thus, according to Miliband, 'To a much larger extent than appearance and rhetoric have been made to suggest, the politics of advanced capitalism have been about different conceptions of how to run the *same* economic and social system, and not about radically different systems' (Miliband 1973: 67). In the case of the UK, it is worth bearing in mind that although such a consensus provided the context in which race relations and equal opportunity legislation were developed, this consensus was by no means confined to governmental or parliamentary arenas. Its significance for both employers and unions is indicated by their participation and co-operation in a wide range of bodies such as NEDCS, ACAS and industrial tribunals. This involvement, sometimes taken as evidence of *incorporation*, also extended to the work-place – a process regarded by some commentators of the period as part of a 'new realism' which marked the end of ideology and which resulted inevitably from industrial progress: 'Consensus develops wherever industrialisation is successful. The labour force becomes committed to and settled into the web of rules, the surrounding structure. The sense of protest subsides. The enterprise managers, left to their own devices, push less hard' (Kerr *et al.* 1973: 266).

Even if the 'new realism' perceived by Kerr and his associates was later displaced by a very different 'new realism', the context of work-place consensus, marked by the pattern of work-place relations identified in the Donovan Commission's report of the mid-1960s, provided a suitable medium in which to interpose in the 'web of rules' first, a pressure to cease any overt racial discrimination and, subsequently, guidelines intended to reduce gender and racial inequalities.

Of the values within the consensus, perhaps the most significant for the emergence and shaping of the concept of equal opportunity was the commitment to full employment initially accepted by the Conservative–Labour coalition government of 1940–45 and subsequently upheld by governments of both parties. In the Employment Policy White Paper of 1944 the government ushered in 'a regime of economic policy making. . .(which had). . .as its central predicate the necessity of full employment. . .Of course full employment was always an ambiguous notion but to be explicitly opposed to it in the 1950s and 1960s was to put oneself almost outside the realms of tolerable argument' (Tomlinson 1983: 49).

In this period, in which much of the immigration from the New Commonwealth (NCW) took place, employment opportunities continued to grow as the decline in many of the older industries was generally more than offset by expansion elsewhere in the public and private sectors.

The commitment to full employment eventually came to be accompanied by a parallel commitment to continuous economic growth which in 1959 was said to be 'newly explicit as an objective of governments' (Radcliffe Report 1959). To the extent that this was achieved, it would make available the resources necessary for dealing with social issues which might otherwise have had a lower order of priority. Both the commitment to full employment and the commitment to economic growth required a further element of consensus – the acceptance of state interventionism. While there were considerable differences about the need for intervention or the extent of intervention in specific cases, in general there was an acceptance that the state could, and should, intervene actively by legislative and other means wherever problems were perceived. In employment this resulted in major intervention over questions such as regional unemployment, training, incomes and resolution of disputes. Thus, when it came to considering how to combat racial discrimination and promote equal opportunity, the interventionist path was well-trodden.

The legislation was also framed in the context of a belief that reductions in economic inequalities, associated with generally rising living standards and a progressive lowering of income differentials, were in turn contributing to a reduction in social inequalities. This was partly related to a supposed *embourgeoisement* of the working class, but in addition was linked to perceptions of a *greatly* increased level of mobility between classes. As Fox has indicated, there was a belief that:

> More and more it becomes possible for talent and hard work to reap their reward through an upward progress in what is sometimes called a meritocracy – a new aristocracy based on individual ability and effort instead of on birth and social rank. . .it offers a view of society as a reasonable and fair system of arrangements within which individuals and groups engage in healthy competition for the good things in life. (Fox 1974: 7)

A belief in an emerging meritocracy in which there was greater opportunity for upwards mobility was strengthened by a number of developments. Among these were educational reforms – which were held to have reduced many of the inequalities in the crucial period of individual learning and development prior to entry into the labour market – as well as changes in industrial organisation. One aspect of the latter was an alleged shift of organisational power away from the owners of capital towards what Galbraith termed 'the technostructure': 'the association of men of diverse technical knowledge, experience, or other talent which modern industrial technology and planning require' (1969: 67). This was one consequence which was believed to follow from changes in organisational size, complexity and concentration, changes which had also required greater formality in the administration and control of work and employment. Thus the shift towards technocratic control offered greater opportunities, as did the combined effects of improved educational provision and more objective – achievement-related – methods of selection and promotion.

In the environment established by those elements of the consensus to which we have referred, it was perhaps reasonable to believe that the problems experienced by the 'new communities' in employment would gradually melt away. That is to say, as the first generation of NCW immigrants acquired relevant skills and experience, and as later generations entered the labour market in more orthodox fashion, so members of the NCW communities would join the upward escalator of economic and social progression. The school system, fairly administered employment organisation – in large companies at least – and other manifestations of the meritocratic society would surely assist this process of assimilation.

This expectation was, perhaps, based on something of a misreading of wider social and economic developments. As Westergaard and Resler point out, a complacency 'characteristic of the 1950s and 60s' gave way 'to a more realistic recognition of continuing obstacles to "equal opportunity" in education; and to a series of attempts to direct policy to reducing them. . .' (Westergaard and Resler 1979: 279). Nevertheless, measures taken against discrimination in the 1968 Race Relations Act and action modestly in support of 'equal opportunities' in the 1976 Act, appeared to leave undisturbed some basic assumptions about employment: namely, that in essence it is meritocratic and fair in organisation and, outside the special cases of race and gender, non-discriminatory.

These and similar assumptions seem implicit in such attempts as there have been in Britain to define the term 'equal opportunity', though as Bindman (1980) points out the term is widely used, but without much precision. According to Bindman,

> In its most limited sense it is used to refer to a policy whose object is solely to prevent unlawful discrimination by the firm or institution that adopts it. In a broader sense it includes giving greater encouragement to members of ethnic minorities to take advantage of opportunities than to others . . . It encourages the acquisition of a fairer or more nearly equal share of the benefits of society for members of ethnic groups who are disproportionately denied them. (Bindman 1980: 319)

McCrudden places more emphasis on the factors of ability and achievement. He sees fair equality of opportunity as requiring 'that those who have the same talent or ability and have the same willingness to use them, should have the same prospects of success regardless of their initial place in the social system, that is, irrespective of the income group, class or racial group into which they happen to be born' (1983b: 29). In the specific context of employment, Seear (1981) defines equal opportunity in employment as meaning 'in plain English, that no one is denied training or a job for reasons that have nothing to do with their competence and capacity' (295).

It is only if one makes certain assumptions about the general nature of employment organisations, and the distribution of opportunities and rewards in employment, that such definitions become operationally conceivable. Even in the era of relatively full employment and economic growth, during which the issue of equal opportunity assumed prominence, the implicit assumptions were unwarranted. For example it is manifestly not the case, contrary to McCrudden's definition of fair equality of employment, that there is a general prospect of success irrespective of the income group or class into which an individual is born. Did the drafters or proposers of the 1975 Sex Discrimination Act or the 1976 Race Relations Act think otherwise?

The prevalence of inequalities in employment becomes clearer if one looks at two areas: the overall structure of labour market organisation and control; and the nature of systems of appointment and promotion.

Consideration of the structure of labour-market organisation and control has for some time been powerfully influenced by the concept of the dual labour market. We have argued elsewhere (Rhodes and Braham 1981) that, in the UK at least, there are considerable grounds for doubting the accuracy of the concept even at a moderately proximate level. As Bohning (1972) and Blackburn and Mann (1979) argue, it is more fruitful to think in terms of disadvantaged *jobs* which are to be found in profusion in firms otherwise similar to the primary sector firms of the segmented model. Within large and small firms, both profitable and marginal, there is likely to be a structure of relatively advantaged and disadvantaged jobs. Within this structure, associated with relative levels of advantage and disadvantage linked to earning capacity, occupational classification, working conditions, lines of promotion, and so on, are clearly defined job territories.

The maintenance of these job territories is not only determined by employers but is also the result of employee action. Employees divided by professional association, trade union, work-place or occupational group, are likely to seek to defend their job territories against other groups of workers. Whether it is men seeking to exclude women from craft occupations, the 'skilled' seeking to exclude the 'semi-skilled', the 'professional' seeking to exclude the 'para-professional' or a work-group resisting changes in duties or recruitment methods, they are all engaged in what amounts to a form of employment discrimination. In seeking to approach the issues of racial or ethnic equal opportunity, it is important to recognise that though there may be qualitative and quantitative differences, they are but one form of a much wider pattern of discrimination and unequal opportunity, operated not just by employers but also by workers against workers.

One of the assumptions associated with employer authority and control is termed by Offe (1976), the 'achievement principle'. This is the idea that there are qualitative differences between employees which can be identified objectively and once identified, utilised to make appointments and decide promotion. This principle would seem to be furthest developed in large

organisations where personnel departments oversee processes of recruitment and promotion based on qualifications, skills, experience and other
measurable criteria. Were such apparently objective criteria the sole arbiter
of occupational placement and mobility, it must be only a matter of time
before suitably qualified members of disadvantaged groups, such as women
and black workers, achieve parity with white male workers.

Why this does not come about may be explained if one considers the concept of 'skill' and its application to describe jobs either by inclusion or
exclusion. Braverman (1974) drew attention to the somewhat elastic nature
of the concept. In non-skilled jobs it is particularly easy for employers to
establish apparently objective entry or promotion requirements which,
though generally irrelevant to the job in question, none the less serve to
exclude, deliberately or not, particular categories of workers. Various
writers have demonstrated how definitions of skill have been manipulated
to exclude women (e.g. Phillips and Taylor 1980; Cockburn 1983). In
some cases they have been excluded by lifting requirements, in others by
insisting that employees accept the firm's right to transfer them from one
location to another. Similarly, black applicants have been restricted or
excluded by language requirements or literacy tests.

Some observers (e.g. Brooks 1975) have argued that black workers are
'least likely to be disadvantaged in large organisations where selection and
promotion are governed by formal criteria and procedures'. But whatever
the intentions of those in control centrally, it is much more difficult to restrict the scope for interpretation and negative stereotyping by those who
actually apply the formal procedures. More generally, Offe suggests that it
is not possible to apply the achievement principle. Identification of
outstandingly good or extremely poor candidates may be relatively simple,
but there is likely to be a sizeable number between whom it is difficult to distinguish. In these cases functional or formal criteria are likely to be overlaid
or even superseded 'by a second level of ascriptive qualifications and . . .
these then become important as an additional criterion for occupational
status and mobility chances' (Offe 1976: 90).

What the achievement principle does, argues Offe, is to form a basis for
legitimation of procedures and to provide a plausible explanation of inequalities between jobs and individuals. Indeed, in firms of all sizes beliefs
about the characteristics of various categories of worker generate considerable potential for discrimination, particularly when they infuse the process
of labour-market control. Thus, for example, a record of frequent job changing can be judged as undesirable in manual workers, but desirable in young
executives. Most pervasive and widespread are assumptions made about
the characteristics and limitations of women workers.

These assumptions have restricted them to a relatively narrow, generally low-level range of jobs and thus may provide an insight into the inequalities which black workers face. Hunt found that,

> a majority of those responsible for the engagement of employees start off with the belief that a woman applicant is likely to be inferior to a man in respect of all the qualifications considered important. The higher the level of the job, the greater the proportion who considered men were more likely to have the required attributes. Assuming identical attributes of both a man and woman applicant, the majority would give preference to a man rather than to a woman for all types of work, with the exception of catering and domestic work, where women were preferred, and office work where the majority expressed no preferences. (Hunt 1975)

Black workers have suffered from a range of adverse assumptions not only about their work capabilities but also about their personal behaviour. It might have been anticipated that such attitudes would have moderated (or at least become more covert) since Patterson (1965) or Daniel (1968) surveyed them, but evidence submitted in 1974 by employers and careers officers to the House of Commons Select Committee and from Smith (1977) attests to their durability. Moreover, such beliefs are discernible across a wide spectrum of work, as studies of applications for white-collar work (Smith 1977) and graduate appointments (Ballard and Holden 1975) indicate.

Closely related to implicit assumptions made by advocates of equal opportunity policies in employment about the nature of the labour market, are the explicit arguments advanced concerning the relationship between equal opportunity, efficiency and the supposed price of discrimination. For example, according to the CRE (1980), 'It is to the advantage of any organisation to have the widest and best choice for selecting its personnel. If staff or potential staff do not have the chance of demonstrating their ability, employers are denied the opportunity of using it.' And though Seear recognises that managers need to be convinced that equal opportunity policies will contribute to their 'primary obligation to society', that is the effective running of a business in order to create wealth and provide goods and services, she concludes that the implementation of an equal opportunity policy is 'another job for competent managers running an efficient and responsible enterprise' (1981: 305). According to Seear, in neither the USA nor in Britain does the law, by requiring equal opportunity, force an organisation to operate with reduced efficiency: the law only demands the removal of a condition which cannot be justified and this should make for better, not worse selection.

However, it is worth noting that the law does not apply to selection procedures which are unfair, or arbitrary in their effects, to *all* applicants regardless of racial group. As Pearn points out in his analysis of indirect discrimination in employment, 'If it is equally "unfair" to everyone it does not matter in law, though of course it would be stupid of an employer to operate inefficient selection practices, *as many seem to do*' (1979: 46–7, emphasis added).

The comment of an American personnel specialist quoted by Pearn that 'Under the law it is okay to be *fairly* stupid, but not okay to be *unfairly* stupid' (1979: 47), therefore seems to us to demonstrate a greater understanding of the *in*efficiency of the labour market than is possessed by many of the advocates of equality of opportunity. Moreover, where efficiency *is* the aim, it does not follow that the result will be 'colour blind' or that otherwise non-discriminatory methods of selection, promotion and dismissal will be adopted. In the first place, *un*equal opportunities in employment do not *per se* testify to a distortion of the labour market; on the contrary, employers in many industries seek cheap labour, whether in the UK or abroad, and thus stand to benefit from discrimination. Indeed, the first generation of black immigrants was widely regarded as a labour supply which could be used to fill jobs which could not be filled from other sources. As one large Bradford manufacturer said, 'If we could interview queues of English men for our vacancies we would not employ any immigrants at all. The plain fact is that we need immigrants' (quoted in Allen *et al.* 1977: 44).

However, more fundamental is the consequence for various categories of workers of the pressures in favour of operational efficiency and the connection between managerial careers and organisational performance. If operational efficiency requires that the best workers available be recruited, that is those from whom the highest return will be obtained, all other things being equal, the most suitable candidate for many jobs will be the one the gatekeeper considers is 'stable', 'dependable' and 'acceptable' – the one who is least likely to disturb the unity and level of work of the existing workgroup. In these circumstances, considerations of efficiency may allow the group characteristics ascribed to individuals a greater rather than a lesser role in deciding to prefer one candidate to another or which among a group of existing employees to dismiss. Given that the requirements of many jobs or the relevance of certain skills and experience are often matters for subjective judgement, it is not always an easy matter to establish that methods of selection are discriminatory.

In this context, it is helpful to visualise the flow of candidates through selection processes in terms of a queue system. An individual's place in the queue will be related not merely to the stated skill, qualification and experience requirements of particular jobs, but also to a combination of the categorisation of a job (e.g. overtly as 'women's work', or, usually, covertly as work suitable for blacks) and to the work characteristics believed by employers to be associated with factors such as age, sex and skin colour.

As Brooks says, 'it is clear that in the queue black workers occupy a place near the back, but not necessarily at the back for most jobs, with most employers' (1975: 2). This is, of course, an oversimplification. Ascriptive qualifications may be less important to some employers than to others. And individuals handicapped by association with unfavourably perceived groups do succeed against more advantaged candidates. In addition, the structure and composition of 'job queues' is modified by the preferences of workers, for example those who are unemployed may not seek certain kinds of jobs for which they might be considered well-qualified.

Despite these reservations, the concept of the queue is consistent with much of the statistical evidence about the characteristics of the unemployed. That is to say, position in the queue is also a consequence of the level of employment; as unemployment increases, so those who are associated with undesirable characteristics and who may thus face discrimination, are pushed towards the back of the queue, particularly the queue for the more desirable jobs.[1] It is striking, however, that discussion of equal opportunity and anti-discrimination legislation and its implementation, rarely appears to take explicit account of prevailing economic conditions and the implications these have for both the general level of employment and the employment prospects of black workers in particular. In part, this may be because it is easier to compare legislation in the USA and the UK (usually to the disadvantage of the latter) in terms of, say, the opportunities for complaint and the kind of evidence of discrimination which is admitted (that is, what is open to those, whether individuals or groups, who claim to have experienced discrimination) rather than in terms of the effect that legislation has, say, on the black–white income differentials and on the black profile of employment and unemployment. More generally, though, what we are suggesting is that the question as to whether equal opportunity measures are well-suited – in principle and/or in practice – to conditions of full employment and economic expansion, may be quite a different question to asking about the prospects for equal opportunity programmes in adverse economic conditions, where the size of the 'cake' to be redistributed is the same or even smaller than in the past.

Migration of labour and capital

Migration and the subsequent movement of migrants within the labour market of the receiving country, should be viewed in the context of processes of adaption, expansion and contraction of the labour force which have been central to industrialisation and capitalist accumulation.

Even in time of depression, organisational and technological changes require continuous adaption and relocation from the work force. In time of full employment, however, unless a reserve supply of labour can be located, there is a tendency for labour costs to increase and, in particular, it becomes harder to attract labour into certain kinds of work, so causing production bottlenecks and threatening continued economic growth.

Ideally, this labour reserve should be prepared to move into areas of labour shortage, whatever the type or location of the job and, equally, be prepared to move out of the work force when unemployment rises to high levels.

Agriculture has long been one of the most significant sources of additional labour in most industrialised countries. But in recent times, perhaps the most important reserve has been in the expansion of the female labour force. For example, in Britain the number of female employees grew from 6.3 million in 1951 to 8.3 million in 1971 (or 42.6% of the economically active work force). Their vulnerability to unemployment in recession was most clearly evident in the period after the Second World War when talk of the vital contribution of women's work to the war-effort was replaced by an emphasis on the 'secondary' nature of women's earnings and the virtues of domesticity.

When labour shortages developed in Britain after the war, recruitment of 'European Volunteer Workers' and, later, of black workers was influenced by the expectation that any economic boom would be short-lived and would recede as the dislocation caused by the war diminished. The option of importing labour thus recommended itself as a solution to an apparently temporary problem; should economic expansion not persist, immigrant workers could return to their countries of origin, just as many of them had done after their war service. In West Germany during the 1960s and early 1970s, this 'mobile labour potential' of migrant workers was referred to as the *Konjuncturpuffer* (boom buffer). That is to say, in time of economic expansion the recruitment of foreign workers saved indigenous workers from the consequences of labour shortages, and in time of economic recession the 'export' of foreign workers cushioned the indigenous labour force against unemployment. In both Britain and West Germany alternative solutions, such as substantial rises in wages in order to tempt indigenous workers back into unpopular occupations, might have seemed less attractive in so far as they might be less easily reversed once the conditions which gave rise to their adoption had ceased.

What was not perceived at the time was that these shortages of labour marked the beginning of a long-term trend which came to affect the economies of most of the industrialised countries of Europe. The prolonged economic boom which lasted in much of north-west Europe from the 1950s to the beginning of the 1970s would probably not have been sustained without migrant labour. Indeed, between 1960 and 1965, according to a UN survey, almost the entire increase in the European labour force was accounted for by immigrant labour. In the period as a whole, migration, together with transfers from agriculture, the arrival of political refugees and an increase in female employment, helped to contain wage costs and expand output. In this sense, migration and economic growth were interdependent.

As the number of migrant workers grew and as they were joined by increasing numbers of their dependents, so becoming transformed into settled communities, the economic conditions which had produced a demand for their labour had given way to low and sometimes negative rates of growth. As it turned out, black immigrants to Britain did not provide the same 'mobile potential' as did *Gastarbeiter* in West Germany, largely because as citizens they were not obliged to depart when their labour was no longer required. But even *Gastarbeiter* did not prove to be as readily 'disposable' as changes in economic conditions seemed to require. Thus, but the mid-1970s, the policies of the *formerly* labour importing countries of Western Europe have veered, explicitly or implicitly, from 'immigration to repatriation' and the new economic orthodoxy became 'capital to men, not men to capital' (Cohen 1980: 14).

In the UK, registered unemployment had started to rise in the mid-1960s (though it is worth pointing out that the 1962 Commonwealth Immigrants Act was passed at a time when the Treasury acknowledged that shortages of labour were restricting economic growth). By 1981 unemployment in the twenty-four OECD countries had reached 26 million and there was a growing belief that high levels of unemployment and reduced levels of economic activity were likely to persist into the next decade.

It is against this background that we turn to an examination of the causes of unemployment in Britain. Our purpose is not to survey the whole range of factors involved – whether at the level of specific industries or geographical areas, or at the level of the impact on Britain of the recession in the capitalist world – but rather to consider only those developments which have particular implications for the employment of black workers and for the implementation of equal opportunity policies.

In general terms, perhaps the most significant of these developments is the current phase of the modifications in the pattern of operation of industrial organisations. In essence, it is clear that during the past twenty or thirty years there have been major changes in the way in which companies function, partly as a result of concentration. Growing numbers of industrial workers are employed by large multi-plant companies which, increasingly, operate in more than one country. The pattern of operations of such firms is less and less likely to be dominated by considerations of a specific national market or national economy and correspondingly more likely to be concerned with calculations related to the global economy. Even large firms such as retailing consortia, which remain mostly, if not entirely, within a national economy, have increasingly become active in the international economy, particularly by sub-contracting work for part or whole products. In addition, a greater number of small firms are similarly participating in international markets. According to Frobel *et al.* (1980), there has come into being a 'new international division of labour', which has superseded that in which Third World countries were principally valued as providers of migrant workers and raw materials. In this new phase production processes can be sub-divided and relocated in order to obtain the optimum combination of labour and capital. Where possible, companies will seek to move production from high-wage economies to economies or economic enclaves where wage costs are low and likely to remain low by reason of a virtually inexhaustible labour supply.

Thus the current era of high unemployment can be seen, in part, as a consequence of relocation of work away from the industrialised countries. Much of the work which has been moved involves those parts of a production process – not necessarily of the production of complete products – in which labour costs are high. This is especially significant for black workers because they are disproportionately concentrated in jobs vulnerable to relocation. Here, Frobel *et al.*'s detailed analysis of developments in the German textile industry may be of particular relevance for black workers in Britain. Frobel *et al.* demonstrate that the number of textile jobs within Germany has declined steadily since the mid-1960s, while German-owned factories have been established in south-east Asia and North Africa. In one case, parts of trousers were cut out on automatic machines in Germany, then flown to a German-owned factory in Tunisia to be sewn together, and finally flown back to Germany to be sold – an illustration of the extent to which production processes can be divided between high-wage, capital-intensive and low-wage, labour-intensive elements.

In this respect it is illuminating to recall the role widely assigned to immigrant workers. They were seen as valuable in so far as they constituted cheap labour, willing to perform less desirable jobs at wage levels at which insufficient local labour would be forthcoming. As Cohen and Jenner (1968) said, they could be seen as approaching the economist's ideal of economic man: constrained by such factors as lack of skill and discrimination to work long and unsocial hours, in poor conditions, in order to earn as much as possible.

However, certain of the advantages which employers were able to derive from 'ghettos' of immigrant workers and low pay were counteracted by, for example, trade union action and the impact of legislation. Legislation and other political and industrial action in the industrialised countries has also been concerned with broader questions of health, safety and environmental protection. Even where such intervention has not affected labour flexibility or availability, it has often contributed to increased costs. For firms located in sectors where profitability or production is declining, and often these are labour-intensive, the advantages to be gained from moving to areas of low-cost labour are obvious. But for more profitable industries as well, relocation to the Third World offers considerable potential for increased profits. Improvements in transport and communications and the fragmentation of the production process have, in effect, relocated the economist's approximation of economic man to less-developed countries where workers are easy to recruit, lay off, or 'let go'. In these countries workers can be more easily controlled or switched from job to job; they may be more willing to undertake work seen in the industrialised countries as hazardous or undesirable; and they will work long hours for less pay and fewer associated benefits than will workers in countries like Britain and Germany. In these circumstances, it is likely that in Britain and other industrialised countries high levels of unemployment will be sustained and downward pressure on both pay levels and other aspects of work conditions, which are seen as cost-related (for example, the implementation of equal opportunity policies) will persist.

Black workers and unemployment

There are, broadly speaking, two sorts of factors which help to explain why individuals face varying chances of becoming unemployed and, once unemployed, why they remain unemployed for varying periods. On the one hand, there are the characteristics of the individuals themselves and, on the other hand, there are general processes of frictional and structural change. Statistical evidence shows quite clearly that particular groups are at risk, first of becoming unemployed and then of remaining unemployed for longer than average periods.

But as far as black workers are concerned we are handicapped in two ways. The Department of Employment does not collect statistics on the size of the black labour force *per se*, and thus the unemployment rates for black workers can only be deduced on the basis of census data or from special surveys. However, at the time of writing, most, if not all, of these surveys refer to the period before 1979, that is, before unemployment in the UK rose dramatically. For example, Dex's study of black and white school leavers, though published in 1983, is based on data collected between 1971 and 1976.

Bearing these qualifications in mind, we can begin by drawing a broad distinction between black unemployment (expressed as a proportion of total unemployment) in the period 1963 to 1970 and that since 1970. With minor interruptions, the 1960s show a recovery from a relatively high level of black unemployment following the dramatic increase in black immigration prior to the passage of the 1962 Immigration Act, to a point in 1970 where unemployment amongst black workers – at about 2½% – was roughly equivalent to the proportion of the total work force which was black. After this, except for the period 1973–75, the relative position of black workers deteriorated progressively (Smith 1981).

A Home Office research study, No. 68 (1982), summarises the main features of black unemployment between 1961 and 1980 as follows: black unemployment rates appear to have been high and considerably more sensitive to changes in economic conditions than the general level of unemployment: 'They rise and fall in response to rises and falls in overall unemployment: but in each case more steeply than the general trend' (Home Office 1982: 21). For example, between August 1979 and August 1980 the number of unemployed black workers rose by 48% as against a 38% rise in total unemployment.[2]

The Home Office study puts forward a number of factors to account for both the high level of black unemployment and its particular sensitivity to changes in economic conditions: (a) that the black population is younger than average and that young people find particular difficulty in securing employment where there are few vacancies; (b) that because of their recent arrival black workers may lack certain skills and qualifications and, in the case of Asians, may have language difficulties; (c) that when the supply of labour is abundant the opportunities to discriminate are increased; and (d) that black workers are concentrated in particular occupations, industrial sectors and sorts of enterprise, 'in particular, they are over-represented in manufacturing, which is contracting, generally, and in insecure, low-status jobs. . .' (Home Office 1982: 24).

Certainly, age affects both the incidence and the duration of unemployment. For instance, with each rise of one per cent in the general level of unemployment, youth unemployment rises by 1.7% (Makeham 1980).[3] Or, taking the period January 1981 to January 1983 as an example, while the percentage of registered unemployed of all ages who had been out of work for more than one year increased by 121%, the figure for those aged under 25 increased by 224% (*Department of Employment Gazette* May 1983: Table S. 34). Given the concentration of the black population in this age-group, it is to be expected that it will be disproportionately affected by these trends. According to figures published by the Runnymede Trust, between 1973 and 1981 the number of unemployed blacks born in the UK increased as a proportion of all blacks unemployed from 3.6% to 13.6% and as a proportion of all unemployed from 0.1% to 0.5% (Runnymede Trust 1981, 16). A number of other studies confirm the high and increasing vulnerability of British-born blacks to unemployment. For example, a study of school leavers in Lewisham revealed that, compared with whites, black school leavers were three times more likely to be unemployed and that those in employment had made more applications, attended more interviews and had taken longer to find work than their white counterparts (CRE 1978c).

There is a further category in which young blacks are probably over-represented that has been identified by Dex (1983) and others. This is the phenomenon of recurrent unemployment:

> Someone who is recurrently unemployed will experience more than one incidence of unemployment over a period, say a year, and while each incidence will be recorded in the Department of Employment's statistics (assuming the person registers), and the duration of each separate unemployed period is recorded, the separate periods are not linked together in the statistics, nor is there a cumulative total calculated. It is possible that a small minority of people, by being repeatedly unemployed, constitute a large proportion of those registered as unemployed at the recorded intervals. (Dex 1983: 41)

Dex's study of West Indian and white school leavers in London and Birmingham collected their individual job histories over five years, through a period of economic fluctuations, beginning in 1971, which ended in economic decline. She found that West Indians were more likely to suffer the consequences of redundancies or dismissals, and that they experienced recurrent unemployment more often than did similarly educated whites. This suggested to her that young West Indians constituted a disproportionately large component of 'a reserve or secondary labour force' (1983: 47). This finding is consistent with the idea that in time of falling vacancies, black school leavers are likely to be particularly disadvantaged given that school leavers generally do not possess skills and experience and, moreover, have qualifications – if any – which may not be particularly relevant to the job in question. Thus ascription may play a greater role than usual in deciding their employment prospects.[4]

The Home Office report referred to above, suggests that of the four causes of unemployment, two – the relative youth of the black workforce and factors associated with 'newness' – will obviously diminish with time.

But in view of the prolonged nature of the current economic recession which began in the mid-1970s, and bearing in mind the phenomenon of recurrent unemployment, the apparently short-term consequences for disadvantaged school leavers may become permanent. That is, a qualitative change may be occurring in the labour force which 'does start to become divided on the basis of mobility and unemployment with West Indians falling disproportionately into the more mobile, more unemployed and less trained category' (Dex 1983: 47), which is shut out of the internal labour market.

Nevertheless, the other two factors – discrimination in employment and concentration in 'insecure' jobs, for example in manual work and in the manufacturing industry – will continue to operate to the disadvantage of black workers. The CRE for example, claims that its own research indicates that 50% of employers continue to discriminate against black applicants (CRE 1982 Annual Report: 3). However, it is to the concentration of black workers in insecure jobs that we wish to turn our attention.

The chief source of being unemployed resides in the category of occupation: thus, during a recession firms are more likely to lay-off, and cease recruiting, the non-skilled. Smith found that an unskilled male manual worker was six times more likely to be unemployed than a male non-manual worker (Smith 1981), a conclusion supported by returns from the 1971 General Household Survey (cited in Nickell 1980: 1784). This disparity is not confined to incidence of unemployment: unskilled male manual workers were found to remain unemployed for longer periods than average.

New Commonwealth immigrants originally settled in areas of the country where job opportunities were plentiful. The contrast between a time when black labour was actively sought and the present levels of very high black unemployment is, therefore, all the more marked. One explanation of the change would be that the industries which once recruited black labour have been particularly affected by contraction and recession.

According to the 1971 census, 47% of black males were employed in manufacturing industry as against 33% of the total male work force. But in general, the distribution of black workers across the 27 Standard Industrial Classifications (SICs) was not vastly different from that of the general population. Moreover, Smith found that most industries gave rise to a degree of unemployment which was roughly in line with their share of the work force. This held whether the work force was taken as a whole, or whether separate analysis was made of the white, West Indian and Asian components. The major exception to this pattern was the association between the decline of the textile industry and the rate of Asian unemployment: in 1971, 22% of unemployed Asian men had been employed in textiles, though the industry only employed 10.5% of Asian men in work (and 2.1% of all men in work) (Smith 1981: 34, 11).

Overall, Smith suggests that the 'extra risk of being unemployed that arises from being an Asian or a West Indian is small compared with the extra risk from being an unskilled manual worker rather than a senior manager or a university professor' (1981: 34, 151). In our view, however, a prior question should be posed, namely what extra risk does an Asian or a West Indian face of becoming an unskilled worker and thus occupying a job particularly vulnerable to unemployment?

To seek to explain the disadvantaged employment position of black workers principally in terms of their concentration in contracting industries, is to misunderstand the genesis of the migration of workers into the industrialised countries of Europe which has occurred after 1945. As Bohning (1972) remarks, 'it is not the economic sector as such but the incidence of socially undesirable jobs that matters and there is practically no sector where there are no badly paid and undesirable jobs'. In the initial phase of their immigration, black workers were undoubtedly required to work in declining industries – as they still are – but their labour was also required in expanding and advanced industries: anywhere that indigenous labour had abandoned *disadvantaged jobs*.

The decline in the number of jobs in manufacturing has been underway since the mid-1960s, and manufacturing's share of total unemployment has been falling for longer still. In 1961 the number of jobs in manufacturing stood at 8.2 million or 36% of total employment, 20 years later the number had fallen by a quarter and represented only 28% of the total (Massey 1983: 19). This decline in employment conceals a changing demand for labour which reflects technological changes – both in product and in production processes. This changing demand for labour in manufacturing industry is often accompanied by geographical relocation, both to Third World countries and to previously non-industrial areas in Britain. Manufacturing industry has moved away from 'its traditional sources of labour in old centres of manufacturing skills' (Massey 1983: 231), that is away from the inner-city areas in which the black population is concentrated, to green sites in areas where the black population is largely absent.

There is also some evidence which indicates that Smith's finding that most industries gave rise to a degree of unemployment more or less in line with their share of the total work force (referred to above), may have been overtaken by the effects of the gathering recession which began in the late 1970s. Whereas between June 1971 and December 1982 employment in all industries and services fell by 6.2%, in almost the same period, October 1971 to March 1983, employment in manufacturing fell by 31.1%. Given the concentration of black workers in manufacturing, this might itself suggest serious implications for the black work force. But as Table 11.1

shows, of the nine manufacturing SICs of whose work force 3% or more was of NCW origin in 1971, no less than six suffered a decline in employment even greater than the average for all manufacturing SICs.

Conclusion

In the context of a labour market characterised not only by high unemployment, but also by a rapid decline in the number of jobs requiring very few skills and a steady (and lately accelerating) decline in the number of manufacturing jobs, it might seem that the creation of effective training and re-training schemes has a potentially vital role in mitigating some of the worst aspects of unemployment for black workers – many of whom have been displaced from manufacturing – and in improving the job prospects of young blacks entering the labour market.

For instance, despite the gulf between vacancies and the level of unemployment (cf. *Department of Employment Gazette* May 1983, for example), according to the Chairman of the MSC, the job-centre network – which accounts for about one-quarter of the job-placing market – placed 1.5 million jobs throughout the UK in 1982. Bearing in mind the continuing level of discrimination gauged by CRE investigations, there is clearly considerable room for improving the chances of black applicants obtaining these jobs.

There are, however, a considerable number of obstacles which stand in the way of attempts to improve the profile of black employment and unemployment. The original distribution of black employment was related largely to the prevailing pattern of demand for labour; once it became established it was to a certain degree self-reinforcing. In so far as assumptions developed about the capabilities of groups on the basis of previous performance, certain categories of work became associated with certain categories of workers. In the case of black workers in Britain, as in the case of migrant workers in France, Germany and Switzerland, they were widely regarded as 'suitable' workers to perform otherwise 'unsuitable' jobs. Bohning (1972) has described this process, accurately, as the 'rigidification' or the 'fossilisation' of the social job-structure. The process can be observed, for example, in the consequences for black workers of the changing demand for labour in the textile industry: 'Asian (i.e. manual) jobs have been lost, but Asians have been regarded as unsuited to fill newly created non-manual vacancies' (Fevre n.d.). For those attempting to improve the employment prospects of black workers, widespread assumptions about the suitability or unsuitability of individuals by virtue of their identification as Asians or West Indians, represent one of the most intractable problems.

But the problems posed by the level and nature of black unemployment

Table 11.1 *The decline in manufacturing employment (selected SICs)*

Standard Industrial Classification (SIC)	Industrial Sectors in which according to the 1971 census 3% or more of the work force was of NCW origin	Total Employment (000s) October 1971	Total Employment (000s) March 1983	Change (000s)	Percentages change
I-XXCII	All industries of services	21,648[a]	20,309[b]	−1,339	−6.2
II-XXI	Index of production industries[c]	9,803	7,014	−2,789	−28.5
III-XIX	Manufacturing industries	7,830	5,391	−2,439	−31.11
III	Food, drink, tobacco	747	576	−171	−22.9
VI	Metal manufacture	545	265	−280	−51.4
IX	Electrical Engineering	794	631	−163	−20.5
XII	Metal goods	568	399	−169	−29.8
XIII	Textiles	574	288	−286	−49.8
XIV	Leather, leather goods & fur	46	28	−18	−39.1
IV	Clothing & footwear	436	251	−185	−42.4
XVI	Bricks, pottery, glass, cement, etc.	299	194	−105	−35.1
XIX	Other manufacturing industries	333	223	−110	−33.0

a   June 1971
b   Dec 1982
c   Not seasonally adjusted
Source: *Department of Employment Gazette*, June 1976 and May 1983

are only a part of a much wider set of social problems. The importance of race should not be exaggerated: unemployment magnifies racial inequalities – all categories of black workers face added risks – but it magnifies other inequalities as well: thus fair equality of opportunity, in McCrudden's definition, is an even more remote prospect than previously. What hope, then, is there that black disadvantage in the labour market can be alleviated when the general level of unemployment promises to remain at a high level? Without an up-turn in the general economic climate, it seems clear than an improvement in the employment prospects of black workers requires – in some sense – a deterioration in the employment position of other groups. In fact, developments might rather be in the contrary direction: at a time of increasing job competition, attempts are likely to be made by workers and their representatives to strengthen or extend the boundaries and defences of job territories. This process might have no specifically racial intent – it is likely to be aimed at the unemployed irrespective of colour – but it is one that may conflict, none the less, with attempts to reduce black disadvantage.

The current impediments in the path of efforts aimed at achieving equal opportunity in employment are encapsulated in two extracts from the Confederation of British Industry's evidence to the Select Committee which sat in the mid-1970s, before the present levels of high unemployment had been reached. On the one hand the CBI gave voice to the kind of meritocratic principles that we have mentioned earlier. In its view, unemployment did not prevent the pursuit of goals 'to reduce the level of passive discrimination . . . (and) . . . to make arrangements to ensure that everyone concerned has opportunities to get into, first, the high paying areas within a factory, and second, the promotion that they deserve on merit'. On the other hand, the CBI maintained that, 'Employers have a great deal to think about and they are questions of survival and . . . (the removal of discrimination) . . . does not strike them as being in that kind of category. They will therefore, tend to put it off for as long as they can . . . for purely practical reasons . . . it will always be somewhere near the bottom of the pending tray' (evidence to the Select Committee on Race Relations and Immigration, minutes of evidence, Vol. II, 1974, S1434, S1412 and S1413). As we have argued elsewhere (Rhodes and Braham 1981), effective action to overcome the problems of black workers proved difficult enough even when there was excess demand for labour; in conditions of deepening recession and rising unemployment, effective action will be still more difficult, though by no means impossible.

The present recession not only marks a swing away from generalised economic growth to the pursuit of a 'sound economy', unburdened by the weight of formerly key industries, but also a retreat from the sort of consensus that we have discussed previously. That is not to say that equal opportunity legislation will be abandoned, rather that it is seen an interference with the free-play of market forces, and thus downgraded. Similarly, the economic philosophy of the present government accepts – even requires – the abandonment of the consensual goal of full employment. The implications of government policy are not, however, confined to the unemployed. It is increasingly argued that the current level of unemployment benefits creates a 'floor' below which wages will not fall. The pursuit of a sound economy may require, if this argument is accepted, that this floor should be lowered in order that all wages should be reduced so that workers will begin to 'price themselves back into work'. Clearly such a policy will most seriously affect those in poorly paid jobs, a category in which those black workers in employment are over-represented.

In these circumstances the 'colour blind' consequences of a changing economic climate and of government economic policy – particularly in their impact on the job prospects of black workers – have outweighed and will continue to outweigh the 'colour conscious' effects of equal opportunity policies. If this is so, it may turn out that the focus of debate is not so much about how to achieve equal opportunity, but rather how to shore up the existing economic profile of black workers or, indeed, to prevent it deteriorating from its present position.

12

Equal opportunity and the limits of the law: some themes

RICHARD JENKINS AND JOHN SOLOMOS

As we have already discussed elsewhere, the majority of the papers in this volume were originally presented at a workshop held in the SSRC Research Unit on Ethnic Relations in July 1983. During the presentation of these papers, and the subsequent discussion, a number of themes emerged as being clearly of importance in the eyes of most participants. Following the workshop, one of the organisers (Jenkins) drew up a list of these themes and circulated it to those people who had attended the meeting for their comments. On the basis of that consultative exercise this brief concluding chapter has been written. Although it is authored by the volume's editors, it is, in many senses, the collective product of all those who contributed, either in writing or verbally, to the original meeting.

The limitations of legal intervention

The notion that there are definite limits to the effectiveness of the law was central to the contributions of a number of participants; indeed, it would probably be true to characterise this as the central thread unifying the proceedings, running through all of the discussion. However, as one might expect, there was a considerable degree of diversity with respect to the particular aspects of the general theme highlighted by individual contributors.

Perhaps the best place to start this discussion is with the nature of British common law. It has been extensively commented upon elsewhere[1] that British common law, with its emphasis upon individual rather than collective dispute settlement, is a fundamentally unsuitable vehicle for the achievement of public policy goals such as the removal of unfair discrimination in employment. Some authors, such as Lustgarten (1980; this volume), have argued that the inadequacy of British law in this respect, by comparison with the much more 'political' law of the United States, for example, necessitates the de-emphasis of legal intervention and the adoption of an essentially administrative approach to the problem on the part of the state. Regardless of the political likelihood of such a strategy being adopted – and we shall discuss this in the next section – there was considerable discussion of the problems attached to the successful achievement of a transition from legal to administrative intervention.

A more specific problem with the contemporary legal approach to discrimination is the increasing complexity of the law, in particular the burgeoning case-law affecting discrimination cases. A similarly urgent, and related, problem in the eyes of some participants is the apparent withdrawal of the judiciary from the complexities of matters relating to discrimination in employment, leaving the field to the mercy of Industrial Tribunal members who are themselves frequently far from expert in either the law or discrimination-related issues.

There may, of course, be problems of a different nature with the detailed framing of the law, in particular the 1976 Race Relations Act. Many of these have been highlighted by the Commission for Racial Equality (CRE) in their consultative paper, *The 1976 Race Relations Act – Time for a Change?* (1983a) and more recently in *Review of the Race Relations Act 1976: Proposals for Change* (1985). A good example of this kind of problem, mentioned in that document and also discussed in this volume, is Section 32(3) of the Act, which appears to permit an employer, having satisfied certain conditions, to abdicate responsibility for the discriminatory behaviour of his or her employees (Commission for Racial Equality 1985: 20; Jenkins, this volume). There appears to be little doubt that this sub-section is unhelpful and should be repealed; the same could doubtless also be said for other sections of the Act.

In the sphere of discrimination in employment, a further difficulty can be discerned in the tradition of voluntarism which has, for a long time now, characterised British industrial relations (Clegg 1979: 289–344). Despite varying degrees of government intervention in the field of industrial relations, this continues to limit the effectiveness and legitimacy of the legal regulation of industrial relations. In this respect, it must also be acknowledged that the intervention in this field which has been attempted by the post-1979 Conservative United Kingdom government has either strengthened the legal hand of employers with respect to their dealings with organised labour, or weakened some of the legal rights of the individual in the labour market.

Questions of legitimacy and the extent and nature of state intervention are, of course, much more than narrowly legal issues. They must be mentioned in this section, if only to remind the reader that, although British law may be less overtly political in its operation and consequences than, for example, American law, it is nevertheless a political phenomenon, both in its framing and its interpretation. The politics of equal opportunity and anti-discrimination interventions are the subject of the next section.

Politics and state agencies

The question of the political legitimacy of the notion of equal opportunity (and, conversely, of the view of black people as alien outsiders, unentitled to full membership in the polity) is central to any appraisal of the analyses and arguments put forward in this book. This is a question which must be viewed in context, against the background of a considerable shift at the national political level in the United Kingdom away from the consensus of 'Butskellite' interventionism and a managed economy in the Keynesian sense. At best, as argued by Solomos in his chapter above, the issue of equality of opportunity has become transformed into an exercise in 'symbolic politics'. At worst, the very principles underlying the 1970 Equal Pay Act, the 1975 Sex Discrimination Act and the 1976 Race Relations Act are under open threat from the highest levels of government. Thus, although one may in principle support Lustgarten's advocacy of an administrative approach by the state, the present political climate gives one little cause for optimism that this is, in fact, a strategy which is likely to prove effective under contemporary conditions (see e.g. Lacey 1984). This remains our view despite recent developments, such as the decision of the Civil Service in January 1985 to introduce systematic ethnic monitoring, inasmuch taking such a step does not commit government to taking any specific remedial action on the basis of the findings of the monitoring exercise.

It is not, however, simply a question of lack of support for equal opportunity at the elevated level of the political establishment. The research evidence from a wide variety of sources is too compelling to permit any other conclusion than that popular racism remains a phenomenon to be reckoned with; this is certainly the finding of the 1983 British Social Attitudes Survey (Airey 1984: 122–30). This is a major factor contributing to the creation of an environment hostile to equal opportunity and anti-discrimination interventions. It seems unlikely that economic depression and high levels of unemployment can have any effect other than to exacerbate the situation.

Apart from more general considerations, the post-1979 political climate of 'new realism' has had its very specific effects on the Commission for Racial Equality. Examined and interrogated by the House of Commons Home Affairs Committee, under-resourced, and, on occasions, in open conflict with the government (as, for example, in the case of its formal invesigation of the Immigration Service), it could hardly be said to have been whole-heartedly supported by its parliamentary paymasters. Undoubtedly the Commission must bear some of the responsibility for this state of affairs, and it is to be hoped that its reorganisation in 1983 will have done much to blunt the barbs of its critics' arrows. The basic problem, however, that of the current lack of political legitimacy of the Commission's goals and statutory responsibilities, remains intractable, certainly for the time being, and is perhaps the major handicap under which it must attempt to realise those goals and exercise those responsibilities.

A further problem with the relationship between agencies such as the CRE (or, indeed, the Equal Opportunities Commission and the Fair Employment Agency) and central government, lies in their marginality with respect to the basic agenda of government. Instead of equal opportunity impinging upon every aspect of every government department's business, the issue has, by virtue of the creation of specialist 'quangos'[2] with responsibility for dealing with the broad area, been successfully compartmentalised, isolated and marginalised.

However, problems of legitimacy and marginality are not the only difficulties surrounding the CRE. As Solomos has discussed in his chapter, and, indeed, as the Commission's own reorganisation in 1983 implicitly acknowledged, it is apparent that for a number of years following its formation the CRE was plagued internally by dissension and organisational problems. As the unhappy – and involuntary – marriage of the Community Relations Commission and the Race Relations Board, the Commission has in the past experienced problems in setting its own priorities. Such problems do not, however, appear to be peculiar to the CRE; as Darby has argued (this volume), the Fair Employment Agency in Northern Ireland has also found it difficult to decide whether to emphasise promotional enforcement or purely investigatory strategies. Some, at least, of the problems of this nature experienced by these regulatory agencies stem from the breadth of their remit combined with the narrowness of their budgets. Finally, one last problem which these agencies appear to have concerns the criteria they should adopt in order to select targets which will ensure that whichever activities they do undertake will have the maximum public and political impact. These must, of course, be difficult decisions by their very nature; they are made all the more difficult by the urgency with which they are invested as a consequence of budgetary constraints.

Regulatory agencies and legislation are not, however, the only response which the state can make if the goal of enhanced equality of opportunity is accepted on to the policy agenda as an item of some importance. This, indeed, is the central theme of Lustgarten's argument for an administrative approach, as mentioned earlier. In particular, as Rex has argued elsewhere

214 *Richard Jenkins and John Solomos*

(1981), it is important to recognise the significance of the geographical ethnic division of labour. On the one hand, there is the spatial patterning of black settlement in British cities, on the other, the relocation and restructuring of employment away from the inner cities (Massey and Meegan 1982). Taken together, the net result of these two factors is that employment opportunities are increasingly less likely to be available in the areas where black people tend to live.

As a consequence of this situation, state anti-discrimination and equal opportunity interventions, if they are adequately to address the problem, must include within their terms of reference the process whereby new industry and employment is encouraged or subsidised. There are two dimensions to this process which are significant for the promotion of equal opportunity: first, the *spatial*, in this context the distribution of employment opportunities, as discussed above, and second, the *strategic*, in respect to which policy should perhaps increasingly emphasise job creation rather than, as at present, capital investment.

A second area of state policy which is of prime importance for the pursuit of equal opportunity is education and training. This is, in fact, an area which is steadily gaining in importance as successive governments are forced, under the pressure of increasing unemployment, particularly youth unemployment, to intervene ever more directly and massively in the provision of post-school training (see the chapter by Cross in this collection). With respect to equal opportunity, a distinction should be made between two contrasting aspects of training: the removal of discrimination (direct and indirect) in access to training opportunities *in general*, and the provision of *specialized*, compensatory programmes such as industrial language training. Both are important.

In this section, we have briefly discussed, among other things, the organisational problems of state regulatory agencies. Organisational problems are, however, also important in other contexts. In the next section we shall consider some of the issues which emerge from research into equal opportunity initiatives in employing organisations.

Organisations and equal opportunity

So far, we have looked at the content and context of *legal* and *administrative* equal opportunity initiatives, and the obstacles encountered by these strategies. A further strategy which has been identified in this volume is the *voluntary* approach, typically in the shape of organisationally specific equal opportunity policies and programmes (see the chapters by Jenkins, Jewson and Mason, Lee and Young in this volume). In this section we shall briefly summarise some of the obstacles to voluntarist approaches to the promotion of equal opportunity in employment.

In the first place, it is important to recognise the bureaucratic and/or mechanical or technical constraints which are inevitable in the management of any kind of innovation within complex, formal organisations.[3] Introducing change in this kind of social setting is rarely either straightforward or easy and one should not expect an equal opportunity programme to be exceptional in this respect. General factors of this sort notwithstanding, however, there are other more specific obstacles which prevent voluntary equal opportunity initiatives from achieving their desirable impact within organisations.

Certainly the most important of these obstacles – although probably only by a short head – is the lack of support within (white male-dominated) employing organisations for the concept of equal opportunity. Varying in its intensity from lukewarm or half-hearted support, to lip-service, to downright open hostility and opposition, a lack of commitment to the notion of equal opportunity can be found among management, in trade union representatives and on the office or shop-floor. The lack of enthusiasm probably has two sources, the first of which is the climate of popular racism outside (and inside) the organisation, as discussed earlier. More immediately, however, it must also be recognised that inasmuch as the introduction of a degree of genuine equality of opportunity for black workers (or, of course, women) would inexorably reduce the mobility chances of white workers –at whatever the level of employment – it is simply not in the best interests of most white, male employees seriously to support an equal opportunity initiative. Wrench's discussion in this volume of the failure of trade unions to wholeheartedly support the equal opportunity issue is a more comprehensive survey of this problem than can be attempted here. This is, however, a situation which can only be aggravated by a climate of recession and unemployment, in which promotion opportunities, and even the bare fact of employment itself, have become something of a scarce resource.

A further barrier to the promotion of equal opportunity is the characteristic informality and lack of accountability of many organisational employment procedures. Research has indicated that this is true of many aspects of the recruitment process: short-listing, interviewing and the actual making of the selection decision.[4] As a consequence of this lack of accountability, the recruiting process becomes opaque and it is impossible adequately to monitor decision-making. The most obvious shortcoming in organisational procedures in this respect is undoubtedly the continuing resistance of most employers to the introduction of monitored record-keeping. Bearing in mind that some recruitment procedures, most conspicuously, perhaps, 'word-of-mouth' recruitment (see Lee and Wrench 1983), may be indirectly discriminatory, this is clearly a problem of considerable significance. At best, the chronic absence of accountability within organisations makes it difficult to understand or justify selection decisions once they have been made; at worst, however, the organisational space is created wherein blatant racism can operate with a degree of impunity. However, it is important to emphasise, as do Jewson and Mason in their contribution to this collection, that the increased formalisation of employment procedures is not a sufficient response to the problems posed by racism and discrimination.

Moving away from the general character of employment procedures, the chapters by Jenkins, Jewson and Mason, and Young illustrate the limitations in the nature and content of equal opportunity policies within organisations. These limitations stem from a number of sources, including some of the factors discussed immediately above; in addition, however, the lack of useful guidance afforded by the relevant legislation must be recognised as a major obstacle to the successful formulation and implementation of equal opportunity policies.

On top of this, the importance of organisational politics, in particular the weak position of the personnel function in most organisations with respect to access to resources and influence, should also be mentioned. As the 'natural custodians' of equal opportunity initiatives and the management function which can lay some claim to distinct professional skills in the broader area of employment policies and practices, their role in tackling discrimination and the promotion of equal opportunity should, ideally, be crucial. The unfortunate fact that they appear to lack the appropriate degree of organisational authority adequately to fulfil that role must, therefore, be a matter for some concern.

Finally, as Lee's chapter illustrates, the importance of training provision within organisations should not be forgotten in any discussion of equal opportunity. As with the earlier discussions of state training policy, it is necessary to distinguish clearly between different aspects of training in this context. There are three different issues here: the need to guarantee equal access to all types of training opportunity for black workers (and women); training *for* equal opportunity as an integral aspect of organisational equal opportunity policies and programmes; and industrial language, or other specifically compensatory training.

It is precisely the complex inter-relation between these three levels which has been lost in many of the initiatives premised on 'racism awareness training', 'human relations training' and other forms of intervention based on personalised definitions of racism (see Gurnah 1984, Sivanandan 1985). The arguments presented in this volume highlight the need to look at racism as inherently embedded in institutional, political and organisational structures, rather than the result of consciously racist ideas as such.

It should, perhaps, be emphasised at this juncture that, in considering topics such as organisational employment procedures and the provision of training, it is apparent that the distinctions which have been drawn between

egal, administrative and voluntarist approaches to equal opportunity
become increasingly difficult to delineate with any clarity. In areas such as
these the influence of differing strategies for change one upon the other renders attempts at simple categorisation, necessary though they may be,
something less than straightforward. Perhaps the most obvious example of
this overlap of approaches can be discerned in the field of national training
policy, as discussed by Cross in his contribution to this collection.

Contexts of intervention

Throughout the two days of the workshop's proceedings, speaker after
speaker emphasised that the pursuit of equal opportunity and attempts to
attack discrimination in employment, should not be examined in isolation
from a variety of other issues and situational or contextual factors. Some of
these issues and contextual factors have already been discussed; four topics
in particular appeared to be the most important.

The first of these is the current recession in the national and international
economies. Within this broad category, a number of specific issues were
raised as of significance. Unemployment, in particular, has been convinc-
ingly demonstrated to be a disproportionate burden for the black working
class (Smith 1981). Heightened competition for available jobs has enabled
employers to be increasingly choosy in many areas. Furthermore, in response to a glut of job-seekers on the market, employers appear to be
increasingly resorting to the internal labour market, or 'word-of-mouth'
social networks as a means of disseminating vacancy information. It can be
argued that both of these factors are detrimental to the endeavours of black
job-seekers in particular (Jenkins *et al.* 1983). All of these things strike
directly at the heart of the notion of equal opportunity.

Less obviously, perhaps, but no less tellingly, a number of other
recession-related factors have conspired together to influence the situation.
The increased power of employers in the industrial relations sphere, the
diminished power of trade unions which is a corrollary to this (combined,
perhaps, with an increasingly ethnically defensive stance on the part of
some local trade union memberships, as documented by Wrench in his contribution to this volume), and the strains and difficulties attendant upon the
restructuring of many work-places, all come together to put the issue of
equal opportunity, at best, very low upon the policy agendas of both
managements and trade unions.

More generally, it must be recognised that the capitalist labour market is
a fundamentally discriminatory (in the neutral sense of the word) social
arena; some job-seekers are chosen, some are not. Routine recruitment and
selection are all about discriminating between competitive candidates on

the basis of a variety of criteria; some of these criteria are formally bureaucratically rational, many more are not. Inequality is an intrinsic part of the system whereby individuals are recruited to jobs. This general inequality, based upon class stratification and the wage relationship, is the constraining context of the pursuit of equal opportunity for disadvantaged groups in the population. Without social change on a currently unthinkable scale this situation is to say the least, unlikely to improve. Inequality of opportunity for black workers is thus, in one sense, an aspect of the inequality of opportunity experienced by all job-seekers, although not all, of course, experience this inequality as disadvantage.

A third aspect of the broad social context of equal opportunity and anti-discrimination initiatives has already been mentioned in a number of places above. Racism in society, as an ideology which is both deeply-rooted and has a pervasive existence outside the sphere of employment and the labour market, is a major brake upon the legitimate aspirations and goals of black people in Great Britain and elsewhere. Although to reiterate the matter in detail here would be redundant, in the light of the discussion elsewhere in this volume, the importance of racism as an obstacle to the pursuit of equality of opportunity cannot be under-estimated.

Finally, another contextual issue which recurred during the group's discussions concerned the difficulty attached to making generalisations, given the heterogeneity of the organisational and economic settings of employment. There were two specific aspects of this which speakers highlighted. The first of these was the significance of organisational diversity: employing organisations and trade unions differ widely one from another with respect to their bureaucratic structures, informal networks and cultures, management styles, economic situations, political positions and membership. As a result it may be misleading to talk blithely about 'equal opportunity' in a general sense, as if it actually means, in practical terms, something similar in all (or even most) employment settings.

The second issue concerning generalisation relates back to the earlier discussion of the spatial or geographical division of labour. In particular, the economic climate varies from one part of the country to another, and from industry to industry. What might, for example, easily be possible in a high technology company in the relatively prosperous south east, would be likely to create considerable problems of resources, if nothing else, for a struggling metal manufacturing group in the depressed West Midlands. Lest it be thought that we are here 'offering excuses' for the failure of much of British industry to take any interest in the promotion of equal opportunity, this is emphatically *not* the case. However, in order to understand that failure it is necessary to first understand, as comprehensively as possible, something of the complexities of the contexts of its occurrence.

Closing remarks

It should be clear from the other contributions to this volume, as well as from this concluding chapter, that a wide range of issues and themes was raised in the course of the workshop. Most of these topics have already been addressed in the course of the above discussion. There remain, however, two outstanding issues which have yet to be considered – much less, as problems, resolved – and given their undoubted importance it is perhaps fitting that they should provide the substance for the collection's closing remarks.

Most centrally, it must be admitted – if indeed it is permissible to talk in such terms – that most of the discussion and analysis in this volume, regardless of its political or philosophical orientations, is offered from a 'white perspective'. This is in reflection of the fact that the arguments of the workshop revolved around the question: what can a white-dominated society do in order to promote and ensure the extension of equality of opportunity to its black citizens? And this, of course, *is* a vitally important question. Racism, discrimination and the denial of equal opportunity are problems which have their roots in white society; racism is a *white* problem, although it is a problem *for* blacks, in much the same way that gender discrimination, although a problem for women, is largely one of men's making. However, most advances towards the elusive goal of equal opportunity for black ethnic minorities have rested, to a greater or lesser degree, upon the struggles of black people. This is no less the case in Great Britain than in the United States, and it is too important an issue to be overlooked. One of the less optimistic general conclusions which can be confidently drawn from the contributions to this volume is that, certainly in the present climate, the white majority in Britain are unlikely, if left to their own devices, to do much about the social and economic disadvantage experienced by their black neighbours. If that is the case, then autonomous black political action may be the only effective source of pressure for change. This seems to be the lesson of the 1981 urban protests, and the more recent outbursts of protest during September and October 1985.

It is noticeable that each of these periods of protest has been followed by a number of rhetorical shifts in official policy, calls for more 'positive action' to ensure equality of opportunity and promises of more secure and fundamental attacks on discriminatory processes. The limits of the actual changes achieved as a result of such shifts in policy remain to be explored, and cannot be specified without a better understanding of the roots of popular protest in contemporary Britain.

Moving away from questions of the appropriateness of particular strategies for change, there is one final issue to be raised, more as an open question than anything else. Already discussed in the editors' introduction to this volume and by a number of the contributors, it remains a matter of the greatest importance. Quite simply, what do we in fact mean when we talk about 'equal opportunity'? Throughout the workshop's proceedings, there was a tendency for speakers sometimes to use the expression as if 'everybody knows what it means'. This is also the case in the papers collected in this volume; as editors and authors, we are as guilty as anyone else in this respect. However, mindful of the (sometimes contentious) arguments surrounding notions such as 'positive action', 'reverse discrimination' and the 'fair shares approach',[5] we are inclined to insist that everybody does *not* know what everybody else means with respect to the idea of equal opportunity. Does it simply mean an absence of illegitimate discrimination, or should it be construed in a more radical fashion? This is not the place to attempt to answer such a question. It may, however, be exactly the place to emphasise that equality of opportunity remains a fundamentally contested notion in our society. If we are to advance academic and political debates beyond their present (often confused) states, perhaps the best place to start might be by reconsidering some of the core notions which we at present appear largely to take for granted.

Notes

2 **Lustgarten: Racial inequality and the limits of law**

* This article was first published in the *Modern Law Review*, vol. 49, 1986. It has undergone many changes as critical comments made me re-think and develop various ideas. Earlier versions were given as a seminar paper at the Research Unit on Ethnic Relations, then at Aston University, and as a public lecture at the Law Faculty of Liverpool Polytechnic. I am grateful also to the Industrial Law Society for the opportunity to try out these ideas on an expert, non-academic audience, and for the warmth of their reception.

The paper has benefited greatly from a critical reading by Doreen McBarnet, of the Centre for Socio–Legal Studies, Oxford, and by Christopher McCrudden of Lincoln College. Indeed in one sense it is part of an ongoing debate between McCrudden and myself. His article, 'Anti-Discrimination goals and the legal process', in N. Glazer and K. Young (eds), *Ethnic Pluralism and Public Policy* (Heinemann, 1983) is a clear presentation of a view contrary to that expressed here.

I would like to thank all those whose hospitality and commentary have improved the article or made its gestation more pleasant.

1 The Commission for Racial Equality is given powers under the Act to advise, assist and/or represent individual complainants. Under the 1968 Act its predecessor, the Race Relations Board, had the exclusive power to bring legal action. Most successful litigation under the present law has involved CRE support.

2 In 1982, 200 cases heard in industrial tribunals produced only 30 successes, a proportion markedly lower than 25% achieved in the staple of those tribunals, unfair dismissals. From 1977 to 1982, discrimination complaints won only 106 cases. These data come from the CRE 1983e: 9.

3 Many of the scathing criticisms of the CRE in the Report of the House of Commons Select Committee on Home Affairs (1981) were justified. However, the courts have severely restricted the Commission's ability to conduct formal investigations by their interpretation of the relevant statutory provisions in cases such as *CRE* v. *Amari Plastics* (1982) Q.B. 265; *Hillingdon Borough of London* v. *CRE* (1982) A.C. 779; and *CRE* v. *Prestige Group Ltd.*, (1984)

221

1 W.L.R. 335. These legal obstacles were wholly ignored in the Select Committee Report.

4 The Policy Studies Institute Report (Daniel and Stilgoe 1978) reported that most personnel managers and others who would be responsible for implementation of the Act had only the vaguest idea of its substance, and had done nothing to change their practices in light of it. It is possible that a similar survey conducted in 1985, particularly with the Code of Practice in force since April 1984, would reveal considerably greater awareness. See also, K. Young and N. Connelly (1981), documenting widespread ignorance and inaction in many local authorities, who under S.71 have an explicit statutory responsibility to eliminate discrimination and promote equal opportunity.

5 Expressed most openly in the Court of Appeal judgments in *Ojutiku* v. *MSC* (1982) I.C.R. 661; and *Mandla* v. *Dowell Lee* (1983) Q.B. 1. The *Hillingdon* case, supra n. 3, manifests the same attitude more subtly.

6 Notably in the CRE Consultation Document, supra n. 2., and in the strengthened *Review of the Race Relations Act: Proposals for Change*, adopted by the Commission after the consultative process and published in July 1985.

7 E.g. in the articles extracted or cited in L. Friedman and S. Macaulay (eds)(1979); R. Schwartz, and J. Skolnick (eds)(1970) and C. Campbell and R. Wiles (eds)(1979). A good review of the findings and analytical shortcomings of various 'law and social change' theorists may be found in Cotterell (1984, chap. 2). The essay by William Evan, 'Law as an instrument of social change' in A. Gouldner and S. Miller (eds)(1965) is suggestive, but is either speculative or based on extrapolations of one specific instance. A very common flaw is the creation of 'models' which either state the very obvious or are vague to the point of vacuity, e.g. the twelve-factor model of Maxmanion and Sabatier 1981, p. 89.

8 E.g. the doctrine of *res ipsa loquitur* or the sort of presumption used in *McGhee* v. *National Coal Board* (1972) 3 All E.R. 1008, a case of breach of statutory duty.

9 As in *Khanna* v. *Ministry of Defence* (1981) I.C.R. 653; *Wallace* v. *South Eastern Education and Library Board* (1980) I.R./L.R. 193 (N.I.) and *Oxford* v. *DHSS* (1977) I.R.L.R. 255.

10 Although county courts hear housing discrimination cases, there have been only about a score of these in seven years. Discrimination law is essentially employment law, within the domain of Industrial Tribunals, with appeal on questions of law to the Employment Appeal Tribunal.

11 I base this statement on the admittedly arbitrarily selected sample provided by the editors of the Industrial Relations Law Reports.

12 (1910) 2 K.B. 1021.

13 *Hollington* v. *Hewthorn and Co. Ltd* (1943) K.B. 587.

14 RRA 1976, S.56 (1)(c). See *Bayoomi* v. *British Rail* (1981) I.R.L.R. 413.

15 See *Albermarle Paper Co.* v. *Moody*, 422 U.S. 405, 419 n. 11 (1975).

16 E.g. In *re Pergamon Press* (1971) Ch. 388; *Norwest Holst Ltd* v. *Department of Trade* (1978) 3 All E. R. 1280, both Court of Appeal decisions.

17 *Laker Airways Ltd.* v. *Department of Trade* (1977) Q.B. 643.

18 *Department of the Environment* v. *Fox* (1980) 1 All E.R. 58; *Knight* v. *Attorney General* (1979) I.C.R. 194; *Daley* v. *Allied Suppliers Ltd* (1983) I.C.R. 90.

19 *Kirby* v. *Manpower Services Commission* (1980) 1 W.L.R. 725. This, and the three cases cited in the preceding footnote, were all E.A.T. decisions.
20 Finally decided in the affirmative by the House of Lords in *Mandla (Sewa Singh)* v. *Dowell Lee* (1983) 2 A.C. 548.
21 In the *Hillingdon* case, supra n.3.
22 In the *Amari Plastics* case, supra n.3.
23 I would not quarrel in principle with McCrudden's view that legal action may be a useful adjunct to political and administrative effort, though I am far less optimistic than he that a group which is politically weak can exercise a louder 'voice' in the courts, which seem to me generally even less responsive to the needs/claims of the poor and lowly. There is also the boomerang problem: when an authoritative legal ruling interprets the statute so as to narrow its scope or application, it may lead to greater future resistance or even abandonment of changes undertaken in the mistaken view that the law, then unsettled, required them. For a general overview of this issue, see T. Prosser, *Test Cases for the Poor* (C.P.A.G. 1983).
24 I pass over the question of how such a political configuration might come about which, important as it is, can be analytically separated from what a government so-minded would be best advised to do.
25 There is of course a large literature on the limits of the administrative process, emphasising the difficulties of implementing policies through bureaucracies, resistance to innovation and the like. There is clearly some truth in it, though the impressive achievement of the present Government in ensuring that the Civil Service machinery is harnessed to achieve the policies it has adopted suggests it has been much exaggerated. Put another way, in my view the importance of political will has been greatly underestimated, particularly by academics who find its simplicity intellectually unsatisfying.
26 Another provision, S.5, permitting race to be the basis of selection where it is a 'genuine occupational qualification', is of much narrower compass and of little importance in enhancing the prospects of blacks in mainstream employment.
27 To simplify discussion, I have ignored the important role that can be played by a trade union committed to remedial policies in formulating, implementing and monitoring them, and not least in justifying them to their members.
28 This can produce the kind of infuriating Catch–22 to which the Court was so insensitive in the *Ojutiku* case, supra n.5. The complainants were denied financial support by the Manpower Services Commission for an executive training course because they lacked experience. If, as they alleged, discrimination in executive-level employment made acquisition of such experience extremely difficult, how is the chain to be broken?

3 **Solomos: The politics of anti-discrimination legislation: planned social reform or symbolic politics?**

1 Feuchtwang (1981) and Gordon (1982) review some of the broader debates about the effectiveness of race-relations legislation. But see also Runnymede Trust (1979 and 1982) for some useful papers that critically analyse central aspects of the post-1976 experience.
2 Apart from the CRE's own response (CRE 1983a), see Layton–Henry (1980), Cross (1982) and Nixon (1982).

3 Lustgarten (1980) and McCrudden (1983a) present alternative perspectives on some of the criticisms.
4 The best overview of the debates, which also contains some detailed criticisms, can be found in Jessop (1982).
5 An overview of the early history of anti-discrimination policies can be found in Freeman and Spencer (1979).
6 The most detailed discussion of these problems can be found in the Select Committee report on *The Organisation of Race Relations Administration* and the supporting evidence (1975). For a critical analysis see Lea (1980).
7 The assumption that the first generation of immigrants were more likely to accept their situation than the second generation of young blacks was a constant theme in official ideologies on anti-discrimination policies; see Sivanandan (1982).
8 This assumption reflects a more general tendency for governments in western liberal democracies to marginalise issues such as 'race' and poverty by giving them 'special' attention. See Friedland (1982) and Offe (1984).
9 Kushnick (1971) discusses this background in some detail.
10 See Lea (1980) and Feuchtwang (1981) for a discussion of these issues.
11 See Lester and Bindman (1971) and Freeman and Spencer (1979).
12 Sivanandan (1982) argues that this constitutes the major difference between the 1965 and 1968 Acts and the 1976 Act.
13 This is clear from Gordon (1982) and Feuchtwang (1982).
14 As a result of the criticisms made by the Home Affairs Committee and others of the formal investigations procedure, the CRE called a temporary halt to all new investigations during 1983 and 1984 in order to allow the ones already started to be completed.
15 See the conclusion to this volume for a brief discussion of research issues.
16 See Benyon (1984) and Parkinson and Duffy (1984) for a discussion of the impact of the riots.

4 Darby: Religious discrimination and differentiation in Northern Ireland: the case of the Fair Employment Agency

1 In addition to the literature cited in this paragraph, see the work of Hewitt (1981), Kelley and McAllister (1984) and Whyte (1983).
2 For the benefit of readers from outside the United Kingdom, a 'quango' is a quasi-autonomous non-governmental organisation.

5 Cross: 'Equality of opportunity' and inequality of outcome

1 I should like to thank Juliet Cook, Pat Dutton, Richard Jenkins and John Wrench for their help with this paper.

7 Jenkins: Equal opportunity in the private sector: the limits of voluntarism

1 Snell *et al.* also review the impact of the 1970 Equal Pay Act; this, however, lies outside the scope of this chapter and is, correspondingly, not discussed.
2 The main report of this research, *Racism and recruitment: managers, organisations and equal opportunity in the labour market* (Jenkins, 1986) contains a fuller discussion of many of the points touched upon in this chapter.

3 According to Snell *et al.* (1981: 91–2) the 1970 Equal Pay Act may have had more impact than the 1975 Sex Discrimination Act; it seems also likely to this author that the latter piece of legislation has had more effect than the 1976 Race Relations Act, although such a suggestion is impossible to substantiate on the basis of present research.

4 This section, and much of the following section, derive from Chapter 7 of the final report (note 2, above), which, in turn, derives from the original paper presented to the workshop on 'Anti-discrimination and equal opportunity in employment' in July, 1983.

5 It should, however, be emphasised that the professional personnel model of 'best practice' is not, in my experience, very influential in actually determining routine employment practices.

6 Trades Union Congress (1981).

7 Home Affairs Committee, Sub-Committee on Race Relations and Immigration, 1981a: 850–73.

8 See, 'Positive action programme at Thames Television', *Industrial Relations Review and Report*, no. 270 (April 1982), 8–12.

9 See Chapters 6 and 7 of the final report of the author's research into racism and recruitment into employment (Jenkins 1986).

10 For a definition of indirect discrimination, see 1976 Race Relations Act, Section 1.1(b).

11 On this particular question, however, the CRE has recently recommended that section 32(3) of the 1976 Act be repealed (1983e: 20); the Commission has also recognised that the repeal of this sub-section might serve to discourage employers from formulating and implementing equal opportunity policies.

12 These contradictions reflect contradictions at the state level, e.g. between the promotional and enforcement roles of the CRE.

13 See, for example, Barker (1981).

14 The extent of racism is well-illustrated in my own research (Jenkins, 1986: 80–115); see also Airey (1984).

8 Jewson and Mason: Monitoring equal opportunities policies: principles and practice

*   This paper is a revised version of our 'Equal opportunities policies at the workplace and the concept of monitoring' published in *New Community*, vol. XII, no. 1, 1984–5. We are grateful to the editor for permission to reprint it.

1 We are aware that there is no theoretically or ideologically neutral terminology available for the analysis of racial and ethnic relations. In this paper we use the term 'black' to refer generically to people of New Commonwealth and Pakistani descent. In doing so we are not seeking to suggest that there are no significant differences among the groups concerned. However, the issues we discuss here are of general application.

2 This is also a view which can be found in the literature. Thus, for example, P. G. Nordlie writes, 'A practical system has been described for quantitatively measuring potential problems with respect to the status of equality of opportunity within an organisation. . .it provides a manager with objective information on where in the organisation and to what extent personnel decisions are resulting in outcomes associated with skin colour. Used over time it can provide a manager with information about change in the status of equal opportunity within an organisation' (1979: 171).

3 Indeed we would argue that the only way effectively to extend the pursuit of equality of opportunity is for the state to take a much greater role in its promotion. This includes not only the further legislation demanded by the EOC (EOC 1980, 1981b) but also commitment of greater resources to the EOC and CRE to enable them to conduct this kind of monitoring. It is interesting here to compare Britain with the USA (Bindman 1980; Meehan 1983).

4 Another version of the same position is that which emphasises the notion of citizenship rather than the free market. An example of this approach was contained in an advertisement on behalf of the Conservative Party which appeared during the 1983 General Election.

5 We might note here that it is frequently not clear what is to be the point of reference for analysis. The implied comparison is between actual distribution and what would have occurred in the absence of discrimination. However, this leaves open the question of whether the comparison should be with: (a) the numbers of black people and women in the nation as a whole; (b) the numbers in the local community; (c) the numbers in the firm; (d) the numbers among applications received, and so on. One could hardly fail to notice that variations in the distribution of black people and women in these different populations is itself an index of structural disadvantage.

6 Jenkins, in the full report of his research (1986), and in private correspondence, has made it clear that he also recognises this point.

7 The terms 'positive discrimination' and 'positive action' are currently used in many different ways reflecting confusions between principles which we are arguing it is crucial to distinguish. For example, Lord Scarman uses the term 'positive discrimination' to refer to practices which we have designated 'positive action' (Scarman 1981). Juliet Cheetham (1982a), in contrast, uses the term to refer to a wide range of practices straddling the distinction we have made. We may also note, here, that we have avoided the American term 'affirmative action'. This is partly because of the differing legal situations in the United States and Britain. More importantly, however, the concept 'affirmative action' blurs the distinction between 'positive action' and 'positive discrimination' and thus conflates the principles underlying these two concepts. For an example of the confusions to which this gives rise, see Kilson (1983). Usha Prashar has noted that such confusions are widespread and represent a serious obstacle to policy formation (1983).

8 It is important to note that what we are arguing here is that ostensibly similar acts are subject to varying definition depending, amongst other things, on context and on the objectives of the actors involved. Nevertheless, we realise that, in a situation of asymmetrical power relationships, some groups may claim a superior capacity to define whilst others are forced into acquiescence which may be said to run counter to their real interests. It is also important to recognise that these relationships are a product of the wider social distribution of power and that there are limitations on the degree to which they may effectively be challenged or dismantled at workplace level. It is precisely for this reason that we advocate a process of collective discussion and definition, in part as an effort to raise consciousness.

10 Wrench: Unequal comrades: trade unions, equal opportunity and racism

* I would like to thank all those people who gave me their comments on an earlier draft of this paper – in particular Paul Edwards, Annie Phizacklea, Terry Rees,

Richard Jenkins, John Solomos, Danny Silverstone and Zig Layton-Henry.

1 Taken from a circular from 'Liberation: the anti-imperialist, anti-racist organisation' announcing a conference, 'Trade unions and the GLC year against racism', 1984.
2 Personal communication with the author.
3 Taken from a circular announcing the first conference for the Black Trade Unionists Solidarity Movement, held in London, June 1983.
4 For a discussion of the implications of the introduction of YTS for trade unions and equal opportunity see Wrench, forthcoming.
5 From H. W. Longfellow *Hyperion* (1839), H. G. Clarke (1848).
6 From George Santayana *The Life of Reason* (1905–6), Constable (1954).

11   Rhodes and Braham: Equal opportunity in the context of high levels of unemployment

1 Conversely, Glazer (1975) argues that in the USA, substantial progress was made during the 1960s in upgrading the black employment profile without the benefit of the legislation introduced in the 1970s.
2 The sensitivity of black unemployment to alterations in the general level of unemployment applies to both male and female workers, though to a varying extent. According to Home Office estimates, West Indian males are worse off than Asian females and Asian males, who are in turn more vulnerable than white workers (Home Office 1982: 21).
3 This trend may have been reinforced by the finding that young males have become relatively more expensive to employ: in the early 1970s their employment costs were less than half those of adult men, whereas by the late 1970s they were almost 60% (Lynch and Richardson 1982: 366).
4 The chairman of the MSC has said that for the majority, unemployment is a matter of relatively short duration, but that there is 'an important minority, nearly one-third, the long-term unemployed. . .people who have been unemployed for at least a year (and) we know that the longer that someone has been out of a job, the harder it is for them to get back into work . . .' (quoted in *D. E. Gazette*, May 1983, 180).

12   Jenkins and Solomos: Equal opportunity and the limits of the law: some themes

1 Hepple 1983; Lustgarten 1980: 234–5; McCrudden 1983a.
2 For the benefit of readers from outside the United Kingdom, this stands for 'quasi-autonomous non-governmental organisations': publicly funded agencies which, although not part of the fabric of central government, may have regulatory functions.
3 See, for example, Burns and Stalker 1961.
4 This was the main focus of the research by Jenkins in the Research Unit on Ethnic Relations (Jenkins 1986).
5 See, for example, Lustgarten 1980: 14–25; McCrudden 1983a: 71–2.

Bibliography

Abbott, S. (ed.) 1971, *The Prevention of Racial Discrimination in Britain*, London: Oxford University Press

Airey, C. 1984, 'Social and moral values', in R. Jowell and C. Airey (eds), *British Social Attitudes: the 1984 Report*, Aldershot: Gower

Allen, S., Bentley, S. and Bornat, J. 1977, *Work, Race and Immigration*, Bradford: University of Bradford School of Studies in Social Sciences

Applebey, G. and Ellis, E. 1984, 'Formal investigations: the Commission for Racial Equality and the Equal Opportunities Commission as law enforcement agencies', *Public Law*, Summer: 236–76

Aronson, E. 1972, *The Social Animal*, London: W. H. Freeman

Baldwin, G. R. 1978, 'A British independent regulatory agency and the "Skytrain" decision', *Public Law*, Spring: 57–81

Ballard, R. and Holden, B. 1975, 'The employment of coloured graduates in Britain' *New Community*, IV, 3: 325–36

Banton, M. 1984 'Transatlantic perspectives on public policy concerning racial disadvantage', *New Community* 11, 3: 280–7

Barker, M. 1981, *The New Racism: Conservatives and the Ideology of the Tribe*, London: Junction Books

Barrett, S. and Fudge, C. (eds) 1981, *Policy and Action*, London: Methuen

Belfast Riot Report 1857, *British Parliamentary Papers*, XXXVI

Ben-Tovim, G. S., Gabriel, J.G., Law, I. and Stredder, K. 1981, 'The equal opportunity campaign in Liverpool', in J. Cheetham *et al.* (eds), *Social and Community Work in a Multi-racial Society*, London: Harper and Row

Bentley, S. 1976, 'Industrial conflict, strikes and black workers: problems of research methodology', *New Community*, V, 1–2: 127–38

Benyon, J. (ed.) 1984, *Scarman and After*, Oxford: Pergamon Press

Bindman, G. 1980, 'The law, equal opportunity and affirmative action', *New Community*, VIII, 3: 248–60

Binstead, D., Stuart, R. and Long, G. 1980, 'Promoting useful management learning: problems of translation and transfer' in J. Beck and C. Cox (eds), *Advances in Management Education*, Chichester: John Wiley

Birrell, D. and Murie, A. 1980, *Policy and Government in Northern Ireland*, Dublin: Gill and Macmillan

Bishton, D. 1984, *The Sweatshop Report*, Birmingham: AFFOR

Blackburn, R. and Mann, N. 1979, *The Working Class in the Labour Market*, London and Basingstoke: Macmillan

Boehringer, G. 1971, 'Discrimination in jobs', *Fortnight*, 14 May

Bohning, W. 1972, *The Migration of Workers in the United Kingdom and the European Community*, London: Oxford University Press

Bourne, J. with Sivanandan, A. 1980, 'Cheerleaders and ombudsmen: the sociology of race relations in Britain', *Race and Class*, XXI, 4: 331–52

Braverman, H. 1974, *Labour and Monopoly Capital*, London: Monthly Review Press

Brewster, C. J., Gill, C. G. and Richbell, S. 1983, 'Industrial relations policy: a framework for analysis', in K. Thurley and S. Wood (eds), *Industrial Relations and Management Strategy*, Cambridge: Cambridge University Press

Brooks, D. 1975, *Race and Labour in London Transport*, London: Oxford University Press

Brown, C. 1984, *Black and White Britain: The Third PSI Survey*, London: Heinemann

Brown, C. and Gay, P. 1985, *Racial Discrimination: 17 Years After the Act*, London: Policy Studies Institute

Burgoyne, J., Boydell, T. and Pedler, M. 1978, *Self Development, Theory and Applications for Practitioners*, Association of Teachers of Management

Burns, T. and Stalker, G. M. 1961, *The Management of Innovation*, London: Tavistock

Cameron Commission 1969, *Disturbances in Northern Ireland*, Cmnd. 532, Belfast: HMSO

Campbell, C. and Wiles, R. (eds) 1979, *Law and Society*, Oxford: Martin Robertson

Castles, S. and Kosack, G. 1972, 'The function of labour immigration in Western European capitalism', *New Left Review*, 73: 13–21

CEDEFOP 1980, *Legislative and Regulations Structure of Vocational Training Systems (FDR, France, Italy, United Kingdom)*, Berlin: CEDEFOP

Central Policy Review Staff 1974, *Race Relations*, unpublished report

Cheetham, J. 1982a, 'Positive discrimination in social work: negotiating the opposition', *New Community*, X, 1: 27–37

1982b, 'Recruitment and education for work with minorities: British and American perspectives', in J. Cheetham (ed), *Social Work and Ethnicity*, London: George Allen and Unwin

Chiplin, B. and Sloane, P. J. 1982, *Tackling discrimination at the workplace: an analysis of sex discrimination in Britain*, Cambridge: Cambridge University Press

Clegg, H. 1979, *The Changing System of Industrial Relations in Great Britain*, Oxford: Basil Blackwell

Cmnd 8455, 1981, *A New Training Initiative: A Programme for Action*, London: HMSO

Cmnd 9135, 1984, *Training for Jobs*, London: HMSO

Cockburn, C. 1983, *Brothers: Male Dominance and Technical Change*, London: Pluto

Cohen, R. 1980, *'Migration, Late Capitalism and Development'*, address to annual conference of Development Studies Association, Swansea, 16 September (unpublished mimeograph)

Cohen, B. and Jenner, P. 1968, 'The employment of immigrants: a case study within the wool industry', *Race*, vol. X, 1:41–56

Commission for Racial Equality 1978a, *Equal Opportunity in Employment: A Guide for Employers*, London: CRE

　1978b, *Monitoring an Equal Opportunities Policy: A Guide for Employers*, London: CRE

　1978c, *Looking for Work – Black and White School Leavers in Lewisham*, London: CRE

　1980, *Equal Opportunity in Employment, Why Positive Action: A Guidance Paper*, London: CRE

　1981, *BL Cars Ltd: Report of a Formal Investigation*, London: CRE

　1982, *Massey Ferguson Perkins Ltd: Report of a Formal Investigation*, London: CRE

　1983a, *Code of Practice: Race Relations*, London: CRE

　1983b, *Equal Opportunity, Positive Action and Young People*, London: CRE

　1983c, *Annual Report for 1982*, London: CRE

　1983d, *Implementing Equal Employment Opportunity Policies*, London: CRE

　1983e, *The Race Relations Act – Time for a Change?*, London: CRE

　1984, *Annual Report for 1983*, London: CRE

　1985, *Review of the Race Relations Act 1976: Proposals for Change*, London: CRE

Commission for Racial Equality/Lancashire Industrial Language Training Unit 1983, *In Search of Employment and Training: Experience and Perception of Redundant Asian Textile Workers*, London: CRE

Compton, P. 1980, 'The other crucial factors why Catholics don't get more jobs', *Belfast Telegraph*, 28 October

Connelly, N. 1985, *Social Services Departments and Race: A Discussion Paper*, London: Policy Studies Institute

Cooper, C. L. and Davidson, N. J. 1982, *High Pressure: Working Lives of Women Managers*, Glasgow: Fontana Paperbacks

Cooper, R. 1981, 'The Fair Employment Agency', in A. Hepburn (ed), *Employment in Divided Societies*, Coleraine: Centre for the Study of Conflict

Cormack, R., Osborne, R. and Thompson, W. 1980, *Into Work: Young School Leavers and the Structure of Opportunity in Belfast*, FEA Paper no. 5, Belfast

Cotterell, R. 1984, *The Sociology of Law: An Introduction*, London: Butterworths

Courtenay, G. 1983, 'Analysis of data from the survey of 1980–81 YOP entrants', unpublished paper, London: SCPR

Coyle, A. 1984, *Redundant Women*, London: The Women's Press

Cross, M. 1982, 'Racial equality and social policy: omission or commission?', in C. Jones and J. Stevenson (eds), *The Yearbook of Social Policy in Britain 1980–81*, London: Routledge and Kegan Paul

　1985a, *The Training Situation of Ethnic Minority Young People in Britain*, West Berlin: CEDEFOP

　1985b, 'Who goes where?: YTS allocations by race', in M. Cross and D. Smith (eds) *YTS and Racial Minorities: Equality or Inequality?* Leicester: NYB

Cross, M., Edmonds, J. and Sargeant, R. 1983, *Ethnic Minorities: Their Experience of YOP*, Sheffield: MSC

Cross, M. and Smith, D. (eds.) 1986, *Black Youth and YTS: Opportunity or Inequality?* Leicester: National Youth Bureau

Daintith, T. C. 1979 'Regulation by contract: the new prerogative', *Current Legal Problems*, 32, 41–64

Daniel, W. and Stillgoe, E. 1978, *The Impact of Employment Protection Laws*, London: Policy Studies Institute

Deakin, N. 1969, 'The politics of integration: policies and practice', paper presented at IRR Annual Conference on Race Relations, Birmingham, September

Department of Employment 1972, *Take 7: Race Relations at Work*, London: HMSO

Dex, S. 1978/9, 'Job search methods and ethnic discrimination', *New Community*, VII, 1: 31–9
1983, 'Recurrent unemployment in young black and white males', *Industrial Relations Journal*, 14, 1:41–9

Dhooge, Y. 1981, 'Ethnic difference and industrial conflicts', *Working Paper in Ethnic Relations*, 13, RUER, Birmingham

Dickens, L. *et al.* 1981, 'Re-employment of unfairly dismissed workers: the lost remedy', *Industrial Law Journal*, 10: 160–75

Donnison, D. 1973, 'The Northern Ireland Civil Service', *New Society*, 5 July

Duffield, M. (forthcoming) *The Rise and Fall of the Indian Shop-Floor Movement: A Hidden History*, Cambridge: Cambridge University Press

Dummett, A. and Dummett, M. 1969, 'The role of government in Britain's racial crisis', in C. Husband (ed), *'Race' in Britain: Continuity and Change*, London: Hutchinson, 1982

Edelman, M. 1977, *Political Language: Words That Succeed and Policies that Fail*, New York: Academic Press

Elliot, M. 1978, 'Government contracts and counter-inflation policy', *Industrial Law Journal*, 7: 120–3

Equal Opportunities Commission 1978, *Equality Between the Sexes in Industry: How Far Have We Come?*, Manchester: EOC
1980, *Fifth Annual Report*, Manchester: EOC
1981a, *Job Evaluation Schemes Free of Sex Bias*, Manchester: EOC
1981b, *Sixth Annual Report*, Manchester: EOC
1982, *Code of Practice: Revised Consultative Draft*, Manchester: EOC
(n.d.), *Towards Equality: A Casebook of Decisions on Sex Discrimination and Equal Pay*, Manchester: EOC

Evan, W. 1965, 'Law as an instrument of social change', in A. Gouldner and S. Miller (eds), *Applied Sociology*, New York: Free Press

Fair Employment Agency 1977–83, *Annual Reports*, Belfast: FEA

Fairley, J. and Jeffrey, P. 1982, *The Training needs of Disadvantaged Groups - Interim Report*, Joint Unit for Research on the Urban Environment, University of Aston in Birmingham

Fenton, S., Davies, T., Means, R. and Burton, P. 1984, *Ethnic Minorities and the Youth Training Scheme*, Research and Development Series no. 20, Sheffield: MSC

Feuchtwang, S. 1981, 'Collective action and English law against racial discrimination in employment', *Politics and Power*, 4, London: Routledge and Kegan Paul
1982, 'Occupational ghettos', *Economy and Society*, 11, 3:251–91

Fevre, R. 1984, *Cheap Labour and Racial Discrimination*, Aldershot: Gower
n.d., *The Labour Process in Bradford*, Bradford: EEC/DES *Transition to Work* Project

Flew, A. 1984, 'The race relations industry', *Salisbury Review*, Winter: 24–7

Foot, P. 1969, *The Rise of Enoch Powell*, Harmondsworth: Penguin

Fothergill, S. and Gudgin, G. 1982, *Unequal Growth: Urban and Regional Employment Change in the UK*, London: Heinemann

Fox, A. 1974, *Man Mismanagement*, London: Hutchinson

Freeman, G. P. 1974, *Immigrant Labor and Racial Conflict in Industrial Societies*, Princeton: Princeton University Press

Freeman, M. D. A. and Spencer, S. 1978, 'Immigration control, black workers and the economy', *British Journal of Law and Society*, 6, 1: 53–81

   1979, 'The state, the law and race relations in Britain today', *Current Legal Problems*, 32: 117–42

Freeman, R. 1983, 'Public Policy and Employment Discrimination in the United States', in N. Glazer and K. Young (eds), *Ethnic Pluralism and Public Policy*, London: Heinemann

Friedland, R. 1982, *Power and Crisis in the City: Corporations, Unions and Urban Policy*, London: Macmillan

Friedman, L. and Macaulay, S. (eds) 1979, *Law and the Behavioural Sciences*, 2nd edn, New York: Bobbs-Merrill

Frobel, F., Heinrichs, J. and Kreye, O. 1980, *The New International Division of Labour*, London: Cambridge University Press

Fryer, P. 1984, *Staying Power: The History of Black People in Britain*, London: Pluto Press

Galanter, M. 1974, 'Why the "haves" come out ahead', *Law and Society Review*, 9, 1: 95–100

Galbraith, J. 1969, *The New Industrial State*, London: Pelican

Ganz, G. 1978, 'Comment', *Public Law*: 333–47

Giddens, A. 1979, *Central Problems in Social Theory: Action, Structure and Contradiction in Social Analysis*, London: Macmillan

Glazer, N. 1975, *Affirmative Discrimination: Ethnic Inequality and Public Policy*

Glazer, N. and Young, K. (eds) 1983, *Ethnic Pluralism and Public Policy*, London: Heinemann

Golding, P. and Middleton, S. 1982, *Images of Welfare*, Oxford: Martin Robertson

Gordon, P. 1982, 'Racial discrimination: towards a legal strategy?', *British Journal of Law and Society*, 9, 1: 127–35

Gough, I. 1979, *The Political Economy of the Welfare State*, London: Macmillan

Greater London Council 1984a, *Ethnic Minorities and the Abolition of the GLC*, London: GLC

Greater London Council, Anti-Racist Trade Union Working Group 1984, *Racism Within Trade Unions*, London: GLC

Greater London Council, Economic Policy Group 1984, *Jobs for a Change*, May, no. 8

Green, R. 1986, 'Racism and the unemployed offender: state responses to black deviance,' in G. L. Lee and R. Loveridge (eds), *The Manufacture of Disadvantage: Stigma and Social Closure*, Milton Keynes: Open University Press

Griffiths, H. 1974, *Community Development in Northern Ireland: A Case Study in Agency Conflict*, Coleraine: New University of Ulster

Gurnah, A. 1984, 'The politics of racism awareness training', *Critical Social Policy*, 11: 6–20

Habermas, J. 1976, *Legimitation Crisis*, London: Heinemann

Halsey, A. H. 1970, 'Race relations: the lines to think on', *New Society*, 19 March: 477–4

Hargrove, E. C. 1983, 'The search for implementation theory' in R. J. Zechauser and D. Leebaert (eds), *What Role for Government?* Durham NC: Duke University Press

Haveman, R. H. (ed.) 1977, *A Decade of Federal Anti-poverty Programmes*, New York: Academic Press

Health Education Council/National Extension College for Training in Health and Race, 1984, *Providing Effective Health Care in a Multiracial Society*, London: Health Education Council/National Extension College for Training in Health and Race

Held, D. *et al.* 1983, *States and Societies*, Oxford: Martin Robertson

Hepple, B. A. 1983, 'Judging equal rights', *Current Legal Problems*, 36: 71–90

Hewitt, C. 1981, 'Catholic grievances, Catholic nationalism and violence in Northern Ireland during the Civil Rights Period', *British Journal of Sociology*, 32, 3: 362–80

Hindell, K. 1965, 'The genesis of the race relations bill', *Political Quarterly*, 36, 4: 390–405

Hitner, T. *et al.* 1982, *Racial minority employment: equal opportunity policy and practice*, Research Paper no. 35, London: Department of Employment

HMSO 1981, *A New Training Initiative: A Programme for Action*, Cmnd 8455

HMSO 1982, The government reply to the Fifth Report from the Home Affairs Committee Session 1980–81, *Racial Disadvantage*, London: Cmnd 8476

HMSO 1984, *Training for Jobs*, London: Cmnd 9135

HMSO 1985, *Education and Training for Young People*, London: Cmnd 9482

Hoel, B. 1982, 'Contemporary clothing sweatshops; Asian female labour and collective organisation,' in J. West (ed.), *Work, Women and the Labour Market*, London: Routledge and Kegan Paul

Hogwood, B. and Gunn, L. 1984, *Policy Analysis for the Real World*, Oxford: OUP

Home Affairs Committee, Sub-Committee on Race Relations and Immigration 1981a, *Racial Disadvantage*, London: HMSO

1981b, *The Commission for Racial Equality*, London: HMSO

Home Office 1975, *Racial Discrimination*, Cmnd 6234, London: HMSO

1977, *Racial Discrimination: A Guide to the Race Relations Act 1976*, London: Home Office

1982, *Ethnic Minorities in Britain – a study of trends in their position since 1961*, Study no. 68

Home Office Research and Planning Unit 1982, *Police Probationer Training in Race Relations*, London, Home Office

Honeyford, R. 1984, 'Education and race: an alternative view', *Salisbury Review*, Winter: 30–2

Hubbuck, J. and Carter, S. 1980, *Half a Chance? A Report on Job Discrimination against Young Blacks in Nottingham*, London: CRE

Hunt, A. 1975, *'Management Attitudes and Practices Towards Women at Work'*, HMSO

Institute of Personnel Management, Joint Standing Committee on Discrimination 1978, *Towards Fairer Selection: A Code for Non-discrimination*, London: IPM

Jenkins, R. 1982, 'Managers, recruitment procedures and black workers', *Working Papers in Ethnic Relations no. 18*, Birmingham: RUER

1984a, 'Acceptability, suitability and the search for the habituated worker: how ethnic minorities and women lose out', *International Journal of Social Economics*, 11, 7: 69–76

1984b, 'Black workers in the labour market: the price of recession', in B. Roberts, R. Finnegan and D. Gallie (eds), *New Approach to Economic Life*, Manchester: Manchester University Press

1986, *Racism and Recruitment: Managers Organisations, and Equal Opportunity in the Labour Market*, Cambridge: Cambridge University Press

Jenkins, R., Bryman, A., Ford, J., Keil, T. and Beardsworth, A. 1983, 'Information in the labour market: the impact of recession', *Sociology*, 17, 2: 260–7

Jenkins, Roy 1967, 'Address by the Home Secretary to the Institute of Race Relations', *Race*, VIII, 3: 215–21

Jessop, B. 1982, *The Capitalist State*, Oxford: Martin Robertson

Jewson, N. and Mason, D. 1984–85, 'Equal opportunities policies at the workplace and the concept of monitoring', *New Comunity*, XII, 1: 124–36

1986a, 'Modes of discrimination in the recruitment process: formalisation, fairness and efficiency', *Sociology*, 20, 1: 43–63

1986b 'The theory and practise of equal opportunities policies: liberal and radical approaches', *Sociological Review*, 34, 2: 307–34

Joshi, S. and Carter, B. 1984, 'The role of labour in the creation of a racist Britain', *Race and Class*, XXV, 3: 53–70

Kahn-Freund, O. 1974, 'On uses and misuses of comparative law', *Modern Law Review*, 37, 1: 1–27

Kelley, J. and McAllister, I. 1984, 'The genesis of conflict: religion and status attainment in Ulster, 1968', *Sociology*, 18, 2: 171–90

Kerr, C. *et al.* 1973, *Industrialism and Industrial Man*, London: Pelican

Kilson, M. 1983, 'In defence of affirmative action: the American case', *New Community*, X, 3: 464–9

Kushnick, L. 1971, 'British anti-discrimination legislation' in S. Abbot (ed.), *The Prevention of Racial Discrimination in Britain*, London: Oxford University Press

Lacey, N. 1984, 'A change in the right direction?: The CRE's consultative document', *Public Law*, Summer: 186–94

Layton-Henry, Z. 1980, 'Commission in crisis', *Political Quarterly*, 51, 4: 441–50

Lea, J. 1980, 'The contradictions of the sixties race relations legislation', in National Deviancy Conference (ed.), *Permissiveness and Control*, London: Macmillan

Lee, G. 1983, 'Implementing equal opportunity: a training perspective', *Equal Opportunities International*, 2, 1: 27–36

1984, *Trade Unionism and Race*, A Report to the West Midlands Regional Council of the Trades Union Congress, December

Lee, G. and Wrench, J. 1980, 'Accident-prone immigrants: an assumption challenged', *Sociology*, 14, 4: 551–66

1983, *Skill seekers – black youth, apprenticeships and disadvantage*, Leicester: National Youth Bureau

Lester, A. and Bindman, G. 1972, *Race and Law*, Harmondsworth: Penguin.
Leys, C. 1983, *Politics in Britain*, London: Heinemann
Little, A. and Robbins, D. 1982, *Loading the Law: A Study of Transmitted Deprivation, Ethnic Minorities and Affirmative Action*, London: Commission for Racial Equality
Lukács, G. 1971, *History and Class Consciousness*, London: Merlin
Lustgarten, L. 1978, 'The new meaning of discrimination', *Public Law*, Summer: 178–205
    1980, *Legal Control of Discrimination*, London: Macmillan
    1982, 'The CRE under attack', *Public Law*, Summer: 229–35
    1983, 'Liberty in a culturally plural society' in A. P. Griffiths (ed.) *Of Liberty*, Cambridge: Cambridge University Press
Lynch, L. and Richardson, R. 1982, 'Unemployment of Young Workers in Britain', in *British Journal of Industrial Relations*, November
Makeham, P. 1980, *Youth Unemployment*, Department of Employment Research Paper, No. 10
Mangum, G. L. 1976, *Employability, Employment and Income*, Salt Lake City: Olympus Publishing Co.
Manpower Services Commission 1977, *Young People and Work (The Holland Report)*, London: MSC
    1979, *Special Programmes Special Needs: Ethnic Minorities and the Special Programmes for the Unemployed*, London: MSC
    1980, *Review of the Second Year of Special Programmes*, London: MSC
    1981a, *The New Training Initiative: A Consultative Document*, London: MSC
    1981b, *A New Training Initiative: An Agenda for Action*, London: MSC
    1981c, *Review of the Third Year of Special Programmes*, London: MSC
    1982a, *Task Group Report*, London: MSC
    1982b, *Annual Report of the Manpower Services Commission 1981/1982*, Sheffield: MSC
    1983a, *Towards an Adult Training Strategy, A Discussion Paper*, London: MSC
    1983b, *Towards an Adult Training Strategy: A Discussion Paper*, Sheffield: MSC
    1983c, *MSC Corporate Plan 1983–1987*, Sheffield: MSC
    1984a, *Survey of YTS Schemes*, Training Division, unpublished
    1984b, 'Ethnic recruitment into YTS in 1983/1984 in Birmingham', Training Division (Birmingham and Solihull Area Office), unpublished paper (October)
    1985a, *Adult Training Campaign: A Guide*, Sheffield: MSC
    1985b, *Adult Training Support for Employers*, Sheffield: MSC
Massey, D. 1983, 'The Shape of Things to Come', in *Marxism Today*, April
Massey, D. and Meegan, R. 1982, *The Anatomy of Job Loss*, London: Methuen
Maxmanian, D. and Sabatier, P. 1981, *Effective Policy Implementation*, Lexington: Lexington Books
McCrudden, C. 1982a, 'Law enforcement by regulatory agency: the case of employment discrimination in Northern Ireland', *Modern Law Review*, 45, 6: 617–36
    1982b, 'Institutional discrimination', *Oxford Journal of Legal Studies*, 2: 303–67
    1983a, 'Anti-discrimination goals and the legal process', in N. Glazer and K.

Young (eds), *Ethnic Pluralism and Public Policy*, London: Heinemann
1983b, *Race Relations Legislation*, Unit 7, Part 2 of E354, Ethnic Minorities and Community Relations: Open University
McIlroy, J. 1982, 'Racism at work: a critique', *Contemporary Affairs Briefing*, 4(2): *passim*
McKeown, M. 1973, 'Civil service discrimination', *Hibernia*, 5 October
Meehan, E. 1983, 'Equal opportunity policies: some implications for women of contrasts between enforcement bodies in Britain and the USA' in J. Lewis (ed.), *Women's Welfare, Women's Rights*, London: Croom Helm
Miles, R. and Phizacklea, A. 1984, *White Man's Country*, London: Pluto Press
Miliband, R. 1973, *The State in Capitalist Society*, London: Quartet
1983, *Class Power and State Power*, London: Verso
Miller, J. 1983, 'Some problems of individual and collective redress in English law', in S. Anderman (ed.), *Law and the Weaker Party*, vol. 2, Abingdon: Professional Books
Moore, R. 1975, *Racism and Black Resistance in Britain*, London: Pluto Press
Mullard, C. 1982, 'The state's response to racism: towards a relational explanation', in A. Ohr, B. Manning and P. Curno (eds), *Community Work and Racism*, London: Routledge and Kegan Paul
Murray, A. 1981, 'Race relations in shop stewards courses: some recent initiatives', *The Industrial Tutor*, 3, 5: 37–46
Murray, A. D. and Chandola, J. R. 1981, 'Training for a multiracial society – A Practitioner's Approach' National Centre for Industrial Language Training, Working Paper no. 26
Murray, D. and Darby, J. 1980, *The Vocational Aspirations and Expectations of Young School Leavers in Londonderry and Strabane*, FEA Paper no. 6, Belfast
National Association of Teachers in Further and Higher Education 1983, *The Great Training Robbery: an interim report on the role of private training agencies with the YTS in Birmingham and Solihull area*, NATFHE, Birmingham Liaison Committee
Nickell, S. J. 1980, 'A Picture of Male Unemployment in Britain', *The Economic Journal*, December: 784
Nixon, J. 1982, 'The Home Office and Race Relations Policy: co-ordinator or initiator?' *Journal of Public Policy*, 2, 4: 365–78
Nordlie, P. G. 1979, 'Proportion of black and white Army officers in command positions', in R. Alvarez *et al.* (eds), *Discrimination in Organisations*, San Francisco: Jossey–Bass
Northern Ireland Economic Council 1981, (abstract in J. Darby, N. Dodge and A. C. Hepburn, *A Register of Social and Economic Research on Northern Ireland*, London: ESRC)
Northern Ireland Office 1973, *Press Notice*, 6 July
Offe, C. 1975, 'The theory of the capitalist state and the problem of policy formation', in L. N. Lindberg *et al.* (eds), *Stress and Contradiction in Contemporary Capitalism*, Lexington: Lexington Books
1976, *Industry and Inequality*, London: Edward Arnold
1984, *Contradictions of the Welfare State*, London: Hutchinson
Ollerearnshaw, S. 1983, 'The promotion of employment equality in Britain', in N. Glazer and K. Young (eds), *Ethnic Pluralism and Public Policy*, London: Heinemann

Osborne, R. 1980, 'Fair employment in Northern Ireland', *New Community*, 8, 1–2: 129–37

Osborne, R. and Miller, R. 1980, 'Why Catholics don't get more jobs – a reply', *Belfast Telegraph*, 14 November

Ouseley, H. 1981, *The System*, London: Runnymede Trust/South London Equal Rights Consultancy

Pannick, D. 1982, 'Class actions and discrimination law', *New Community*, 10, 1: 16–26

Parkinson, M. and Duffy, J. 1984, 'Government's response to inner-city riots: the minister for Merseyside and the task force', *Parliamentary Affairs*, 37, 1: 76–96

Parmar, P. 1982, 'Gender, race and class: Asian women in resistance', in Centre for Contemporary Cultural Studies, *The Empire Strikes Back: Race and Racism in 70s Britain*, London: Hutchinson

Patterson, S. 1965, *Dark Strangers: a study of West Indians in London*, Harmondsworth: Penguin

Peppard, N. 1983, 'Race relations training: the state of the art', *New Community*, XI, 1/2: 150–9

1980, 'Towards effective race relations training', *New Community*, VIII, 1–2: 99–106

Phizacklea, A. 1982, 'Migrant Women and Wage Labour: The Case of West Indian Women in Britain', in J. West (ed.), *Work, Women and the Labour Market*, London: Routledge and Kegan Paul

Phizacklea, A. and Miles, R. 1980, *Labour and Racism*, London: Routledge and Kegan Paul

Pollert, A. 1981, *Girls, Wives, Factory Lives*, London: Macmillan

1985, *Unequal Opportunities: Racial Discrimination and the Youth Training Scheme*, Birmingham: Trade Union Resource Centre

Poulantzas, N. 1978, *State, Power, Socialism*, London: New Left Books

Prashar, U. 1983, 'The need for positive action' in J. Beynon (ed.), *Scarman and After*, Oxford: Pergamon Press

Race Relations Board 1973, *Race Relations Legislation in Britain*, London: Race Relations Board

Radcliffe Report 1959, in J. Tomlinson 1983 *q.v.*, on the workings of the monetary system

Radin, B. 1966, 'Coloured workers and British trade unions', *Race*, VIII, 2: 157–73

Reeves, F. 1983, *British Racial Discourse*, Cambridge: Cambridge University Press

Rex, J. 1981, 'Urban segregation and inner city policy in Great Britain', in C. Peach, V. Robinson and S. Smith (eds), *Ethnic Segregation in Cities*, London: Croom Helm

Rex, J. and Tomlinson, S. 1979, *Colonial Immigrants in a British City: A Class Analysis*, London: Routledge and Kegan Paul

Rhodes, E. and Braham, P. 1981, 'Black workers in Britain: from full employment to recession', in P. Braham, E. Rhodes and M. Pearn (eds), *Discrimination and Disadvantage in Employment*, London: Harper and Row

Richardson, J. J. and Stringer, J. K. 1981, 'The politics of change with special reference to the politics of industrial training policy 1964–1980', *Industrial and Commercial Training*, February: 54–61

Rolston, B. 1978, 'Community development and the capitalist state', PhD. thesis, Queen's University, Belfast
1983, 'Reformism and sectarianism: the state of the union after civil rights' in J. Darby (ed.), *Northern Ireland: The Background to the Conflict*, Appletree: Belfast and Syracuse University Press, NY
Rose, E. J. B. *et al*. 1968, *Colour and Citizenship: A Report on British Race Relations*, London: Oxford University Press
Rose, R. 1971, *Governing Without Consensus*, London: Faber
Runnymede Trust 1974–5, 'Trade unions and immigrant workers', *New Community*, IV, 1: 19–36
1979, *A Review of the Race Relations Act 1976*, London: Runnymede Trust
1981, *Employment, unemployment and black workers*, London: Runnymede Trust
1982, *Racial Discrimination: Developing a Legal Strategy Through Individual Complaints*, London: Runnymede Trust
Ryan, P. 1984, 'The new training initiative after two years', *Lloyds Bank Review*, April: 31–45
Sanders, P. 1983, 'Anti-discrimination law enforcement in Britain', in N. Glazer and K. Young (eds), *Ethnic Pluralism and Public Policy*, London: Heinemann
Scarman, Rt. Hon. The Lord 1981, *The Brixton Disorders 10–12 April, 1981*, Cmnd. 8427, London: HMSO
Schackman, J. 1985, *The Right to be Understood*, National Extension College
Schmitt, D. 1981, 'The consequences of administrative emphases in equal opportunity strategies', paper delivered to the American Political Science Association Annual Meeting, September
Schwartz, R. and Skolnick, J. (eds) 1970, *Society and the Legal Order*, New York: Basic Books
Seear, N. 1981, 'The Management of Equal Opportunity', in P. Braham *et al.*, *Discrimination and Disadvantage in Employment*, London: Harper and Row
Select Committee on Race Relations and Immigration 1975, *The Organisation of Race Relations Administration*, London: HMSO
Shaw, J. 1981/2, 'Training methods in race relations organisations', *New Community*, IX, 3: 437–46
Simpson, J. 1983, 'Economic development: cause or effect in the Northern Ireland conflict', in J. Darby (ed.), *Northern Ireland: The Background to the Conflict*, Belfast: Appletree Press; New York: Syracuse University Press
Sivanandan, A. 1982, *A Different Hunger*, London: Pluto Press
1985, 'RAT and the degradation of black struggle', *Race and Class*, XXVI, 4: 1–33
Slatter, S. St. P. 1974, *The Employment of Non-English Speaking Workers: What Industry Must Do*, London: Community Relations Commission
Smith, D. J. 1974, *Racial Disadvantage in Employment*, London: Political Economic Planning
1977, *Racial Disadvantage in Britain*, Harmondsworth: Penguin
1981, *Unemployment and Racial Minorities*, London: Policy Studies Institute
Snell, M. W., Glucklich, P. and Povall, M. 1981, 'Equal pay and opportunities', *Research Paper no. 20*, London: Department of Employment
Tavistock Institute of Human Relations/Civil Service Department 1978, *Application of Race Relations Policy in the Civil Service*, London: HMSO

Tomlinson, J. 1983, 'Where do economic policy objectives come from?', *Economy and Society*, vol. 12, 1

Torrington, D. *et al.* 1982, *Management and the Multi-racial Workforce*, Aldershot: Gower

Trades Union Congress 1981, *Black Workers: A TUC Charter for Equality of Opportunity*, London: TUC

1982, *Equal Opportunities: Positive Action Programmes*, London: TUC

1983a, *Race Relations at Work*, London: TUC

1983b, *TUC Workbook on Racism*, London: TUC

Wainwright, D. 1980, *Learning from Uncle Sam: Equal Employment Opportunity Programme*, London: Runnymede Trust

Watson, T. J. 1977, *The Personnel Managers*, London: Routledge and Kegan Paul

West Midlands Regional Health Authority 1985, *A Study of Interpreters in the West Midlands Region*, Birmingham, West Midlands Regional Health Authority

Westergaard, J. and Resler, H. 1975, *Class in a Capitalist Society*, London: Heinemann

Whyte, J. W. 1983, 'How much discrimination was there under the Unionist regime, 1921–1968?' in J. O'Connell and T. Gallagher (eds), *Contemporary Irish Studies*, Manchester: Manchester University Press

Wrench, J. (forthcoming), 'YTS, racial equality and trade unions,' in M. Cross and D. I. Smith (eds) *Black Youth and YTS: Opportunity or Inequality?*, Leicester: National Youth Bureau

Young, K. 1983, 'Ethnic pluralism and the policy agenda in Britain' in N. Glazer and K. Young (eds), *Ethnic Pluralism and Public Policy* London: Heinemann Educational Books

1986, 'Metropolis, R.I.P.?' *Political Quarterly*, 57, 15: 36–46

Young, K. and Connelly, N. 1981, *Policy and Practice in the Multi-racial City*, London: Policy Studies Institue

Young, K. and Garside P. L. 1982, *Metropolitan London: Politics and Urban Change, 1831–1981*, London: Edward Arnold

Index

DATE DUE

AP 8 '94			
AP 7 '95			
JU 17 '96			
DE 20 '96			
DE 11 '97			
NO 19 '02			
MY 24 '02			
MY 7 '1			